The Pride of Korean Saga Comics

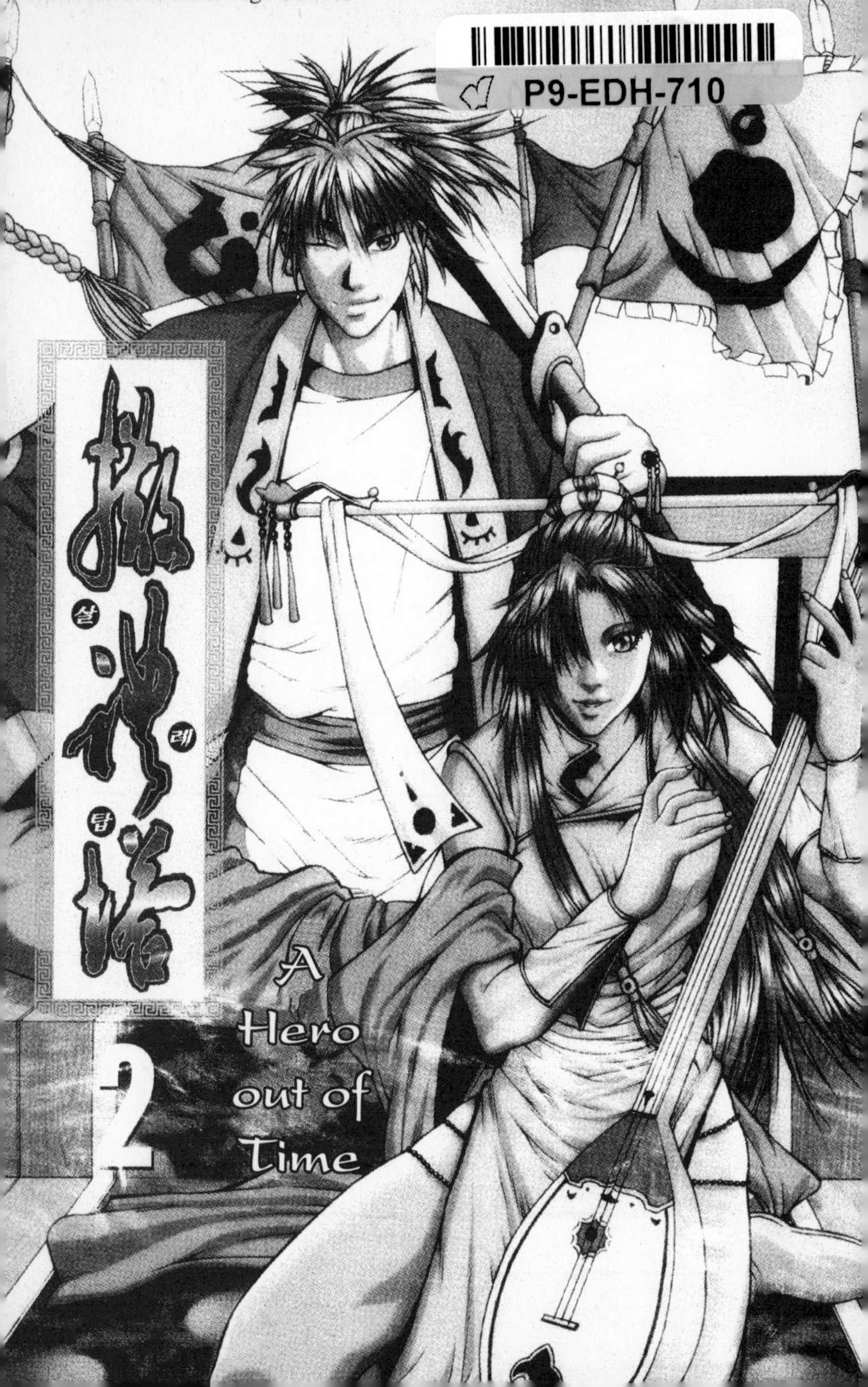
살
례
탑
2
A Hero out of Time

Threads Of Time, Vol. 2
Created by Mi Young Noh

Translation - Jihae Hong
English Adaptation - Luis Reyes
Retouch and Lettering - Derron Bennet
Production Artist - Jose Macasocol, Jr.
Cover Design - Patrick Hook

Editor - Luis Reyes
Digital Imaging Manager - Chris Buford
Pre-Press Manager - Antonio DePietro
Production Managers - Jennifer Miller and Mutsumi Miyazaki
Art Director - Matt Alford
Managing Editor - Jill Freshney
VP of Production - Ron Klamert
President and C.O.O. - John Parker
Publisher and C.E.O. - Stuart Levy

A **TOKYOPOP**® Manga

TOKYOPOP Inc.
5900 Wilshire Blvd. Suite 2000
Los Angeles, CA 90036

E-mail: info@TOKYOPOP.com
Come visit us online at www.TOKYOPOP.com

ISBN: 1-59182-781-7

First TOKYOPOP printing: November 2004

10 9 8 7 6 5 4 3 2 1

Printed in the USA

Threads of Time

Volume 2

By
Mi Young Noh

HAMBURG // LONDON // LOS ANGELES // TOKYO

The Chronicles of Time

High school kendo champion Moon Bin Kim suffered from a recurring nightmare in which he lives as Sa Kyung Kim, the son of a prominent warrior family in 13th-century Korea (Koryo). In the modern day, he is the son of neglectful parents who, from whatever part of the globe they may happen to be, wire him money when he needs it. The nightmares become increasingly more frequent and begin to invade his waking hours, especially the apparition of a girl who seems to be calling out for him.

After a freak accident at the school swimming pool, during which Moon Bin saw the mysterious girl beneath him in the water, pulling him down into dark depths, he found that his nightmare had become more real than he ever imagined. As a hospitalized Moon Bin entered a coma, Sa Kyung Kim emerged from a coma in the past.

But this new consciousness straddles a trasmigratory portal through space in time in which people in his life assume roles in both realities. In the present, his high school's kendo club was battling toward the championships…but in the past, Moon Bin finds himself at the threshold of a territorial dispute with the Mongol Empire.

Genghis Khan has recently died, leaving the great expanse of Asia to his three remaining sons, Chagatai, Ogodei and Tolui. Ogodei, though not the oldest, became the Deh-Khan, ruler of all the Khanates. It was one of Genghis Khan's dying orders to invade Koryo, and the new Deh-Khan intends to do just that. He has chosen a general to lead the invasion of the peninsula—Sali Tayi, one of the stoically fierce fighters in the Mongol army. And to appoint a Chiliarch to accompany Sali Tayi on this path of conquest, the new Deh-Khan has devised a contest of skill, strength and bravery…a contest restricted to male warriors, much to the chagrin of Chagatai's alacritous daughter, Atan Hadas, who longs to show the Mongol world what kind of fighter a woman can be.

contents

Threads of Time

Chapter 6
Atan Hadas and Sali Tayi

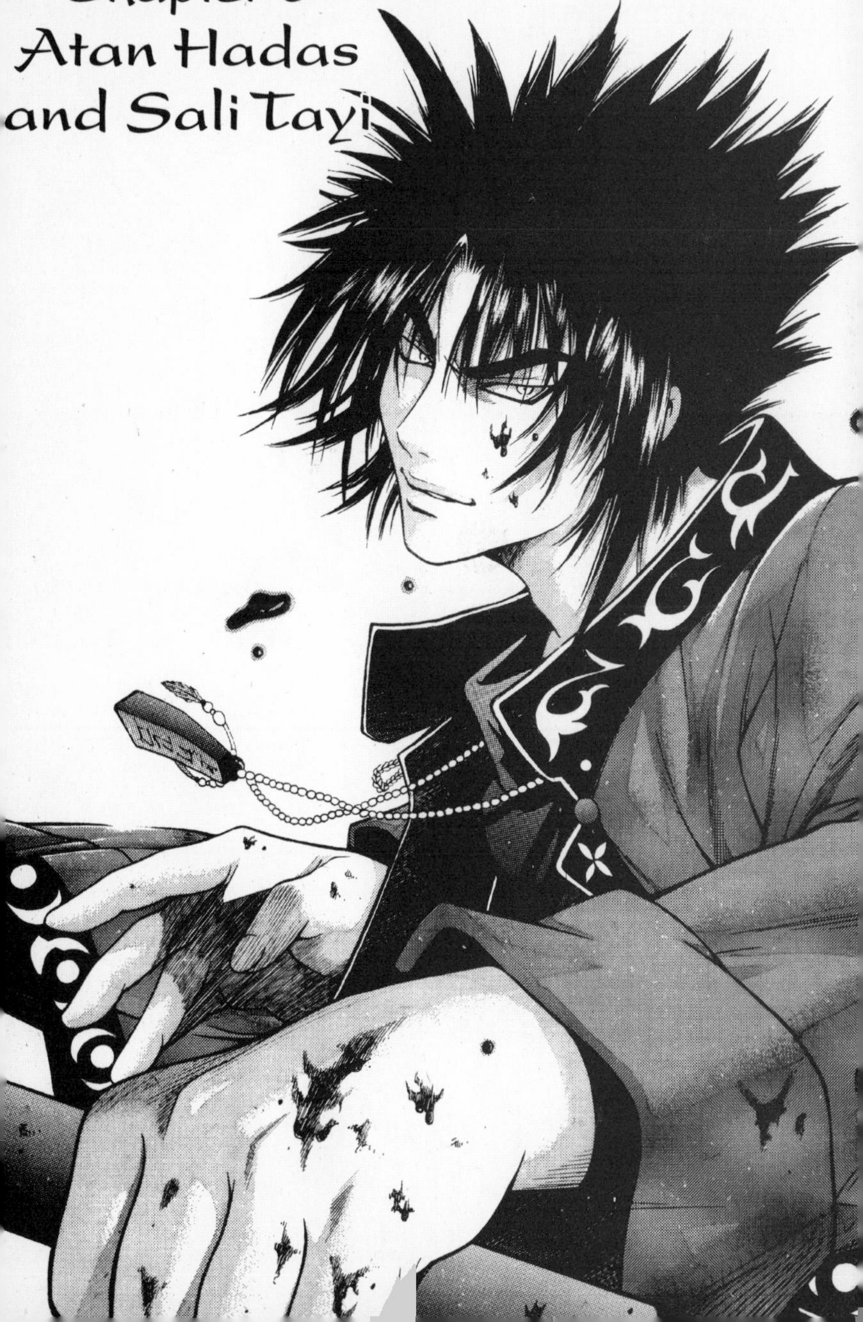

NOW...LET THE COMPETITION BEGIN! CELEBRATE AND ENJOY MY BECOMING OGODEI DEH-KAHN!

UPON THE WINNER, I WILL BESTOW THE TITL AND DUTY OF CHILIARCH

Chiliarch: Commander of a battalion of 1000 soldie

CHILIARCH!

THE CHILIARCH...

THIS IS MY CHANCE!

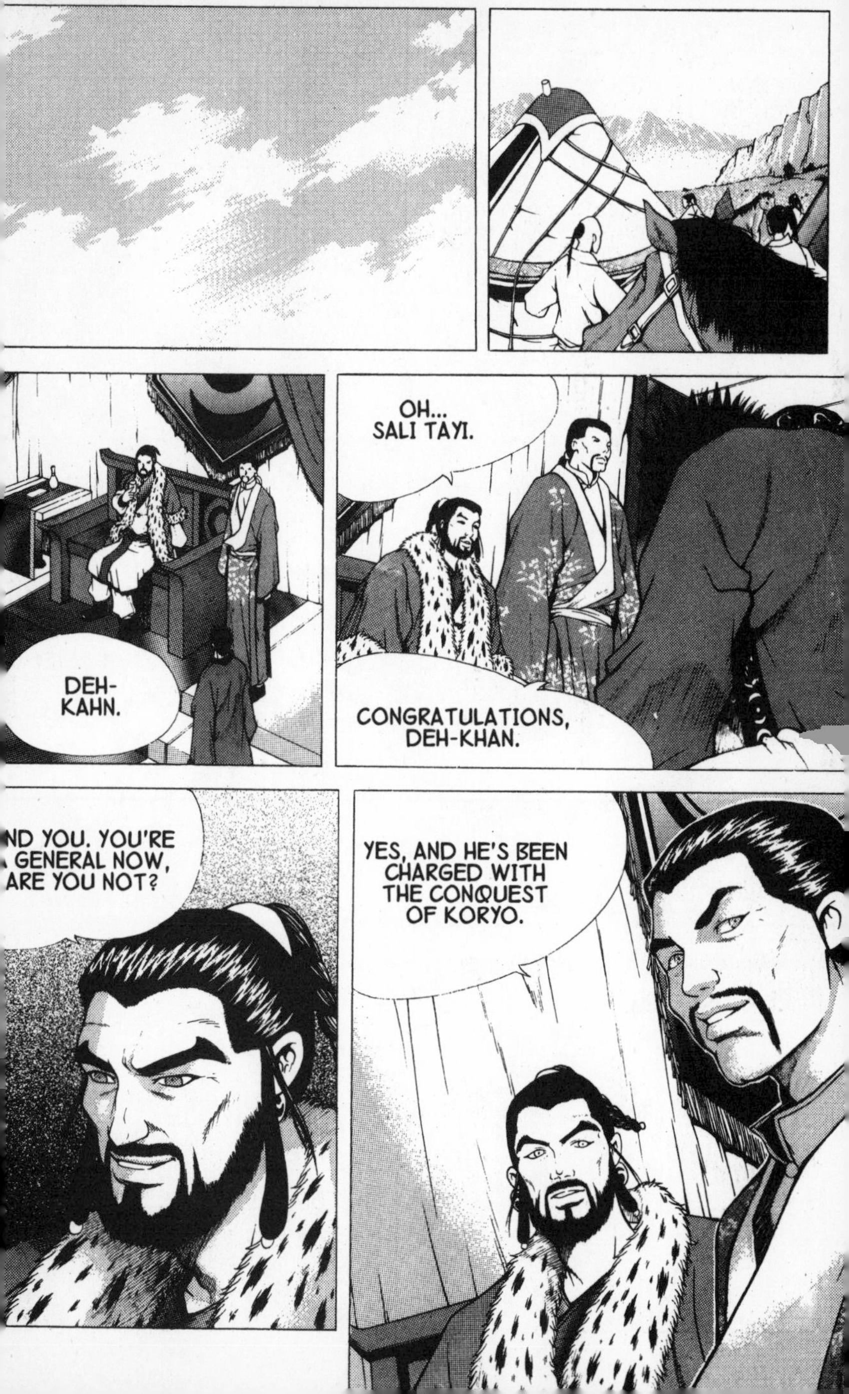
DEH-
KAHN.
OH...
SALI TAYI.
CONGRATULATIONS,
DEH-KHAN.
ND YOU. YOU'RE
GENERAL NOW,
ARE YOU NOT?
YES, AND HE'S BEEN
CHARGED WITH
THE CONQUEST
OF KORYO.

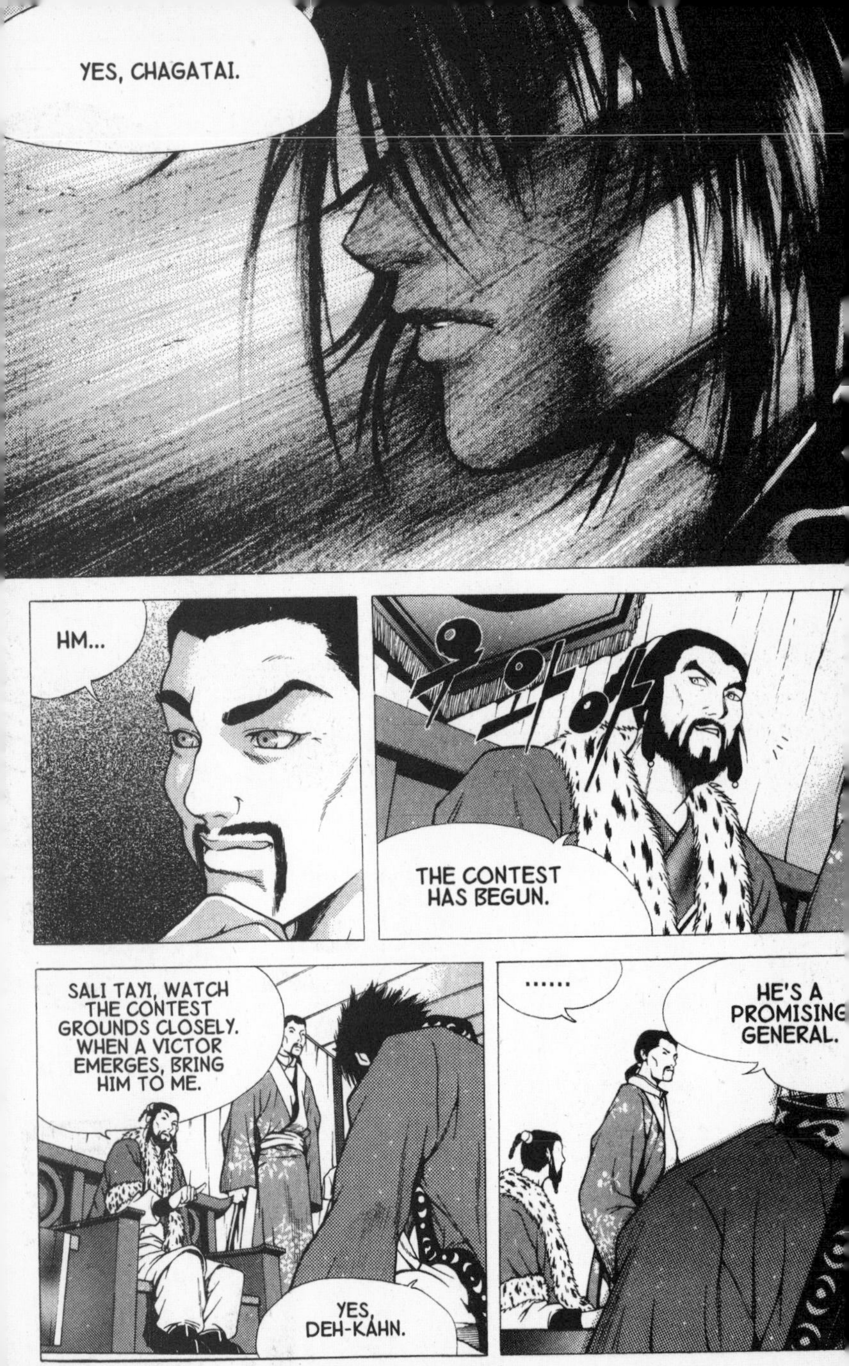
YES, CHAGATAI.
HM...
THE CONTEST HAS BEGUN.
SALI TAYI, WATCH THE CONTEST GROUNDS CLOSELY. WHEN A VICTOR EMERGES, BRING HIM TO ME.
YES, DEH-KAHN.
......
HE'S A PROMISING GENERAL.

AND HOW IS ATAN HADAS? I'VE HEARD GOOD THINGS.

ATAN HADAS IS NINETEEN...AND STUBBORN.

SHE CONTINUES TO DRIVE HER MOTHER MAD WITH HER FOOLISH LONGING TO ENTER THE CONTEST.

Perhaps she is the mistake of our parenting...

BUT, NO MATTER. MY SON WILL EMERGE THE WINNER TODAY.

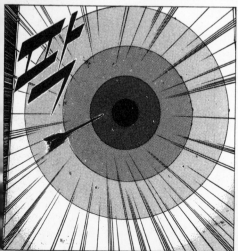

JUST SHORT.

STILL, HE IS QUITE SKILLED.

NEXT CONTESTANT!

DAMN!

SISTER!

HUH?!
WHAT ARE
YOU DOING
HERE?!

......

BECOMING
A BARORHEE.

Barorhee: A warrior

AUGH!
YOU SAID I
COULD WIN
THIS ONE!

Well, I lied.

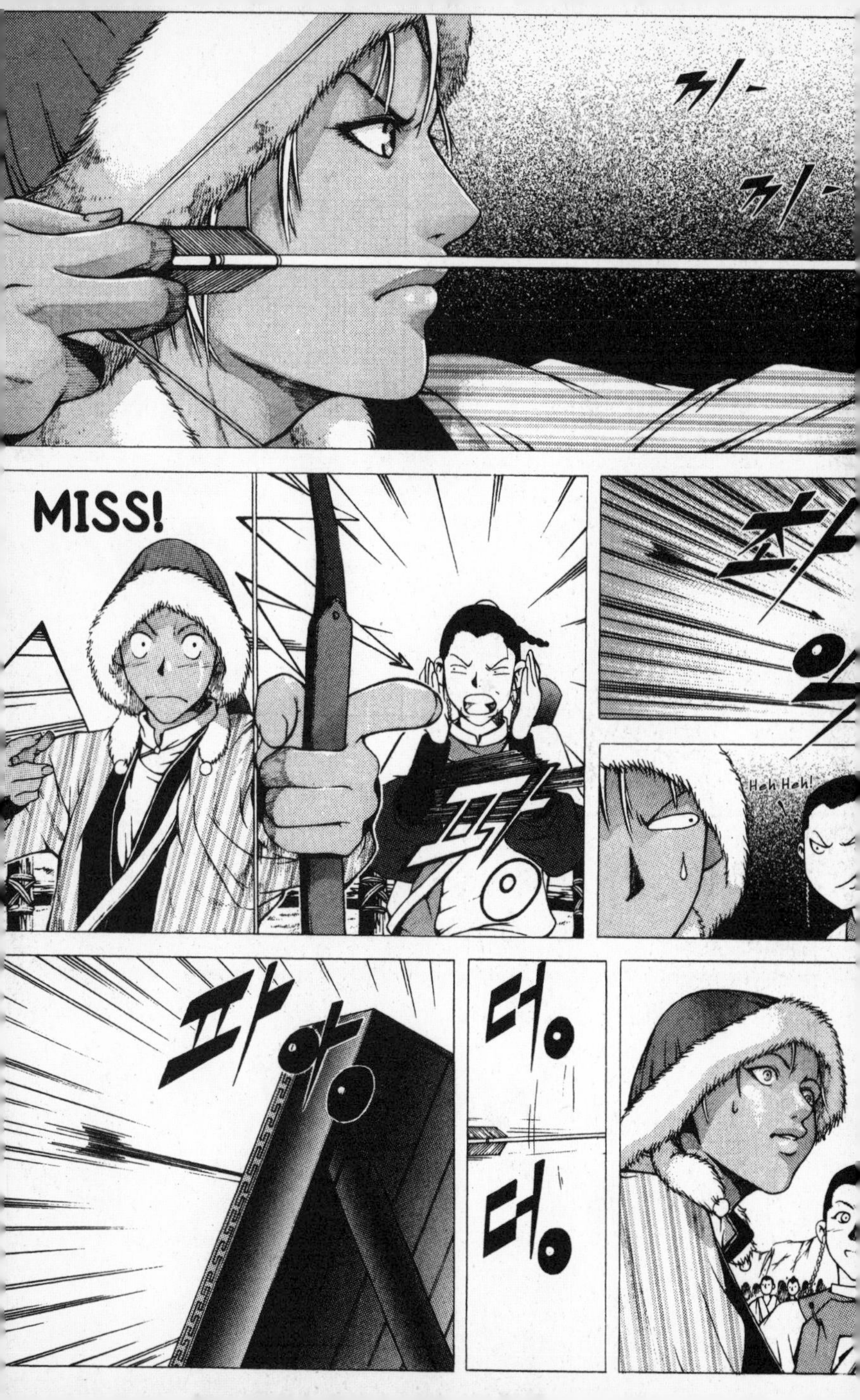
MISS!
Heh Heh!

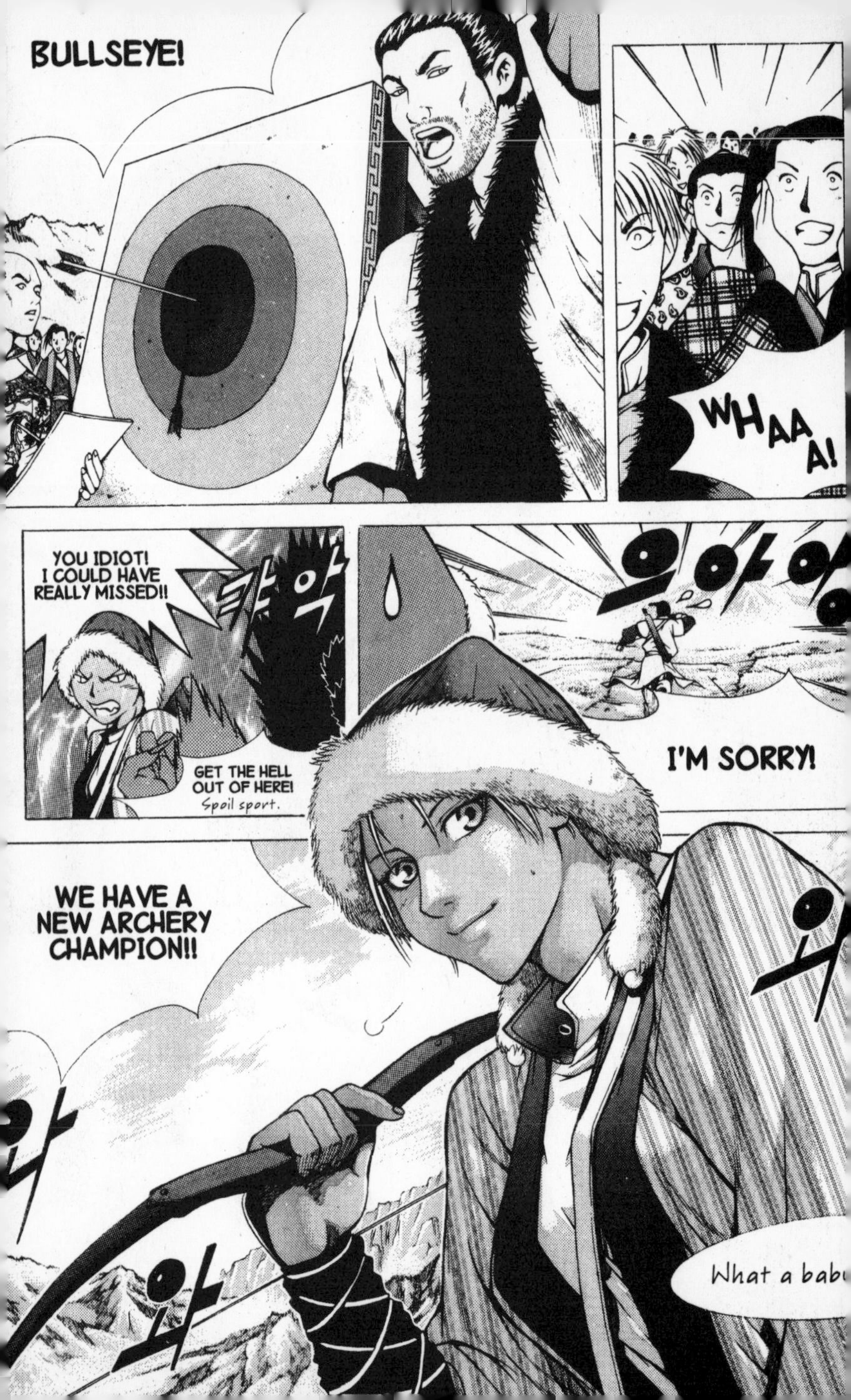
BULLSEYE!
WHAAA A!
YOU IDIOT! I COULD HAVE REALLY MISSED!!
캬악
GET THE HELL OUT OF HERE!
Spoil sport.
와아아아
I'M SORRY!
WE HAVE A NEW ARCHERY CHAMPION!!
What a bab

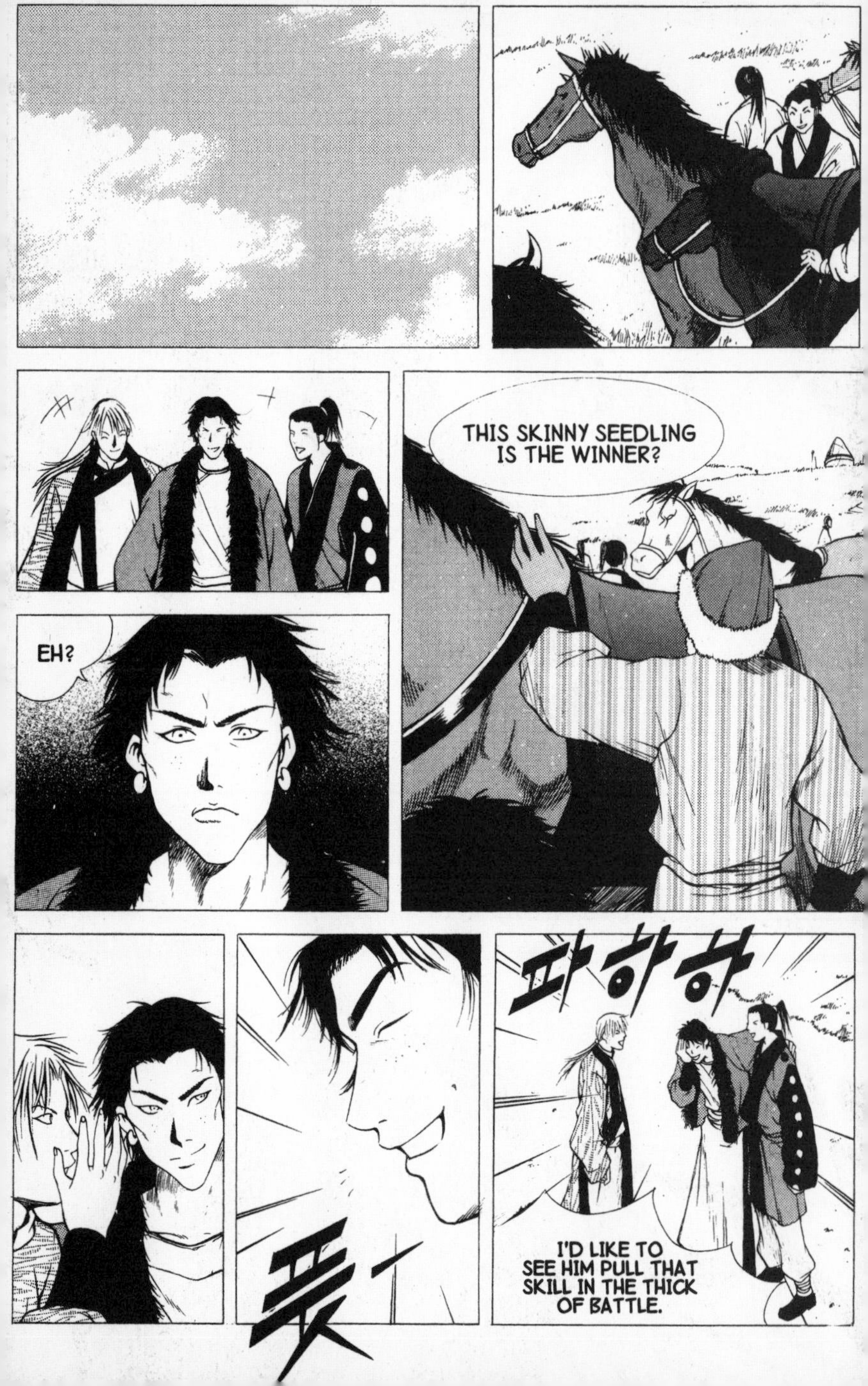
EH?
THIS SKINNY SEEDLING IS THE WINNER?
픗
파하하
I'D LIKE TO SEE HIM PULL THAT SKILL IN THE THICK OF BATTLE.

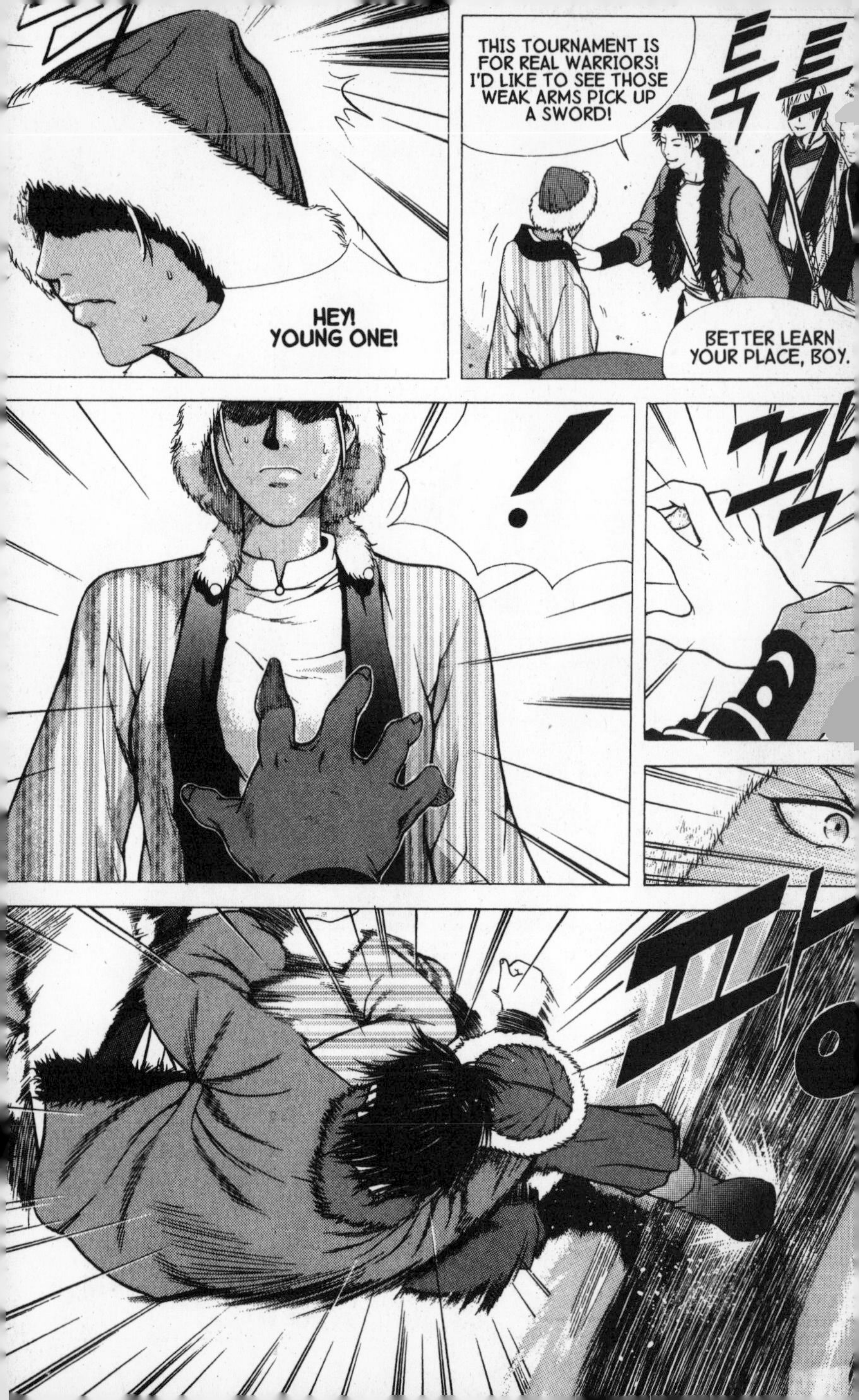
HEY! YOUNG ONE!
THIS TOURNAMENT IS FOR REAL WARRIORS! I'D LIKE TO SEE THOSE WEAK ARMS PICK UP A SWORD!
BETTER LEARN YOUR PLACE, BOY.
!

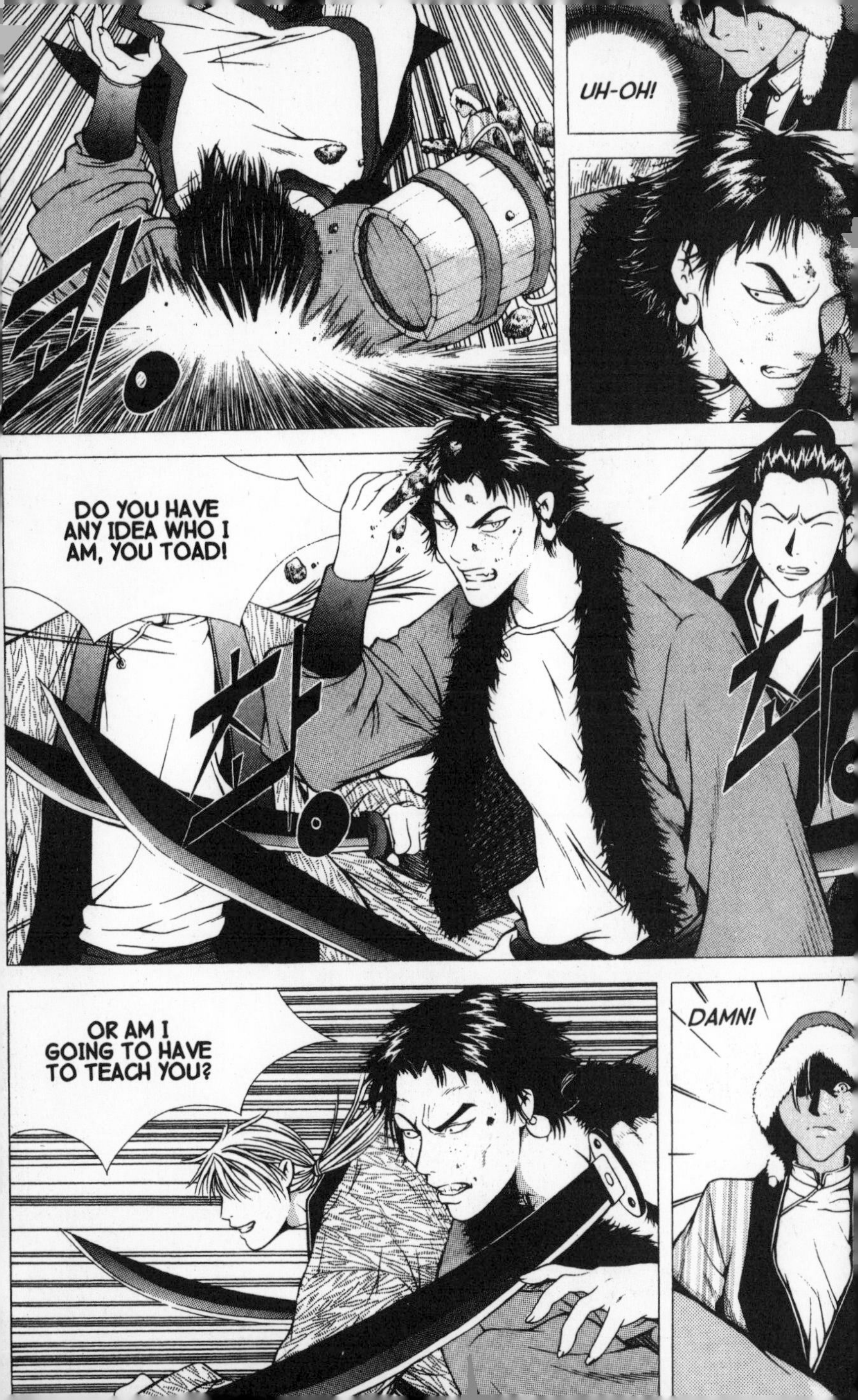
UH-OH!
DO YOU HAVE ANY IDEA WHO I AM, YOU TOAD!
OR AM I GOING TO HAVE TO TEACH YOU?
DAMN!

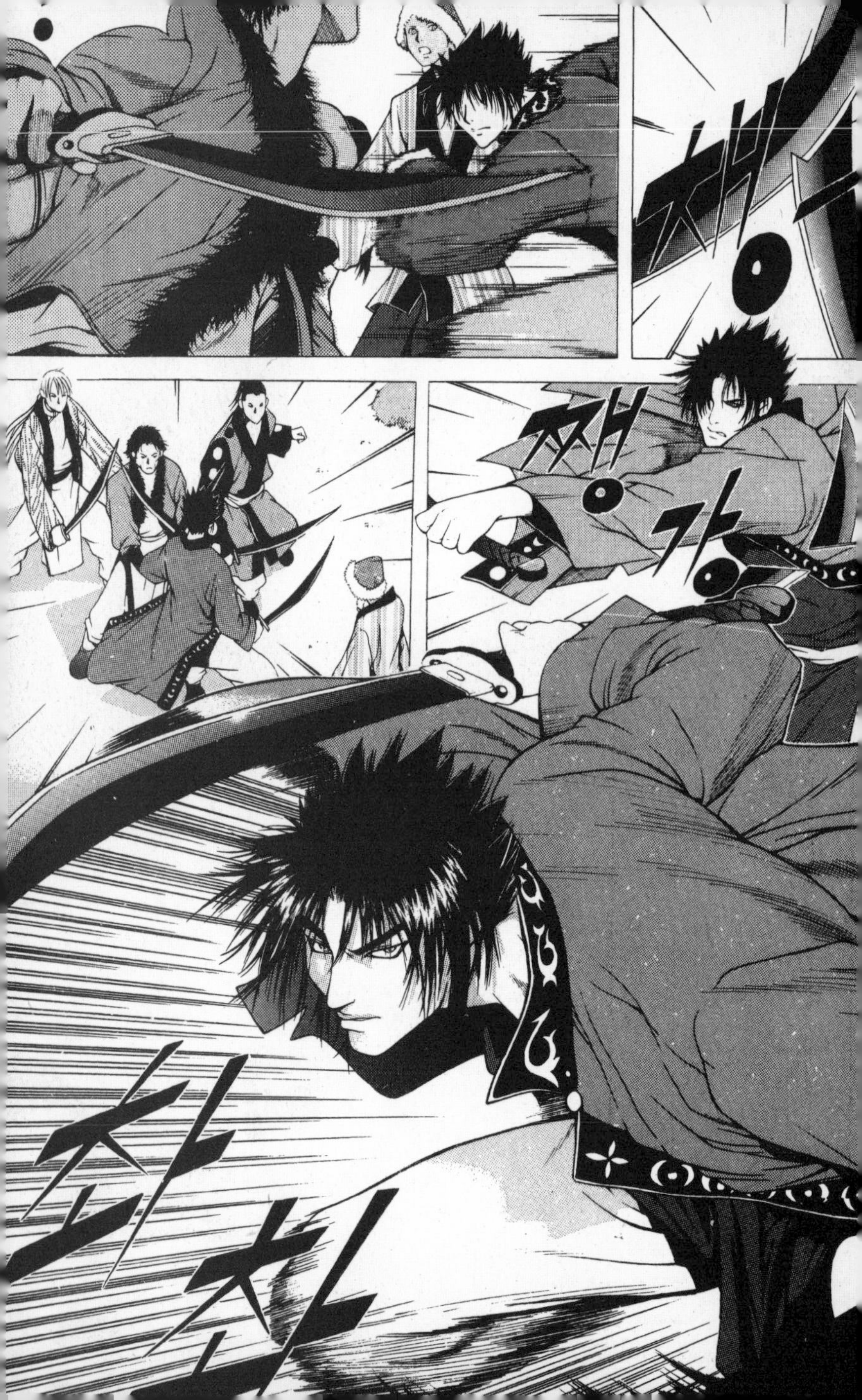

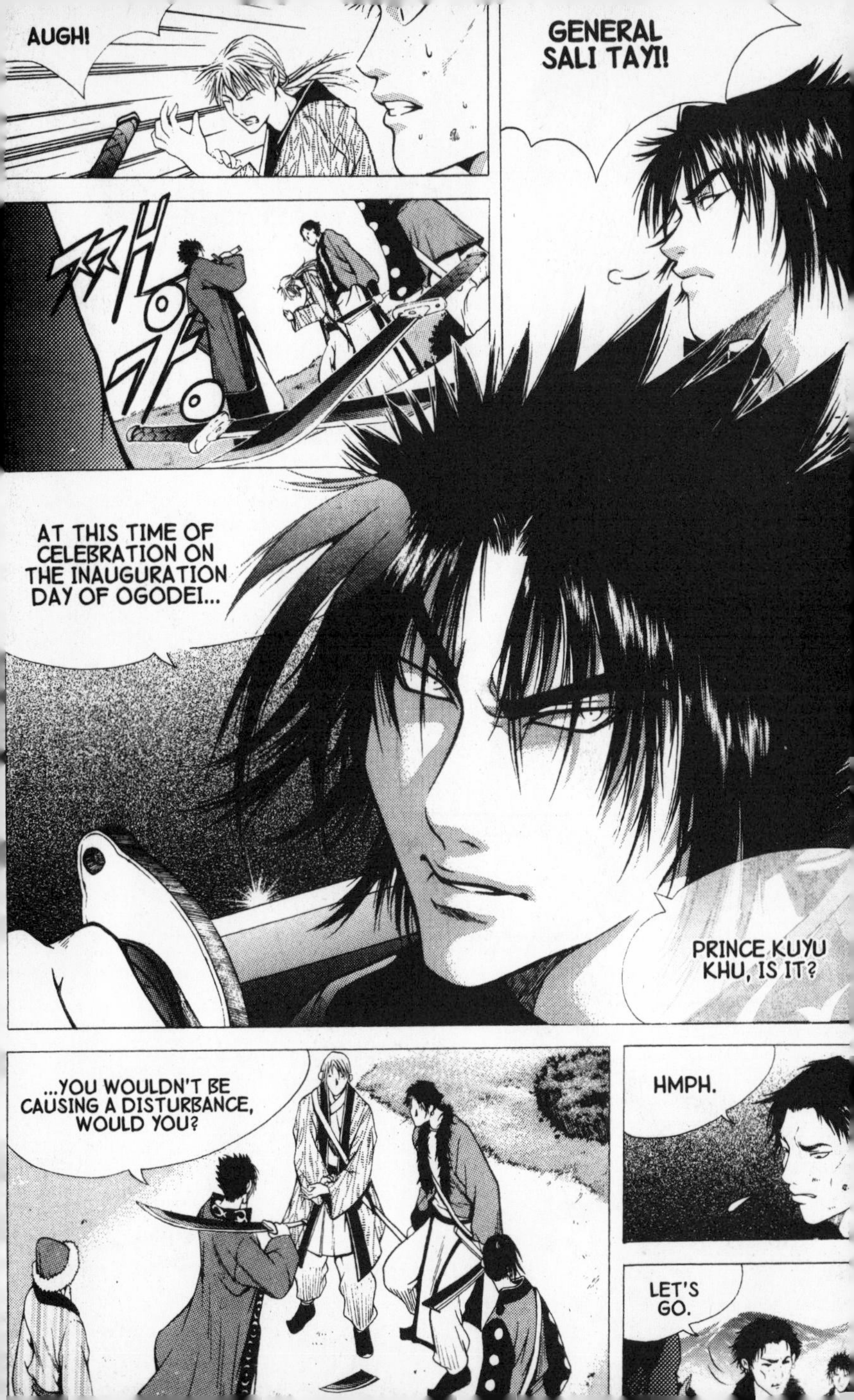
AUGH!
GENERAL SALI TAYI!
AT THIS TIME OF CELEBRATION ON THE INAUGURATION DAY OF OGODEI...
PRINCE KUYU KHU, IS IT?
...YOU WOULDN'T BE CAUSING A DISTURBANCE, WOULD YOU?
HMPH.
LET'S GO.

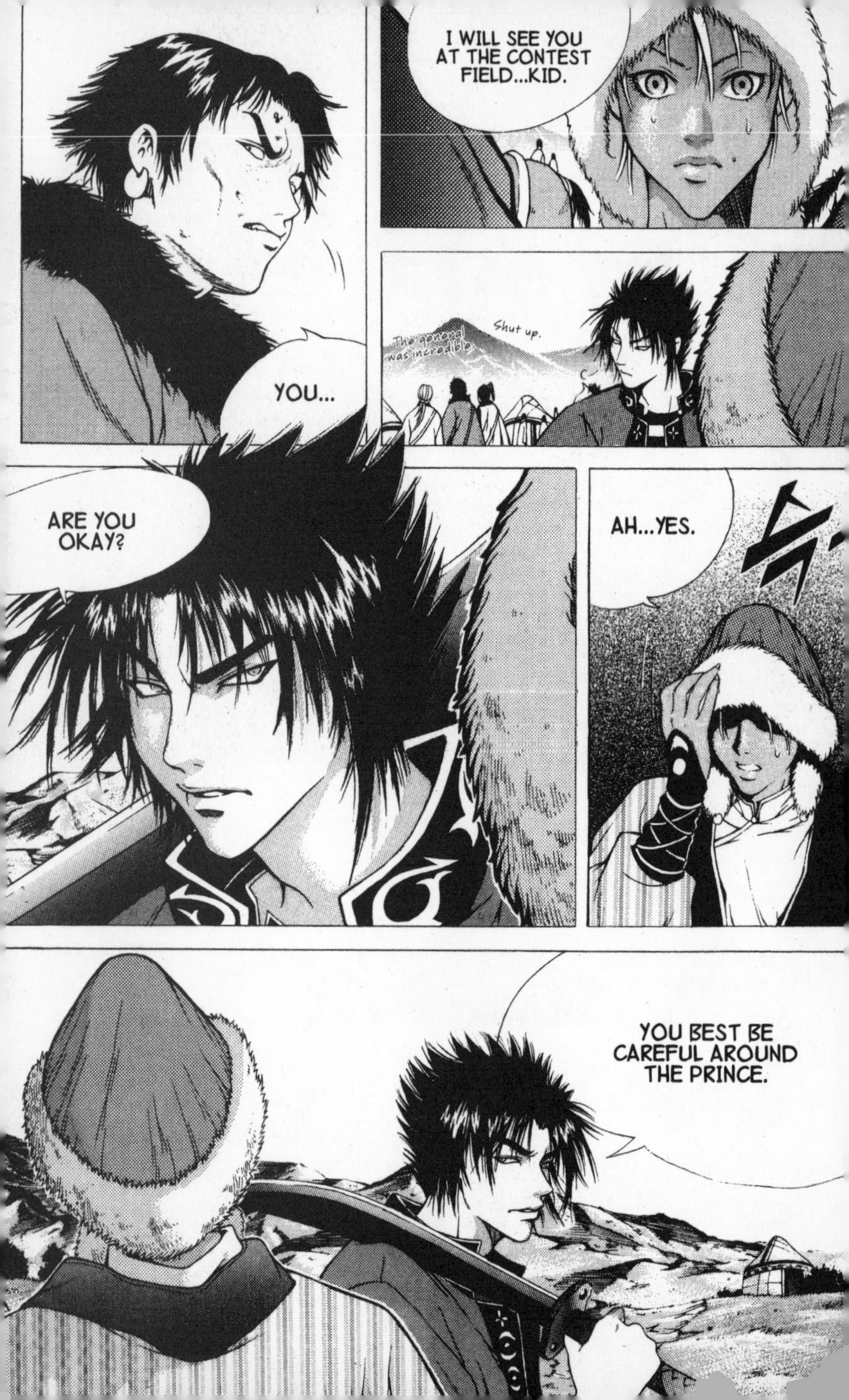
YOU...
I WILL SEE YOU AT THE CONTEST FIELD...KID.
The general was incredible.
Shut up.
ARE YOU OKAY?
AH...YES.
YOU BEST BE CAREFUL AROUND THE PRINCE.

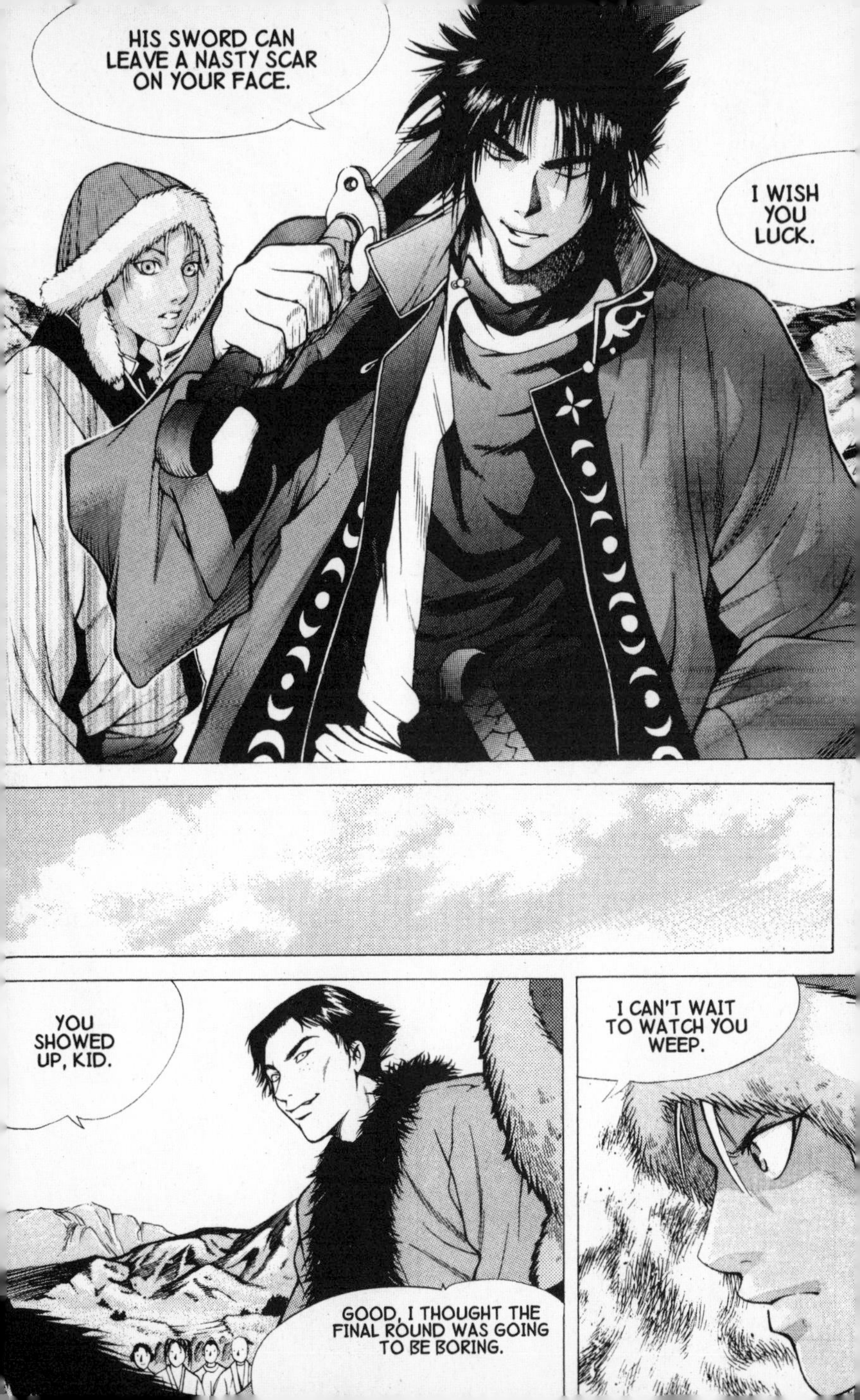
HIS SWORD CAN LEAVE A NASTY SCAR ON YOUR FACE.
I WISH YOU LUCK.
YOU SHOWED UP, KID.
GOOD, I THOUGHT THE FINAL ROUND WAS GOING TO BE BORING.
I CAN'T WAIT TO WATCH YOU WEEP.

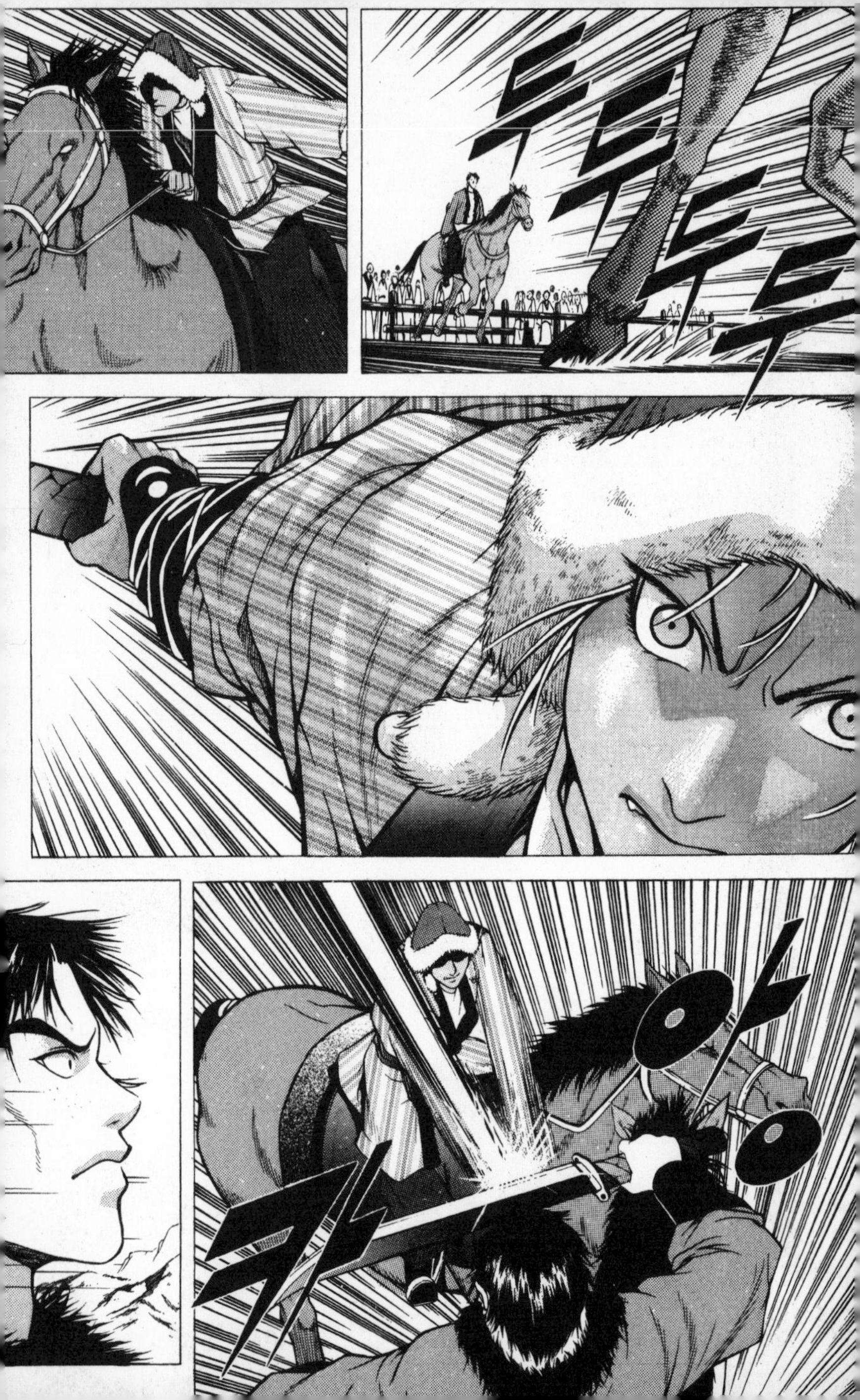

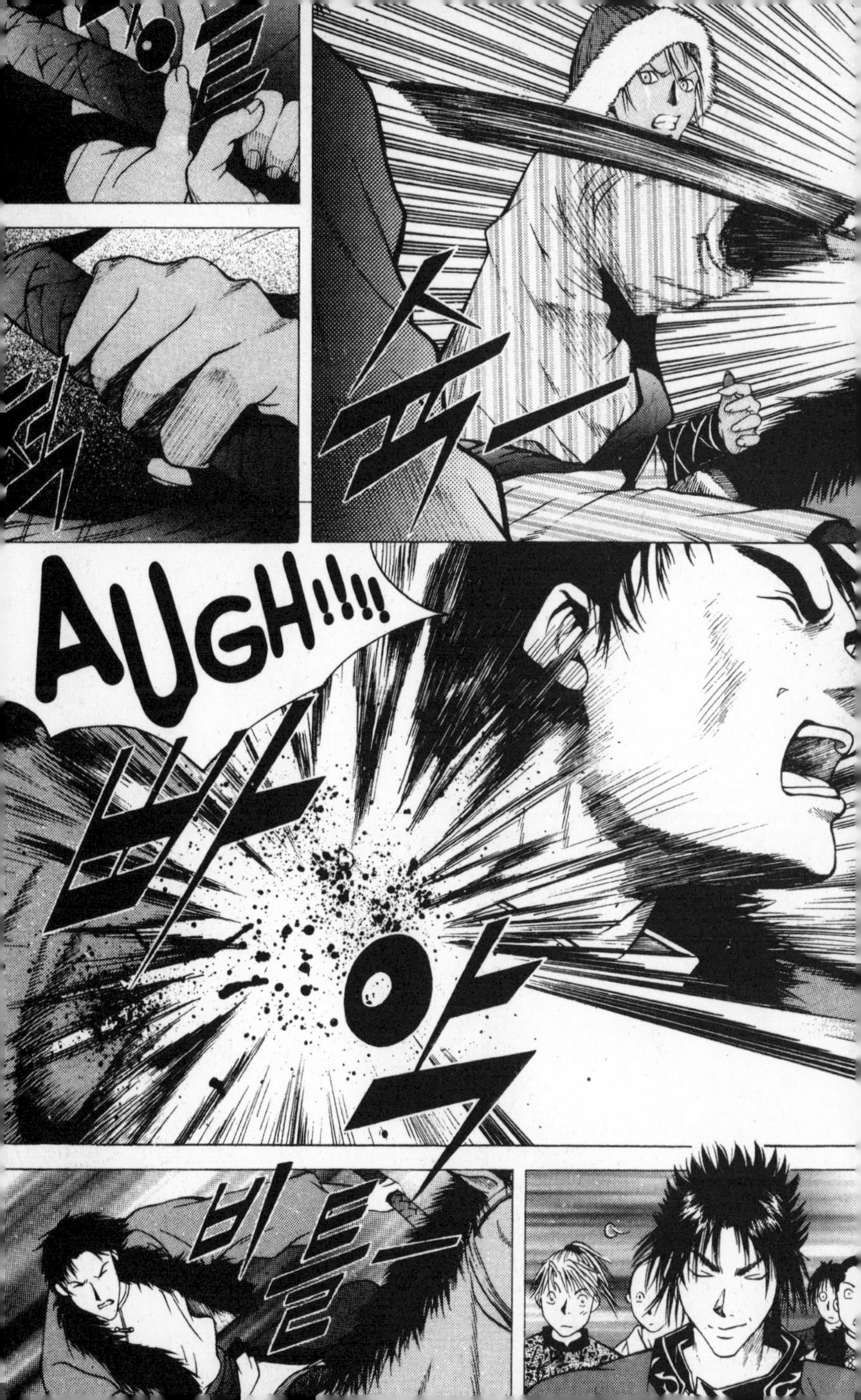
AUGH!!!!

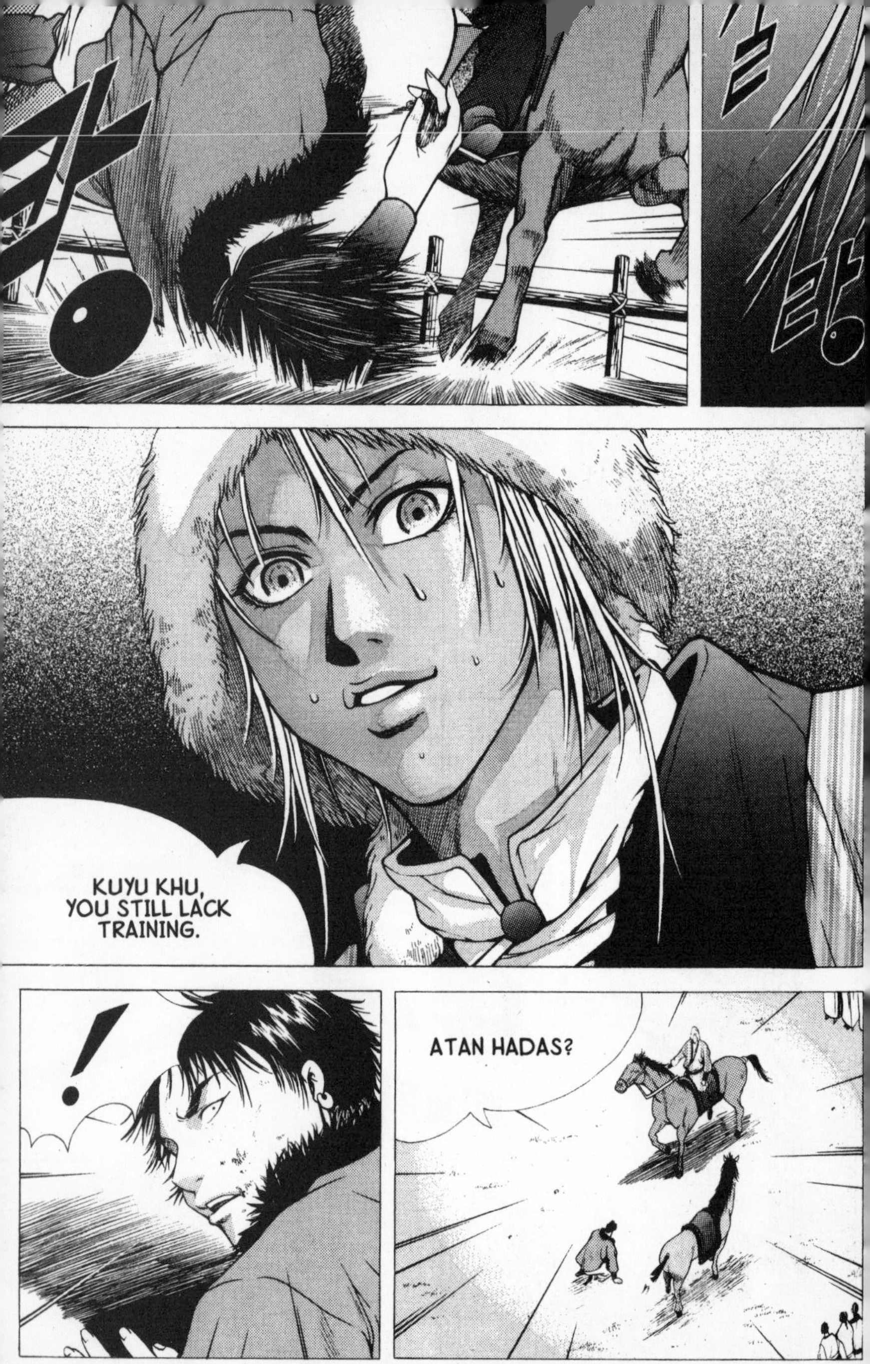
KUYU KHU, YOU STILL LACK TRAINING.
!
ATAN HADAS?

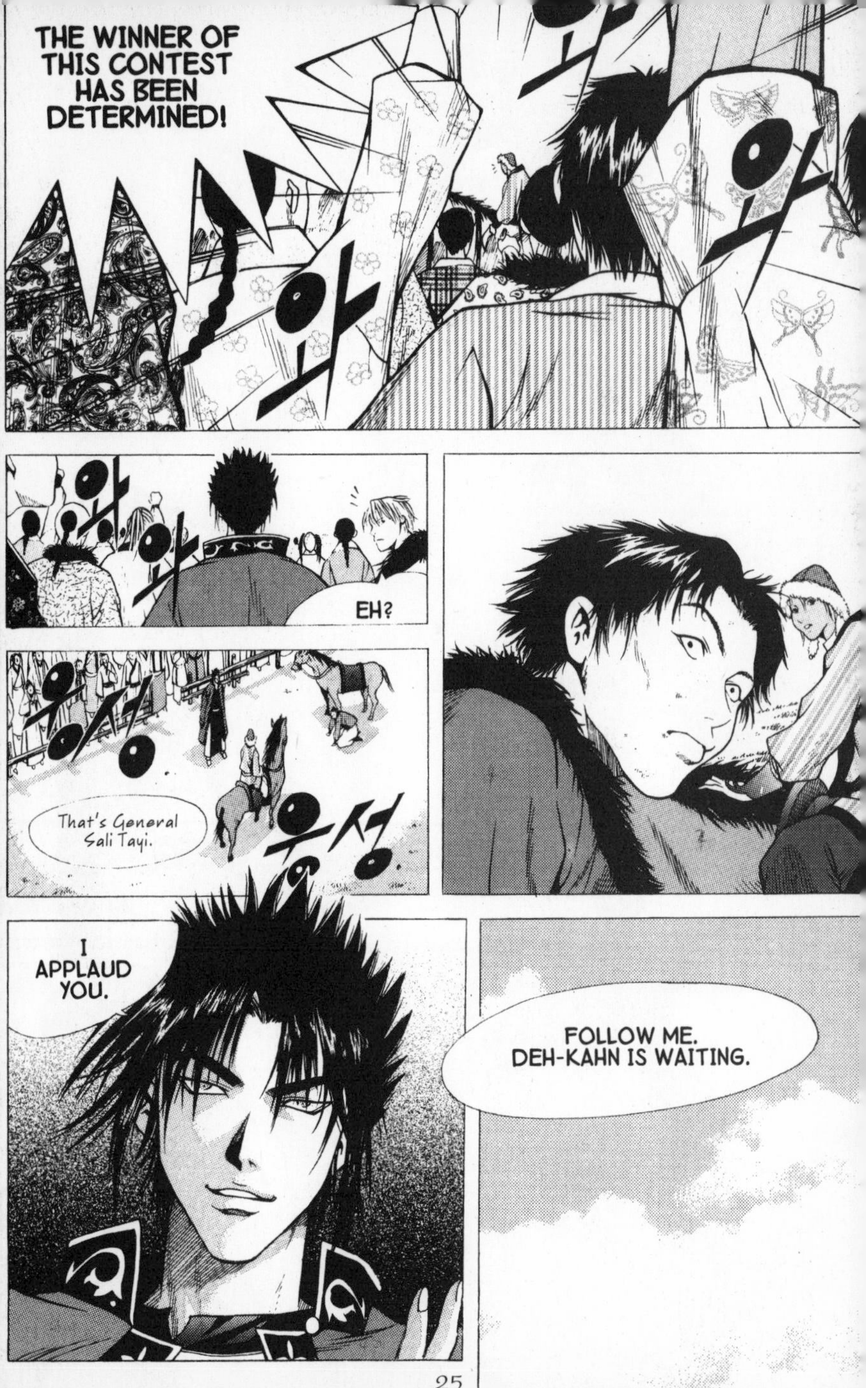
THE WINNER OF THIS CONTEST HAS BEEN DETERMINED!
EH?
That's General Sali Tayi.
I APPLAUD YOU.
FOLLOW ME. DEH-KAHN IS WAITING.

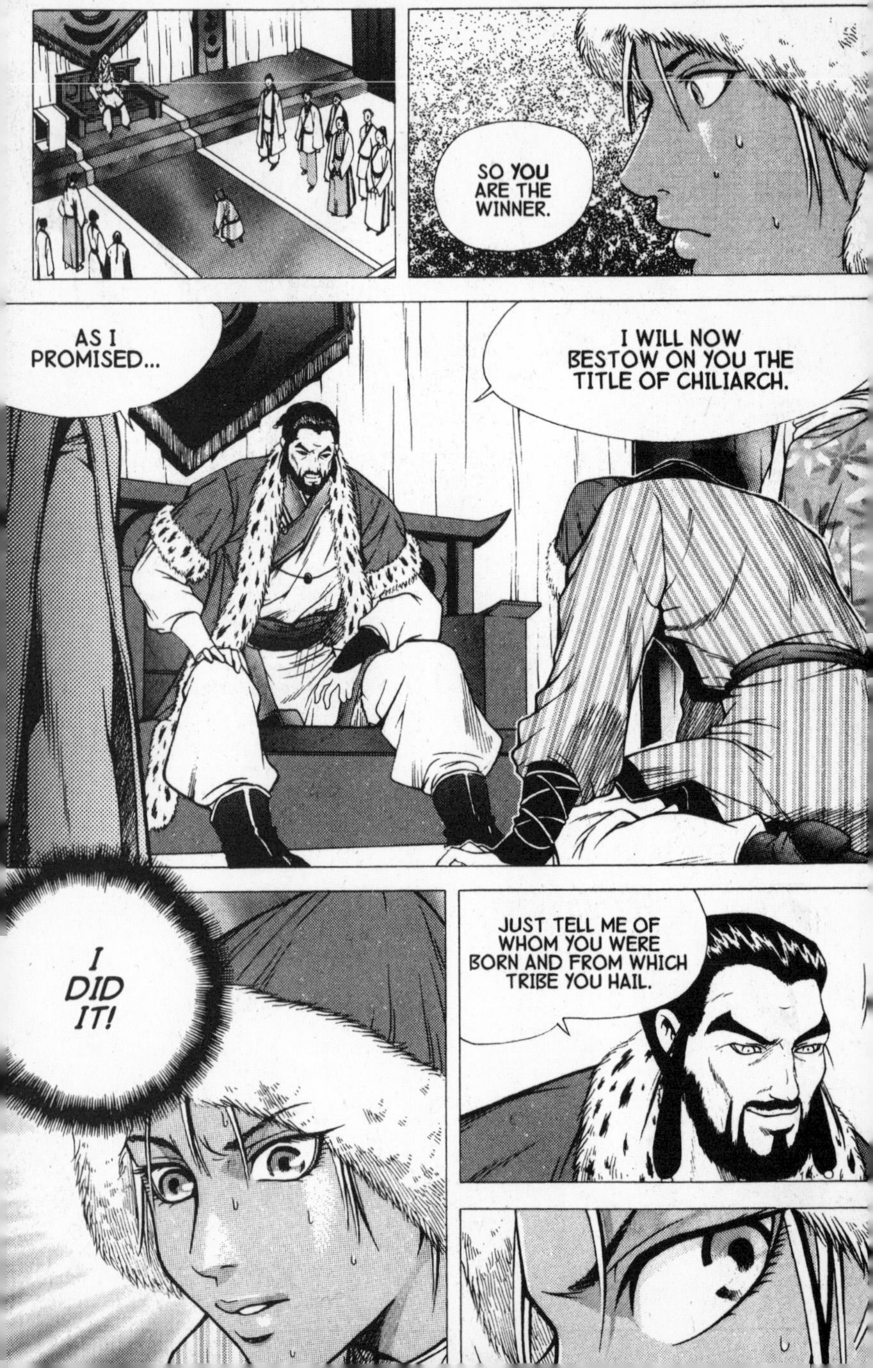
SO YOU ARE THE WINNER.
AS I PROMISED...
I WILL NOW BESTOW ON YOU THE TITLE OF CHILIARCH.
I DID IT!
JUST TELL ME OF WHOM YOU WERE BORN AND FROM WHICH TRIBE YOU HAIL.

FATHER!

FATHER, I AM SORRY.

I...MY NAME...

KUYU KHU?

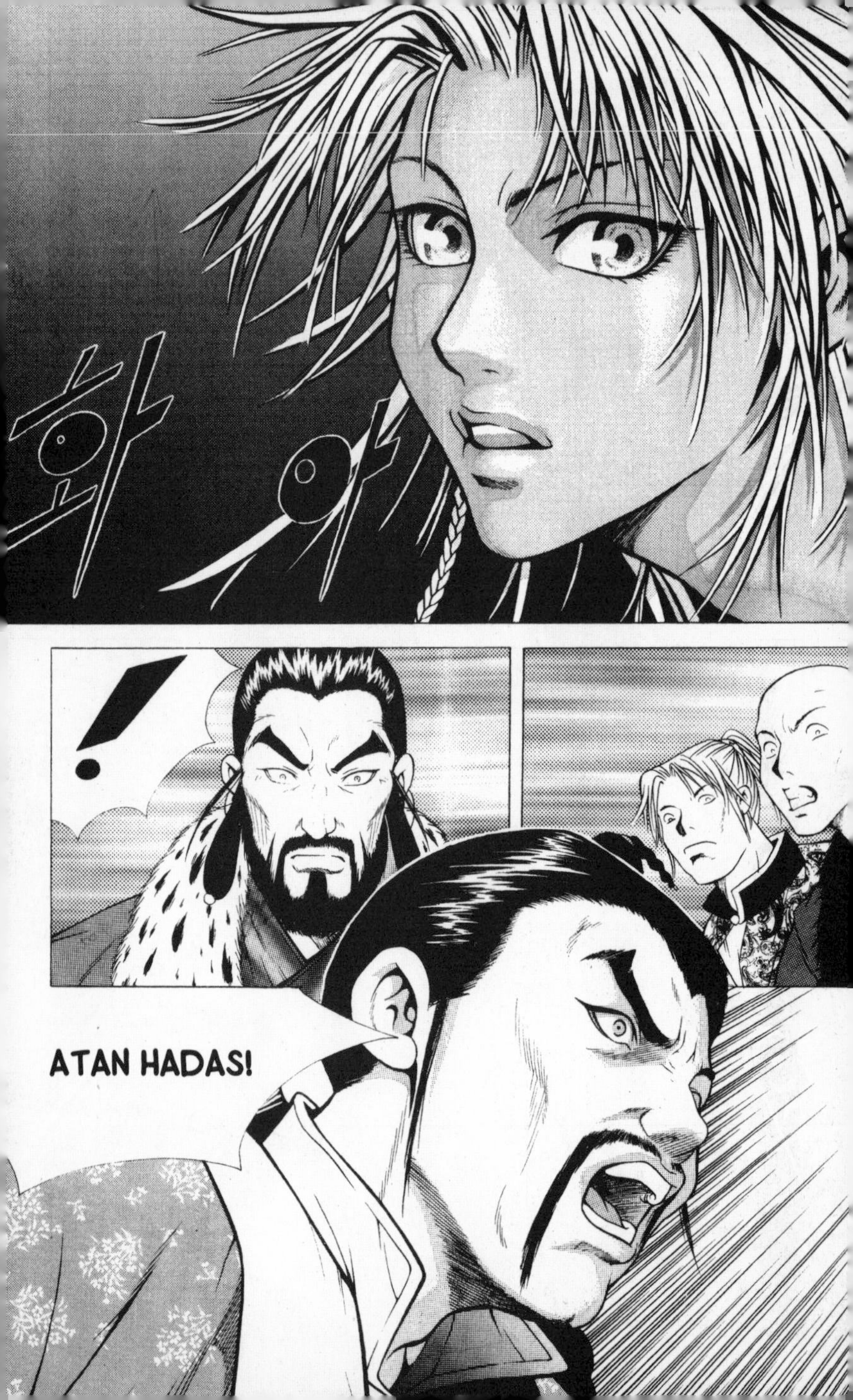
화악
!
ATAN HADAS!

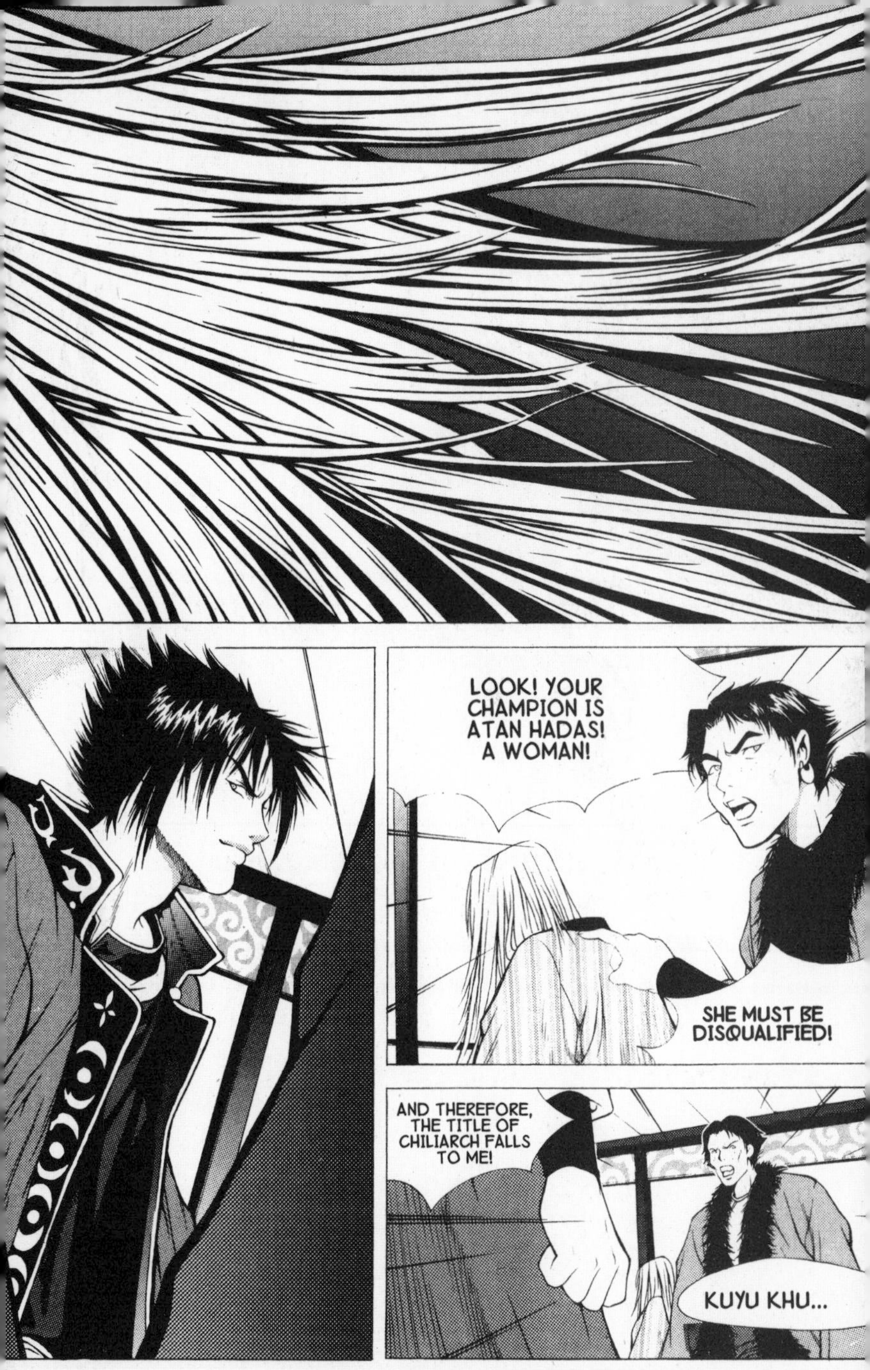
LOOK! YOUR CHAMPION IS ATAN HADAS! A WOMAN!
SHE MUST BE DISQUALIFIED!
AND THEREFORE, THE TITLE OF CHILIARCH FALLS TO ME!
KUYU KHU...

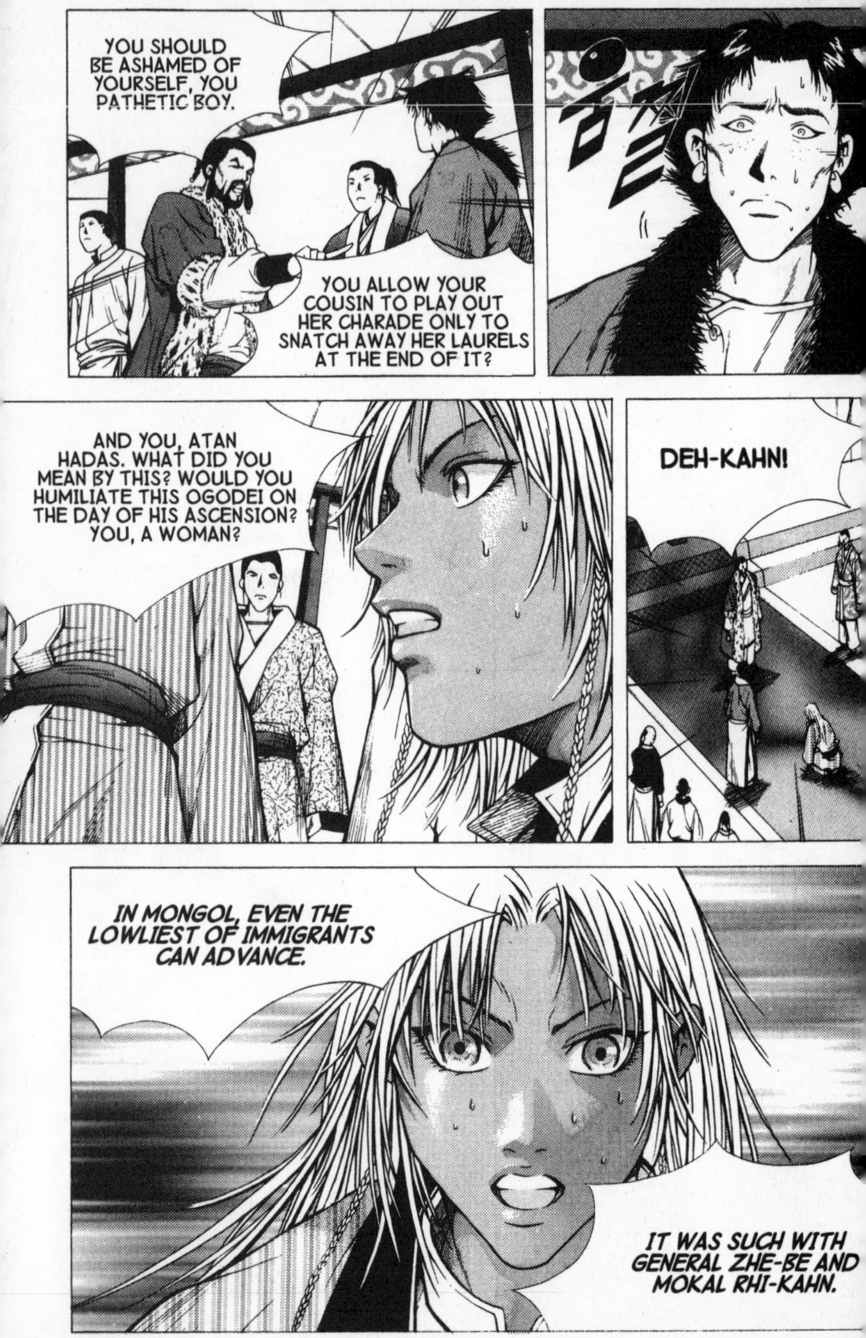
YOU SHOULD BE ASHAMED OF YOURSELF, YOU PATHETIC BOY.
YOU ALLOW YOUR COUSIN TO PLAY OUT HER CHARADE ONLY TO SNATCH AWAY HER LAURELS AT THE END OF IT?
AND YOU, ATAN HADAS. WHAT DID YOU MEAN BY THIS? WOULD YOU HUMILIATE THIS OGODEI ON THE DAY OF HIS ASCENSION? YOU, A WOMAN?
DEH-KAHN!
IN MONGOL, EVEN THE LOWLIEST OF IMMIGRANTS CAN ADVANCE.
IT WAS SUCH WITH GENERAL ZHE-BE AND MOKAL RHI-KAHN.

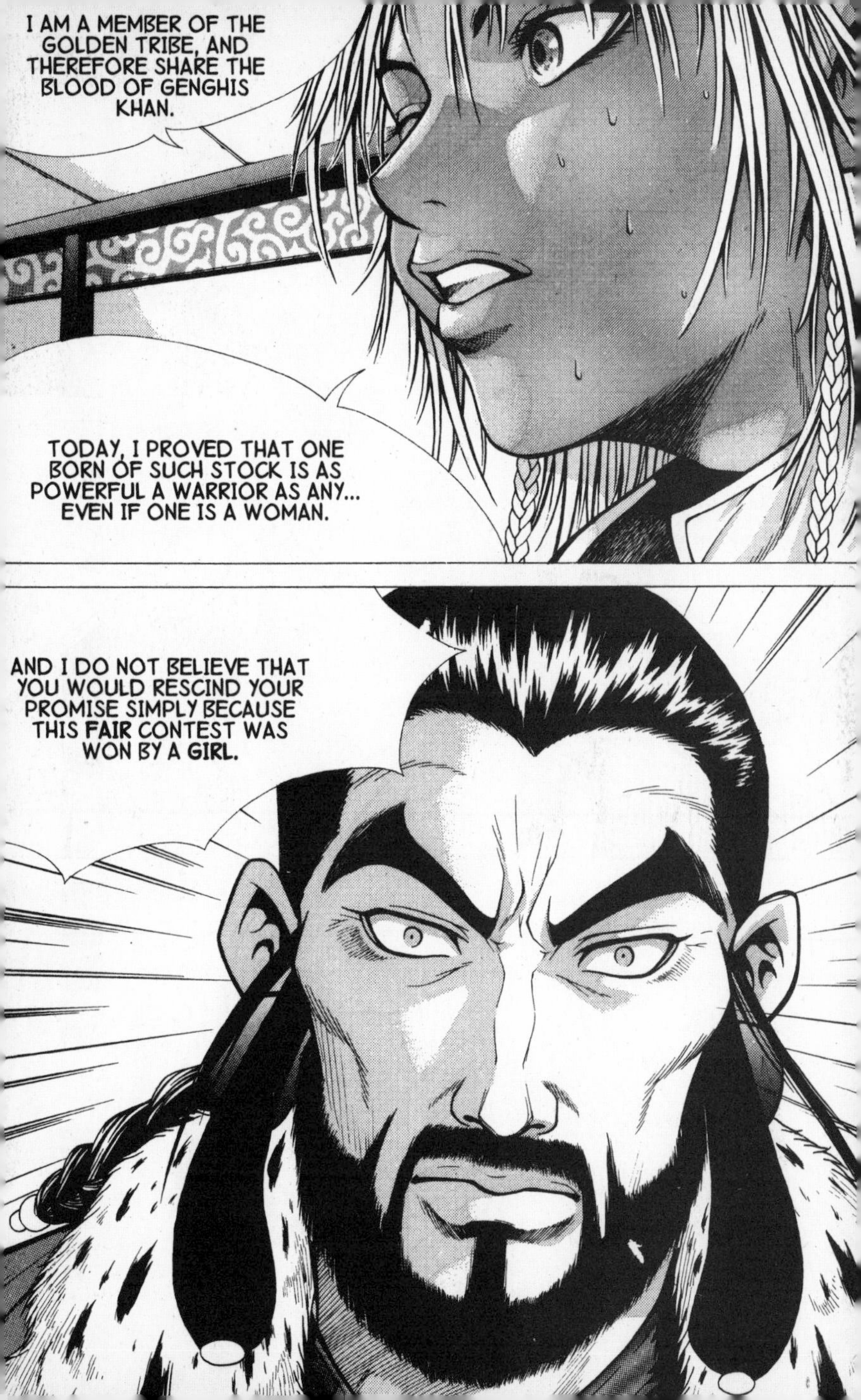
I AM A MEMBER OF THE GOLDEN TRIBE, AND THEREFORE SHARE THE BLOOD OF GENGHIS KHAN.
TODAY, I PROVED THAT ONE BORN OF SUCH STOCK IS AS POWERFUL A WARRIOR AS ANY... EVEN IF ONE IS A WOMAN.
AND I DO NOT BELIEVE THAT YOU WOULD RESCIND YOUR PROMISE SIMPLY BECAUSE THIS FAIR CONTEST WAS WON BY A GIRL.

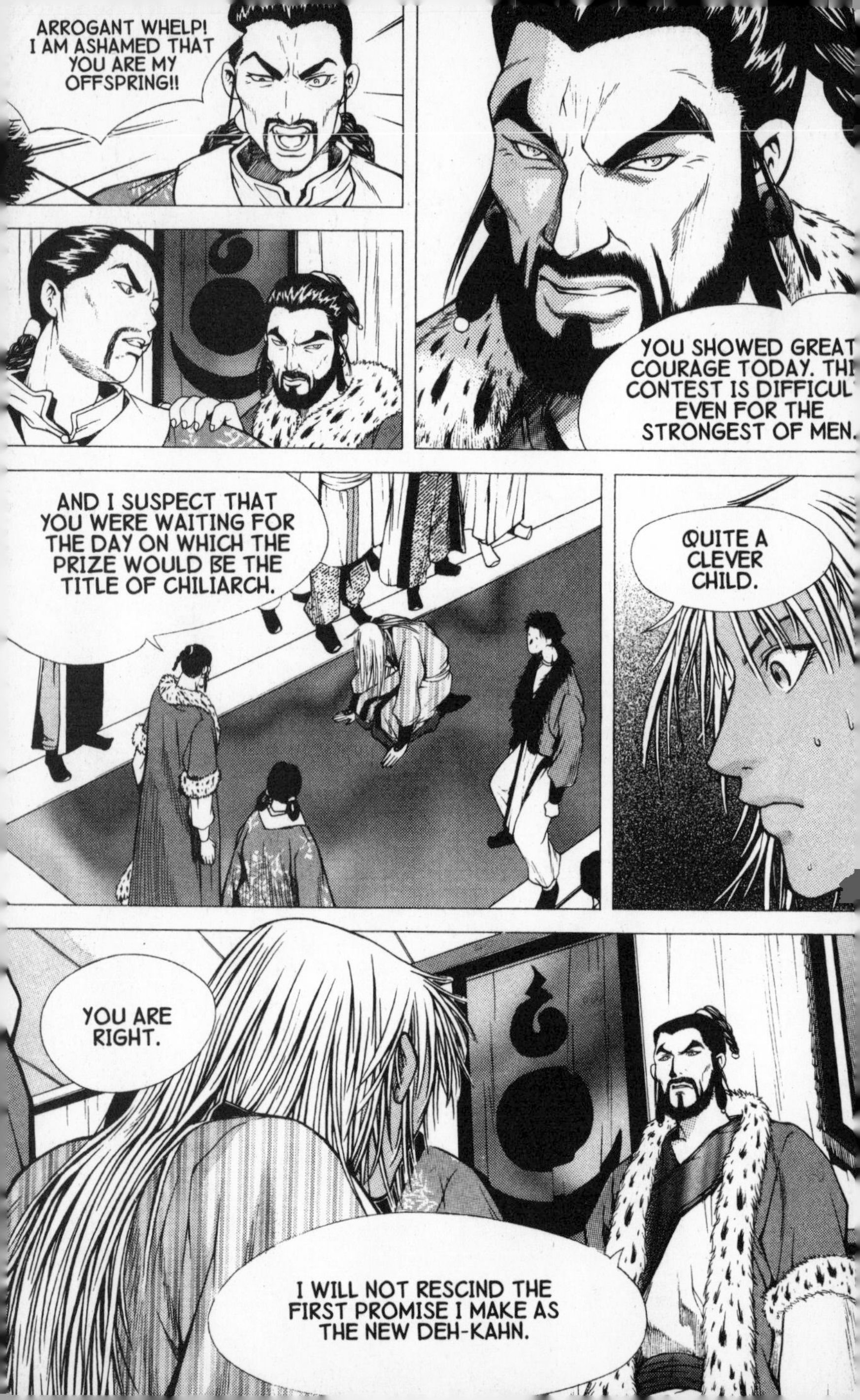
ARROGANT WHELP! I AM ASHAMED THAT YOU ARE MY OFFSPRING!!
YOU SHOWED GREAT COURAGE TODAY. THI CONTEST IS DIFFICUL EVEN FOR THE STRONGEST OF MEN.
AND I SUSPECT THAT YOU WERE WAITING FOR THE DAY ON WHICH THE PRIZE WOULD BE THE TITLE OF CHILIARCH.
QUITE A CLEVER CHILD.
YOU ARE RIGHT.
I WILL NOT RESCIND THE FIRST PROMISE I MAKE AS THE NEW DEH-KAHN.

STILL, I AM YOUR UNCLE. AND I FEAR SENDING MY PRECIOUS NIECE INTO THE FIELD OF BATTLE.

IF YOU WERE TO FIND A PARTNER, I WOULD NOT OBJECT.

DEH-KAHN!

THE GENERAL OF THE KORYO CONQUEST...

AND NEITHER SHOULD YOU, ELDER BROTHER.

SALI TAYI, COME FORWARD.

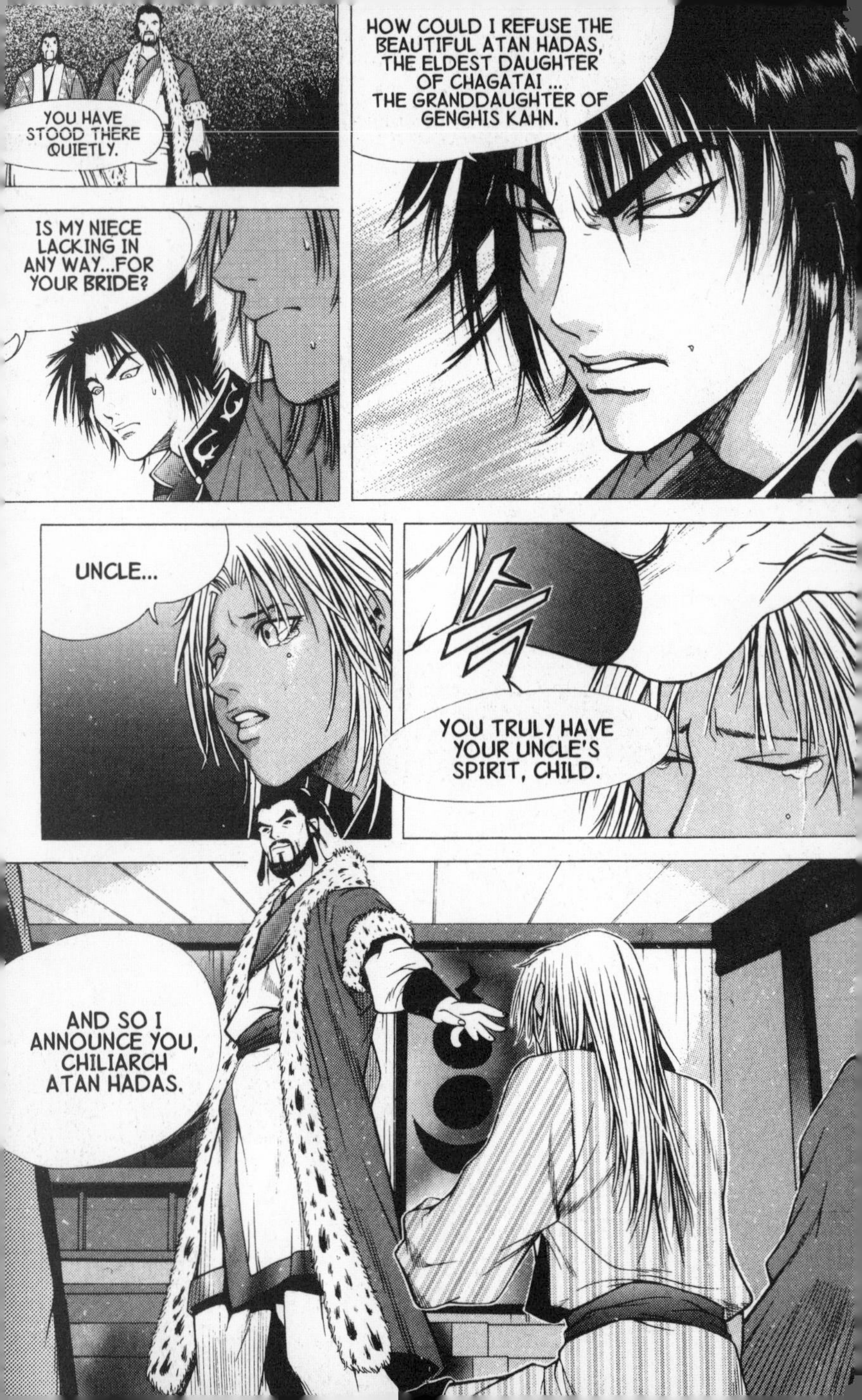
YOU HAVE STOOD THERE QUIETLY.
IS MY NIECE LACKING IN ANY WAY...FOR YOUR BRIDE?
HOW COULD I REFUSE THE BEAUTIFUL ATAN HADAS, THE ELDEST DAUGHTER OF CHAGATAI ... THE GRANDDAUGHTER OF GENGHIS KAHN.
UNCLE...
YOU TRULY HAVE YOUR UNCLE'S SPIRIT, CHILD.
AND SO I ANNOUNCE YOU, CHILIARCH ATAN HADAS.

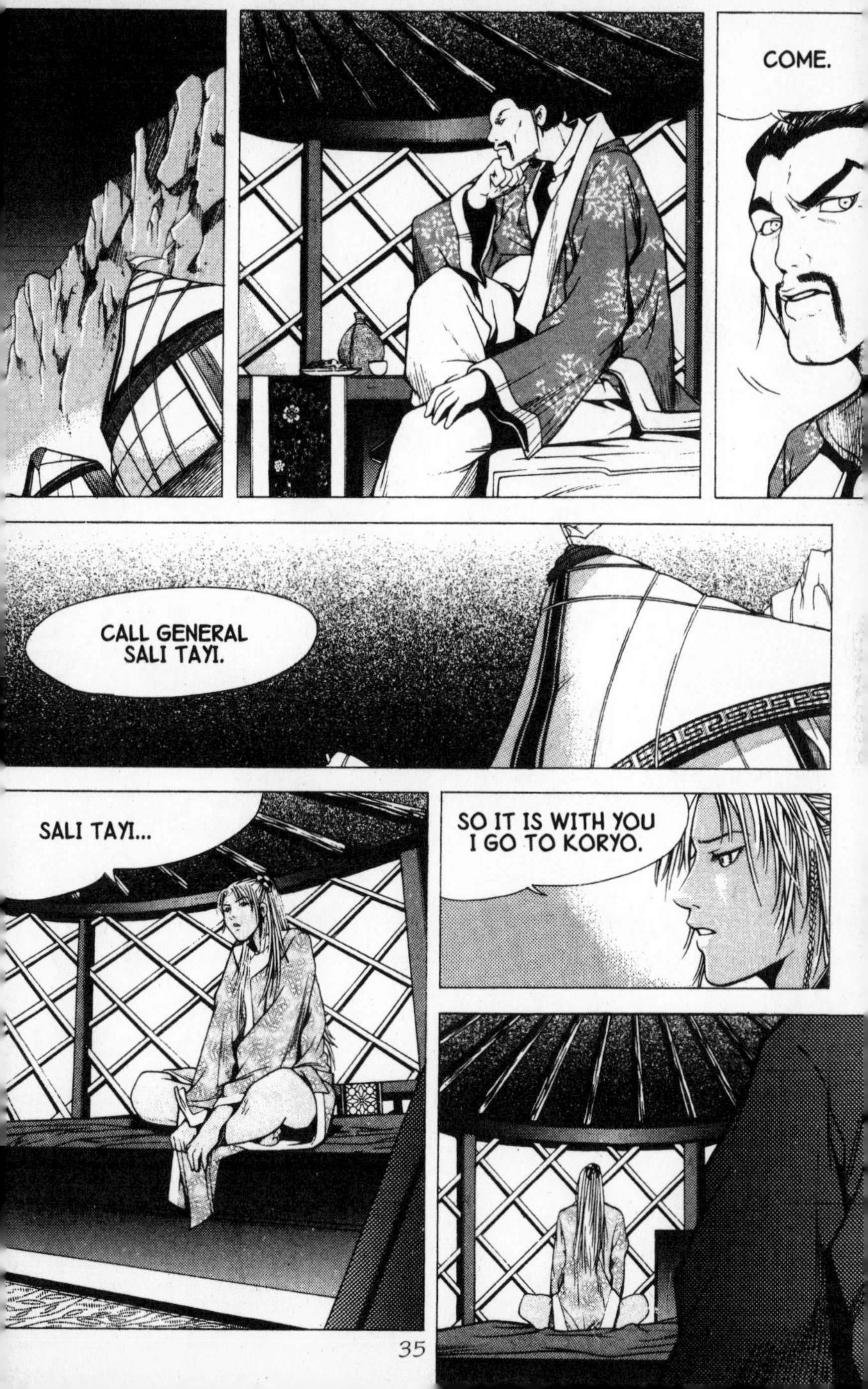
COME.
CALL GENERAL SALI TAYI.
SALI TAYI...
SO IT IS WITH YOU I GO TO KORYO.

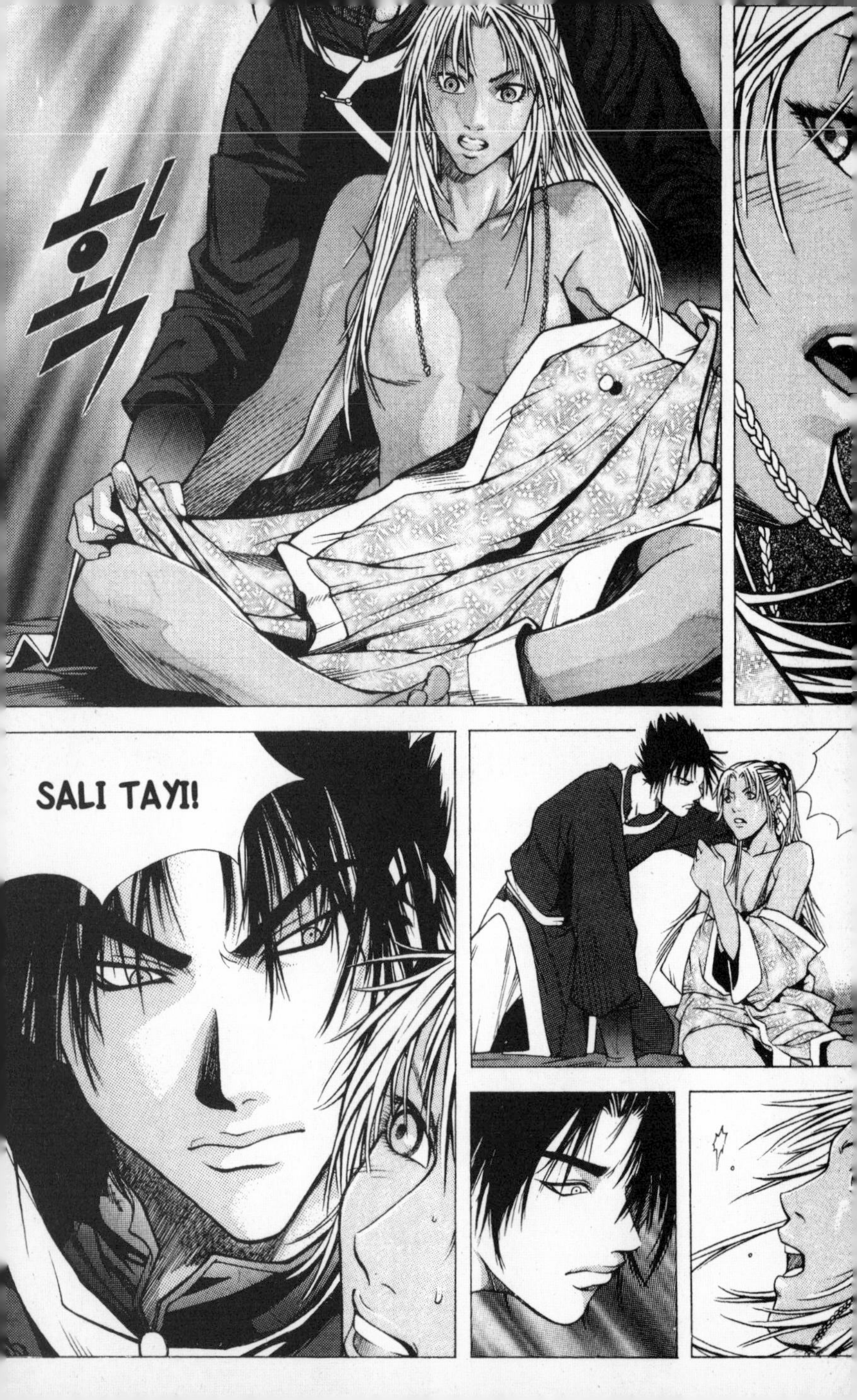
SALI TAYI!

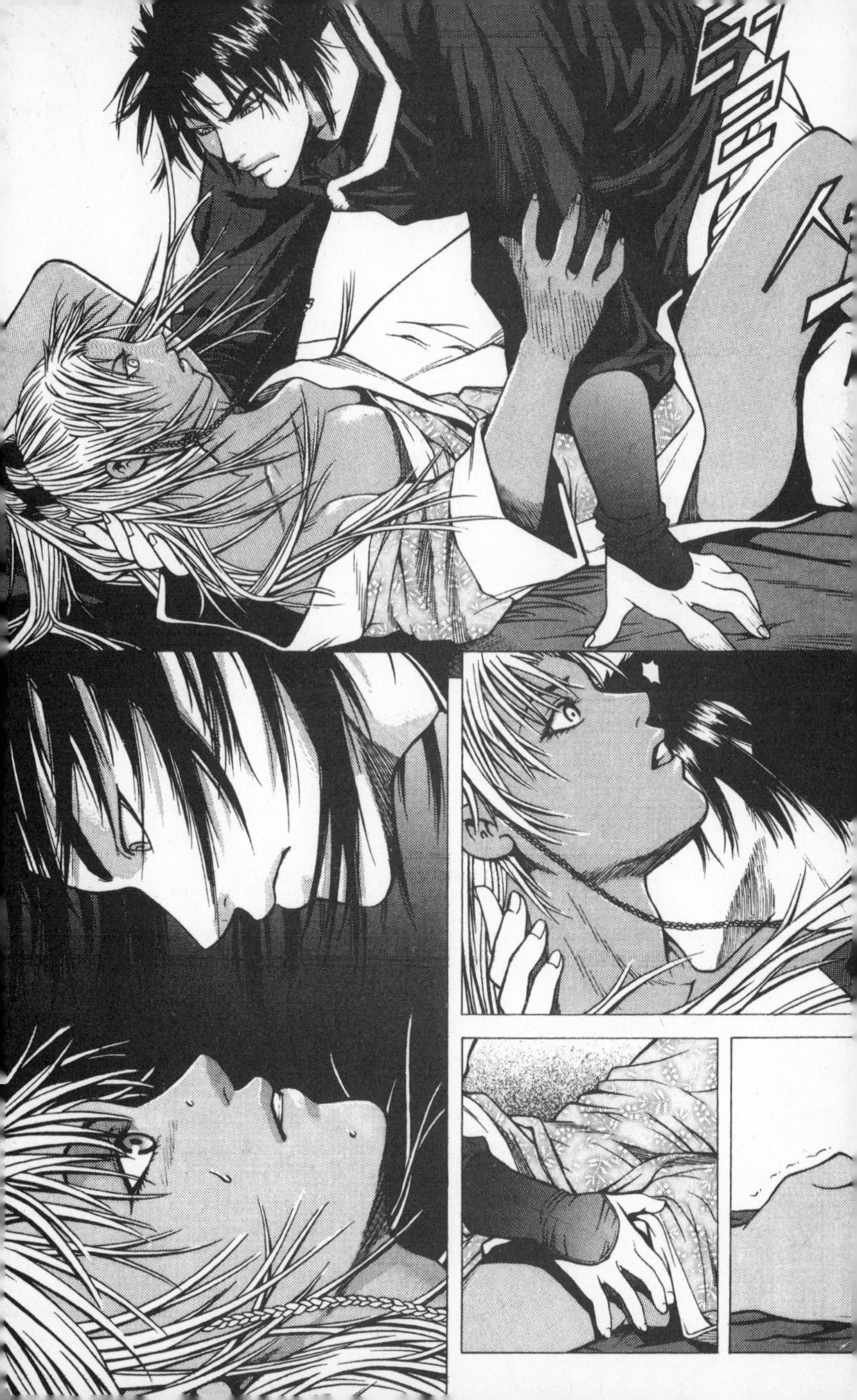

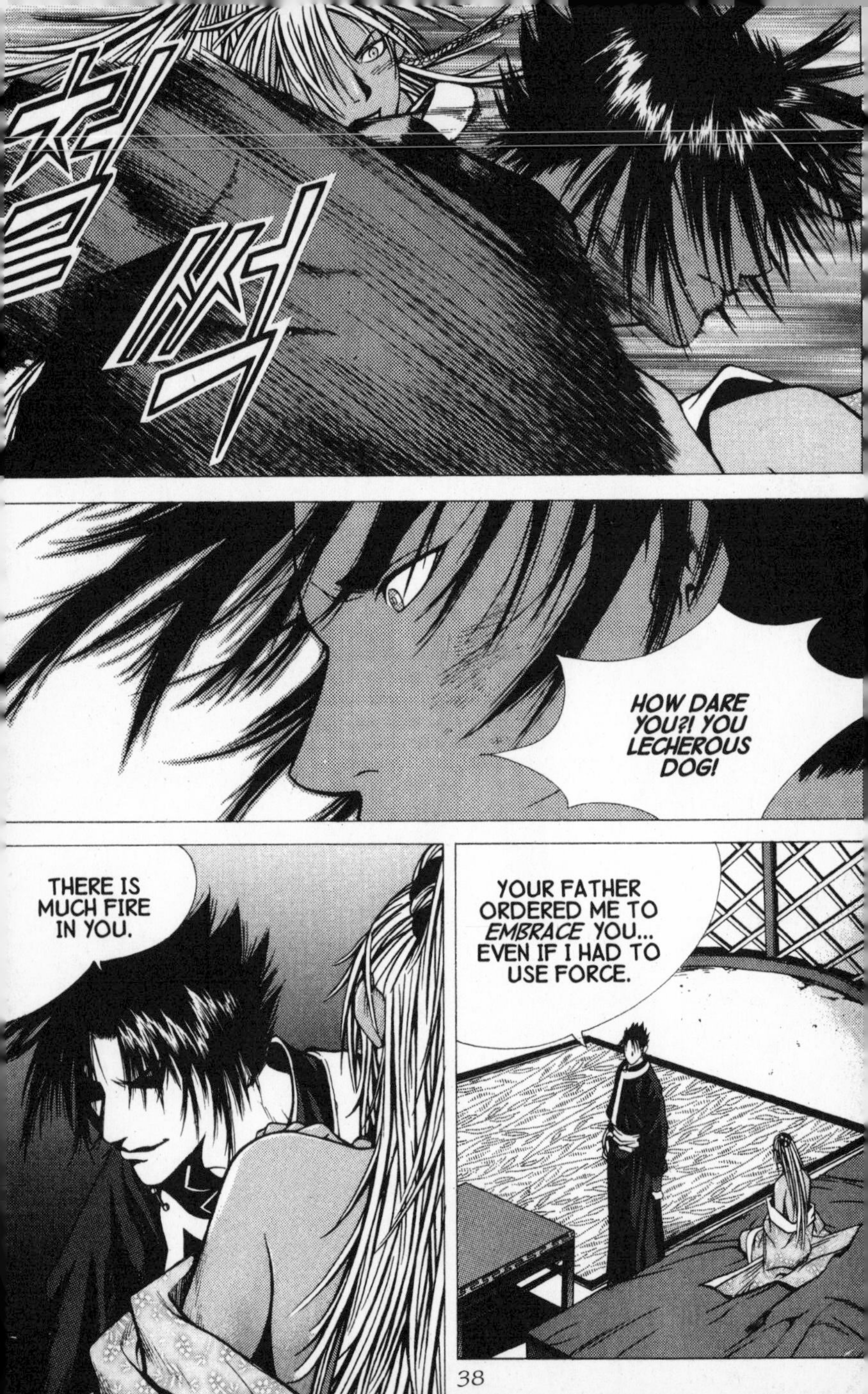
HOW DARE YOU?! YOU LECHEROUS DOG!
THERE IS MUCH FIRE IN YOU.
YOUR FATHER ORDERED ME TO *EMBRACE* YOU... EVEN IF I HAD TO USE FORCE.

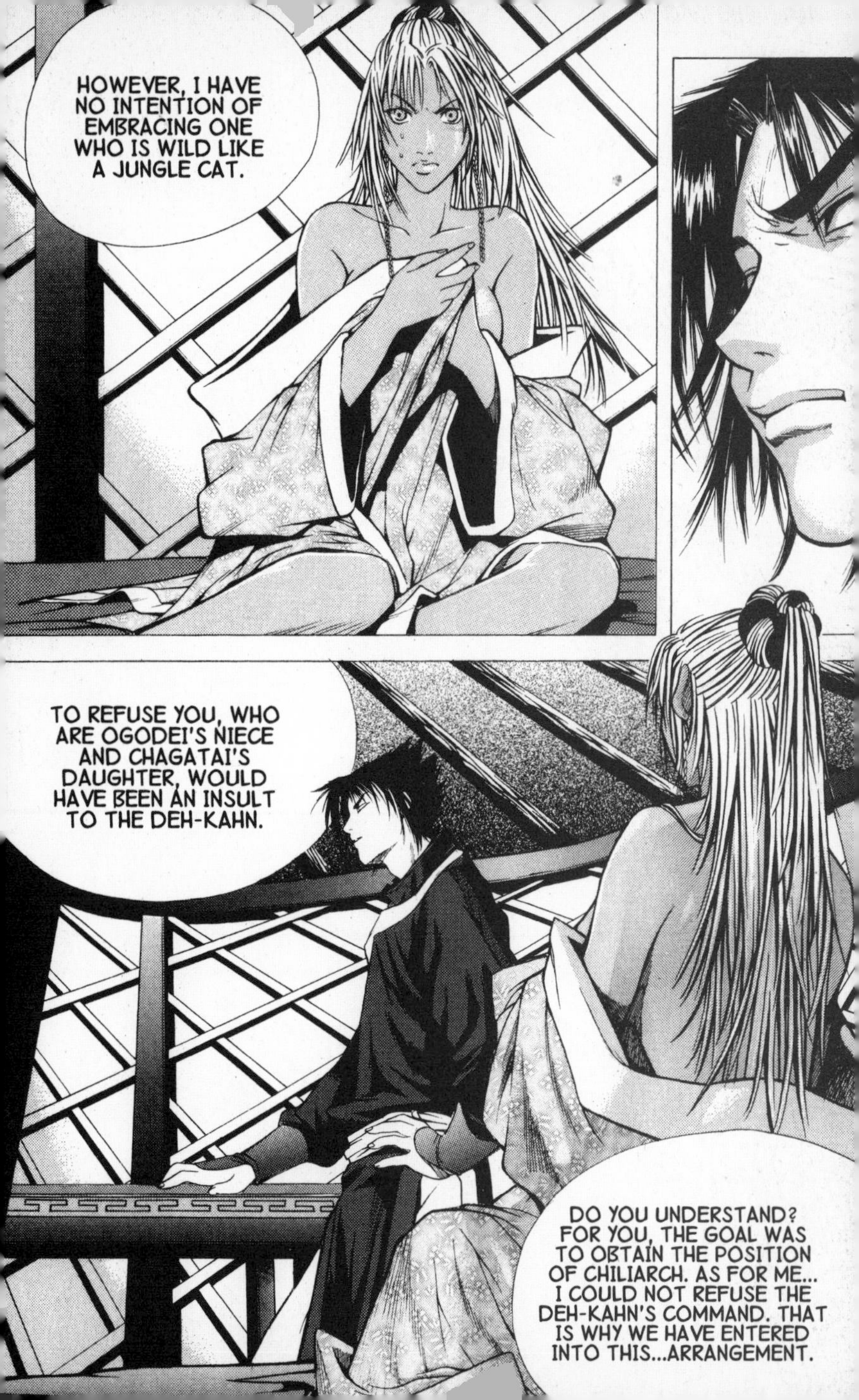
HOWEVER, I HAVE NO INTENTION OF EMBRACING ONE WHO IS WILD LIKE A JUNGLE CAT.
TO REFUSE YOU, WHO ARE OGODEI'S NIECE AND CHAGATAI'S DAUGHTER, WOULD HAVE BEEN AN INSULT TO THE DEH-KAHN.
DO YOU UNDERSTAND? FOR YOU, THE GOAL WAS TO OBTAIN THE POSITION OF CHILIARCH. AS FOR ME... I COULD NOT REFUSE THE DEH-KAHN'S COMMAND. THAT IS WHY WE HAVE ENTERED INTO THIS...ARRANGEMENT.

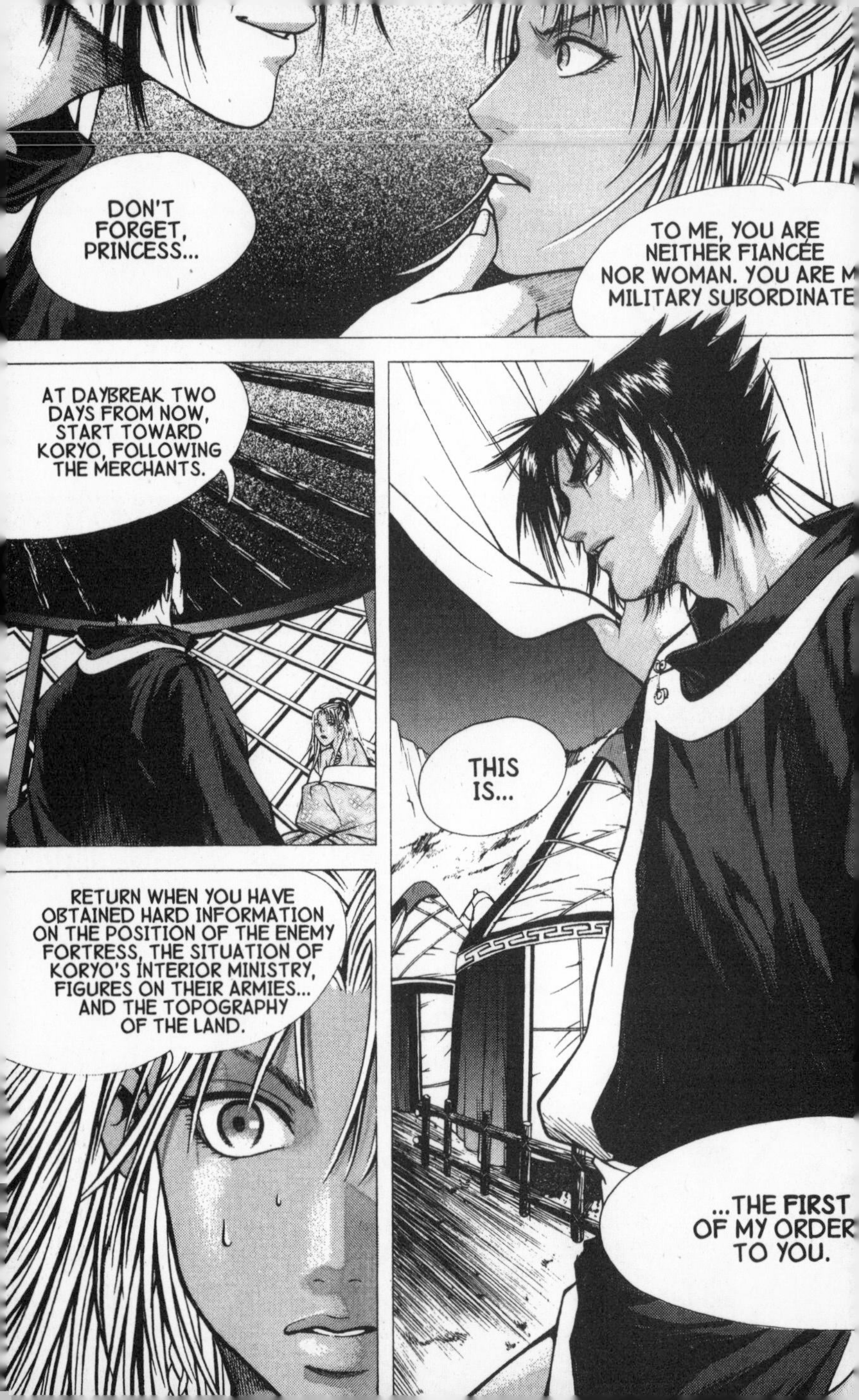
DON'T FORGET, PRINCESS...
TO ME, YOU ARE NEITHER FIANCÉE NOR WOMAN. YOU ARE M MILITARY SUBORDINATE
AT DAYBREAK TWO DAYS FROM NOW, START TOWARD KORYO, FOLLOWING THE MERCHANTS.
RETURN WHEN YOU HAVE OBTAINED HARD INFORMATION ON THE POSITION OF THE ENEMY FORTRESS, THE SITUATION OF KORYO'S INTERIOR MINISTRY, FIGURES ON THEIR ARMIES... AND THE TOPOGRAPHY OF THE LAND.
THIS IS...
...THE FIRST OF MY ORDER TO YOU.

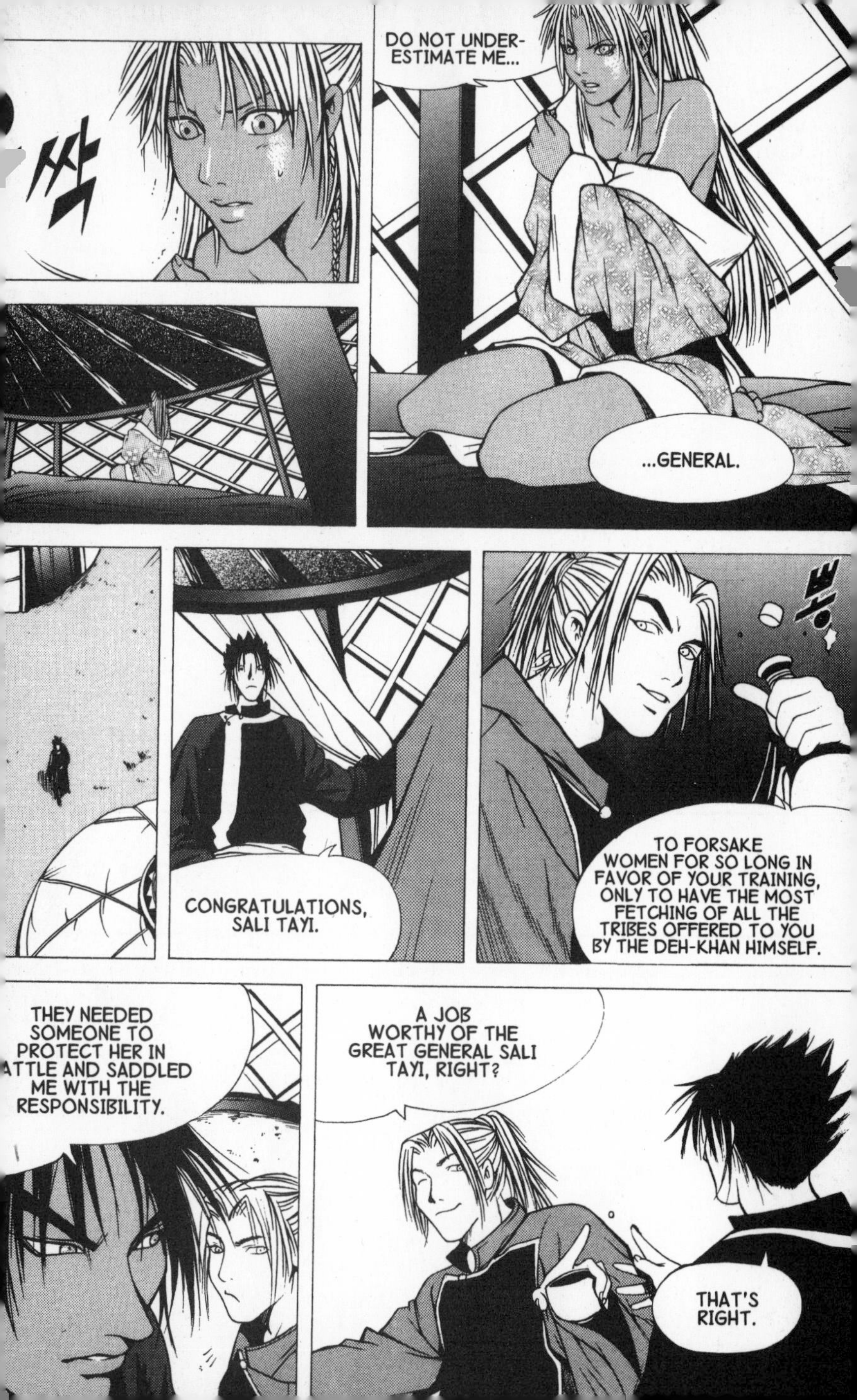
싹
DO NOT UNDER-ESTIMATE ME...
...GENERAL.
CONGRATULATIONS, SALI TAYI.
TO FORSAKE WOMEN FOR SO LONG IN FAVOR OF YOUR TRAINING, ONLY TO HAVE THE MOST FETCHING OF ALL THE TRIBES OFFERED TO YOU BY THE DEH-KHAN HIMSELF.
THEY NEEDED SOMEONE TO PROTECT HER IN ATTLE AND SADDLED ME WITH THE RESPONSIBILITY.
A JOB WORTHY OF THE GREAT GENERAL SALI TAYI, RIGHT?
THAT'S RIGHT.

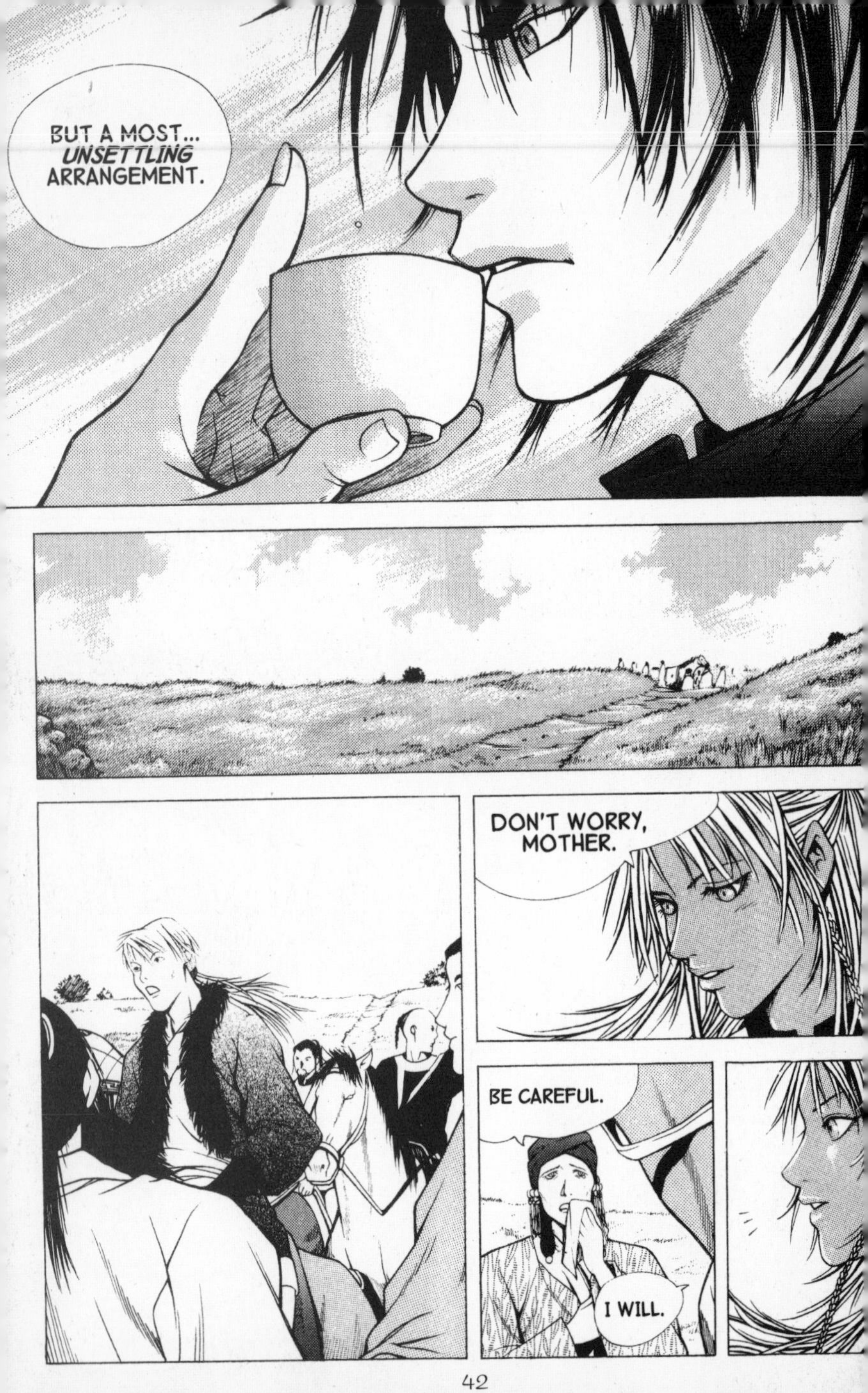
BUT A MOST... *UNSETTLING* ARRANGEMENT.
DON'T WORRY, MOTHER.
BE CAREFUL.
I WILL.

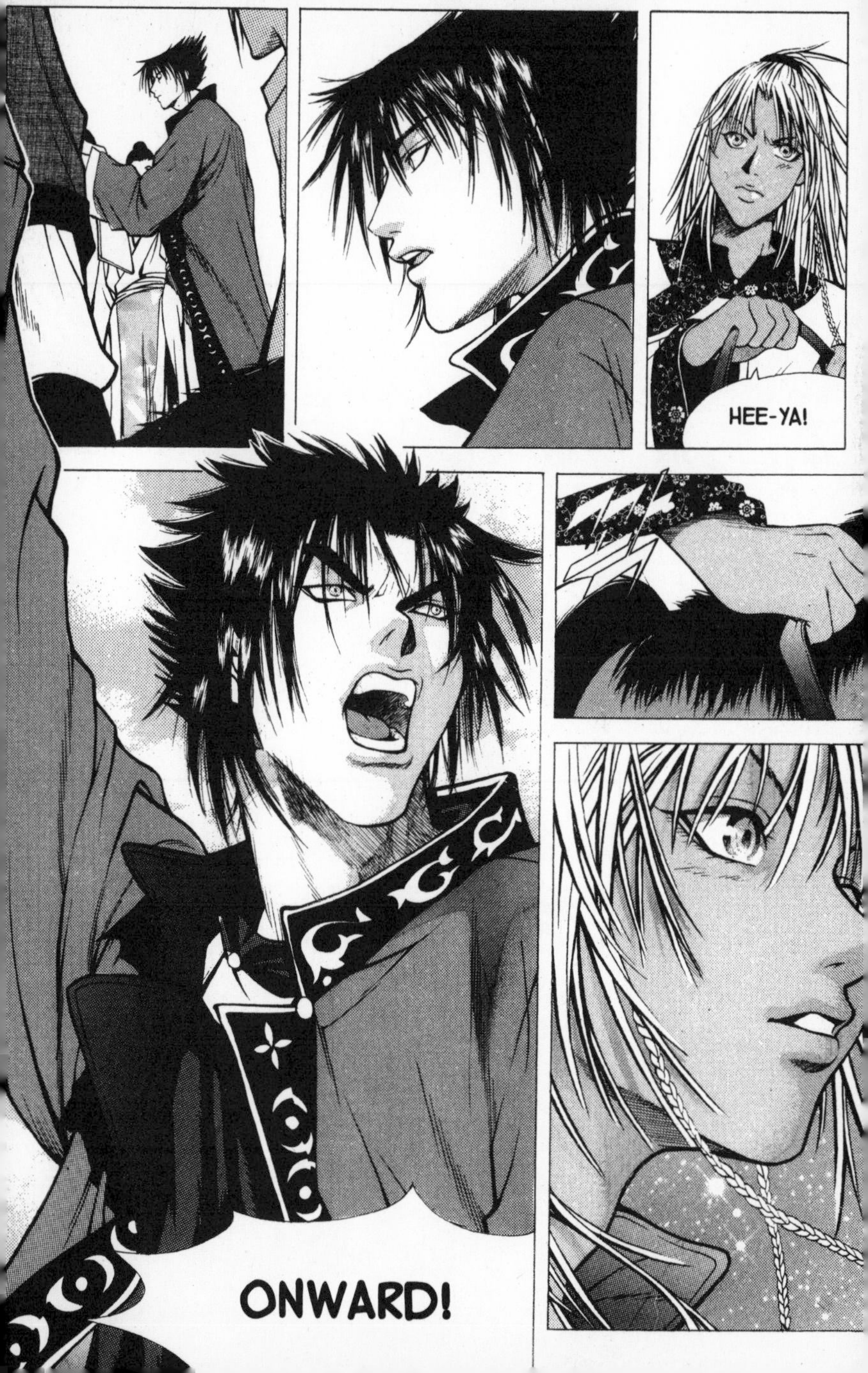
HEE-YA!
ONWARD!

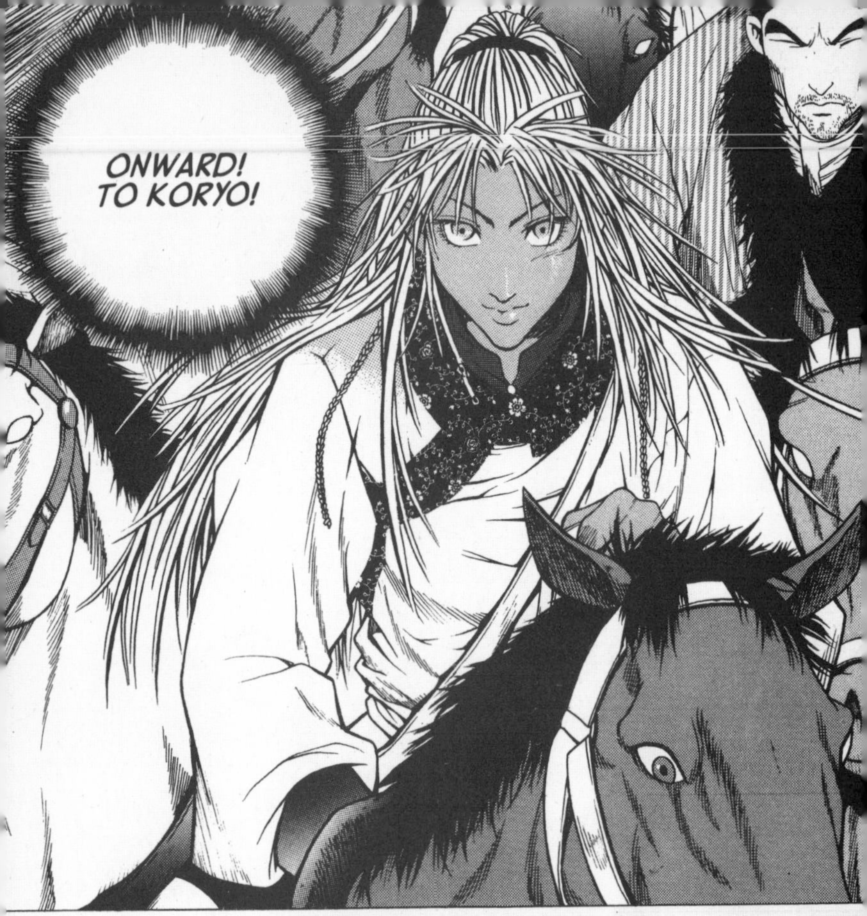
ONWARD! TO KORYO!

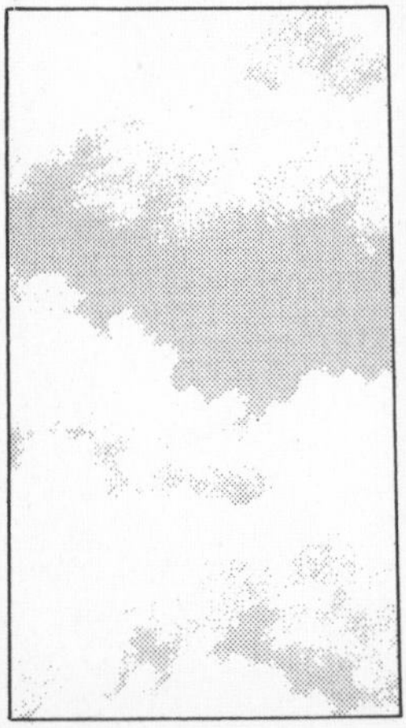

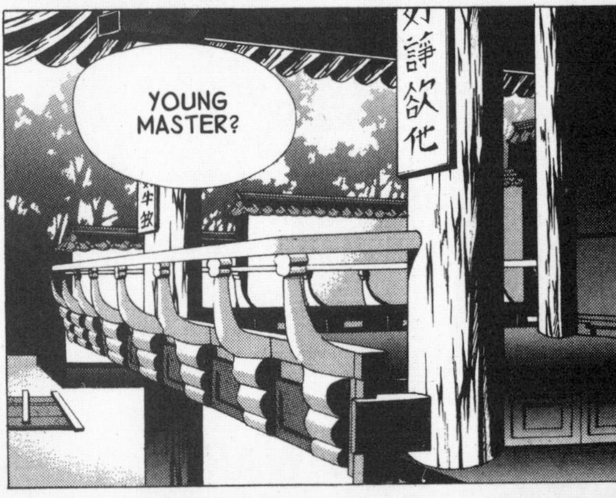
YOUNG MASTER?

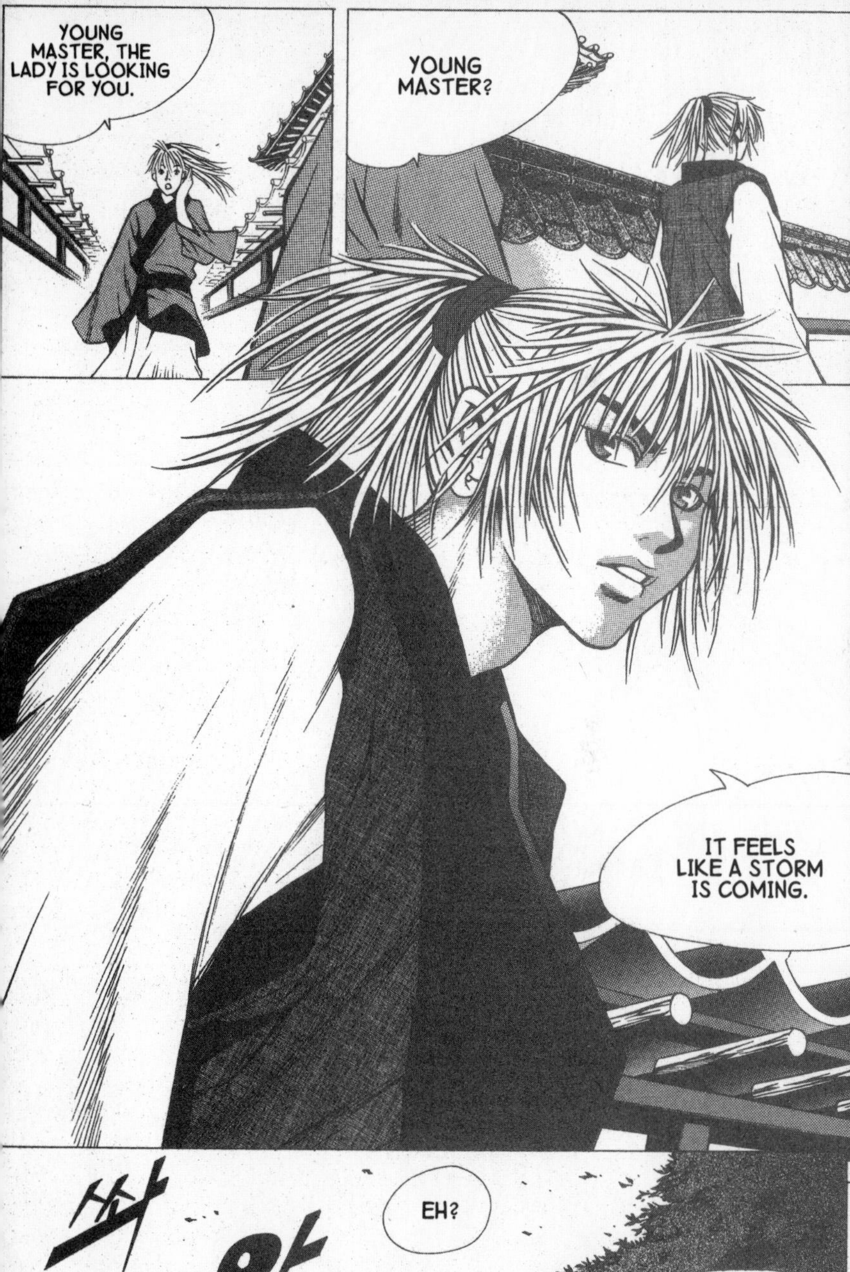
YOUNG MASTER, THE LADY IS LOOKING FOR YOU.
YOUNG MASTER?
IT FEELS LIKE A STORM IS COMING.
쏴
EH?
아

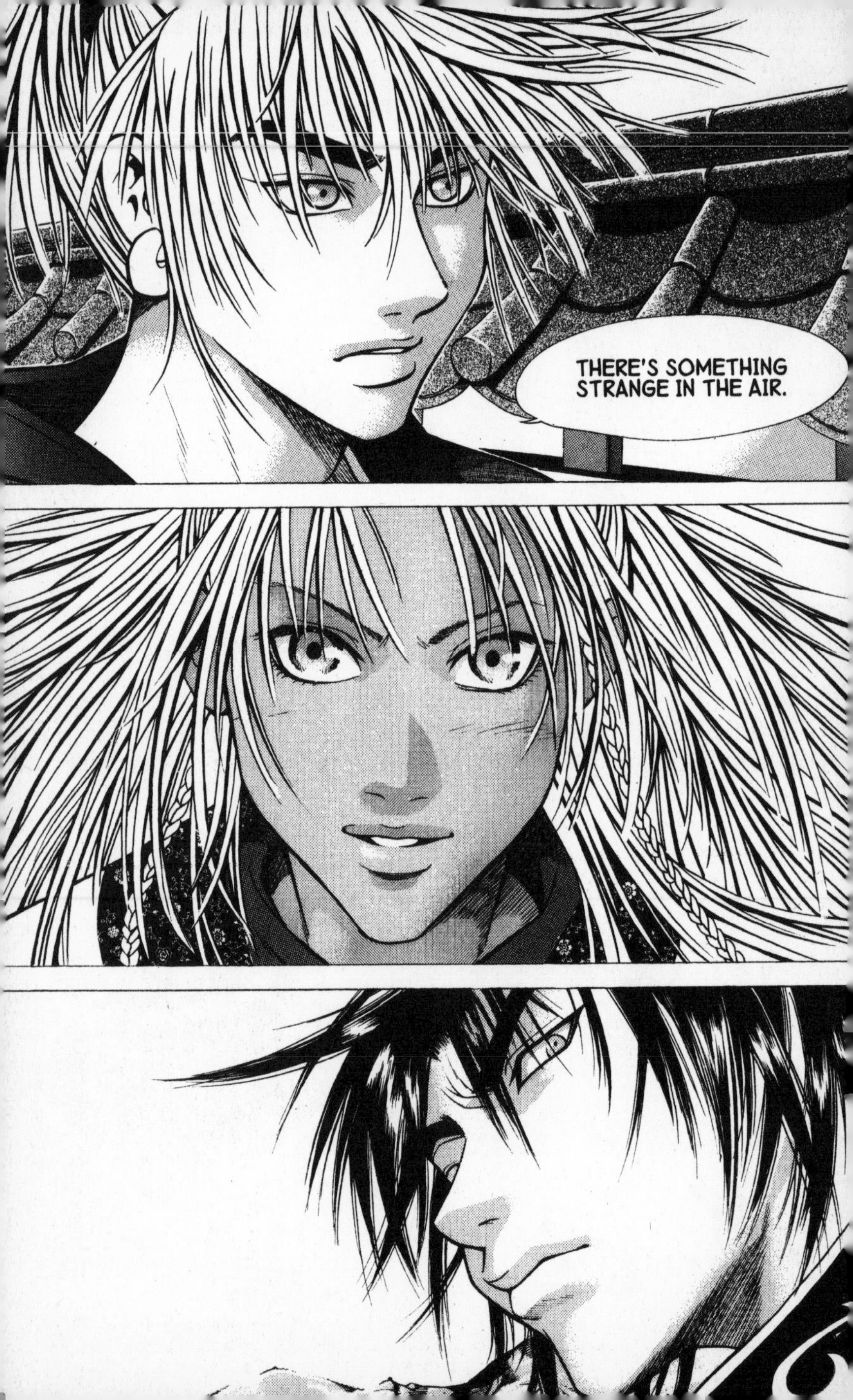
THERE'S SOMETHING STRANGE IN THE AIR.

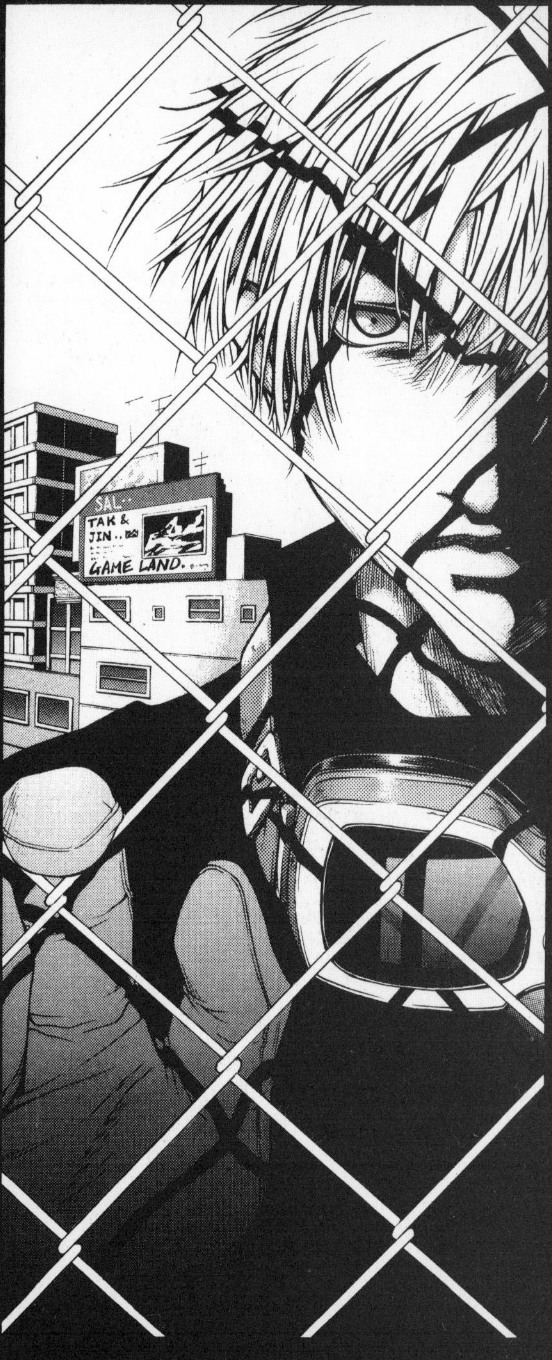
TAK &
JIN ..
GAME LAND.

Chapter 7
A Calling

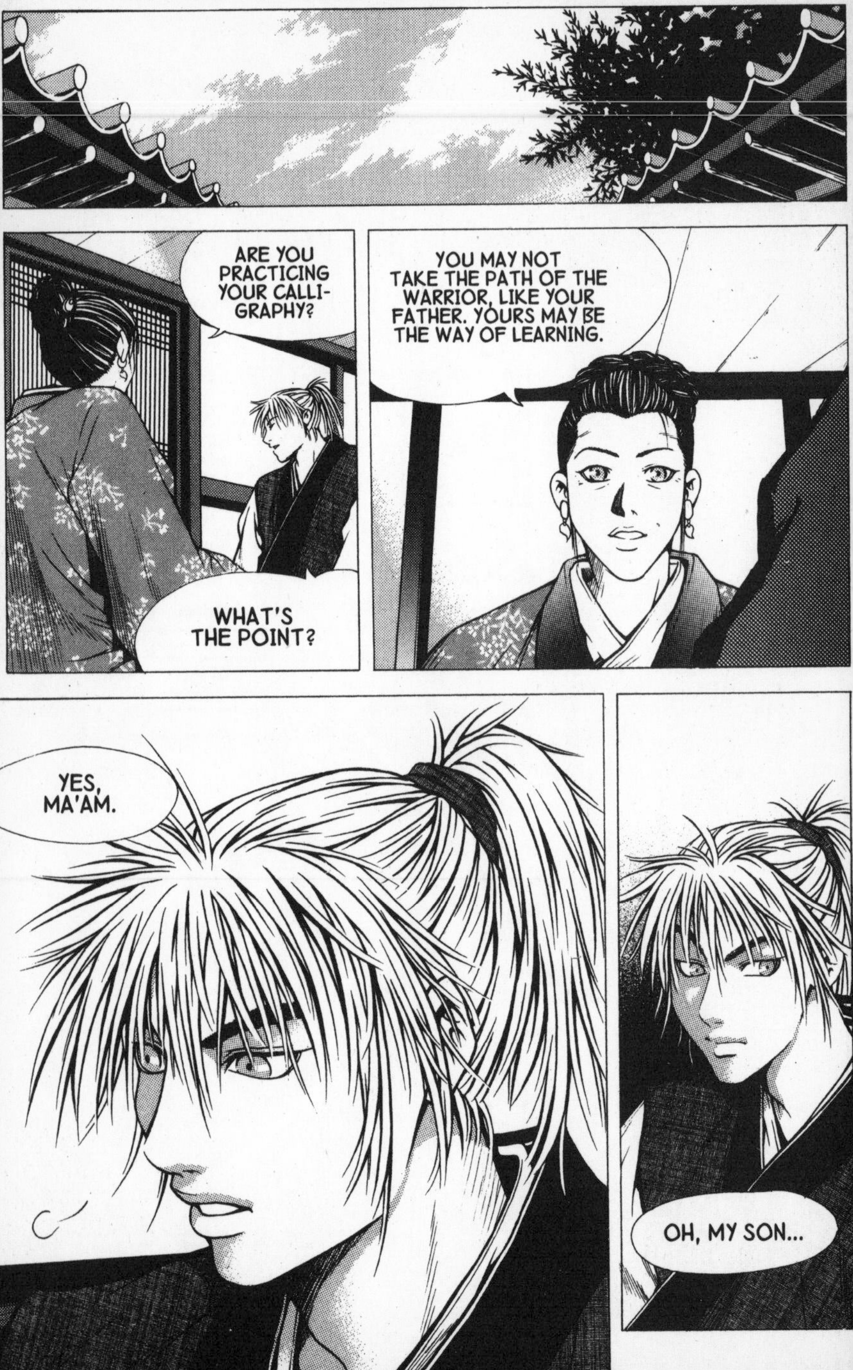
ARE YOU PRACTICING YOUR CALLI-GRAPHY?
WHAT'S THE POINT?
YOU MAY NOT TAKE THE PATH OF THE WARRIOR, LIKE YOUR FATHER. YOURS MAY BE THE WAY OF LEARNING.
YES, MA'AM.
OH, MY SON...

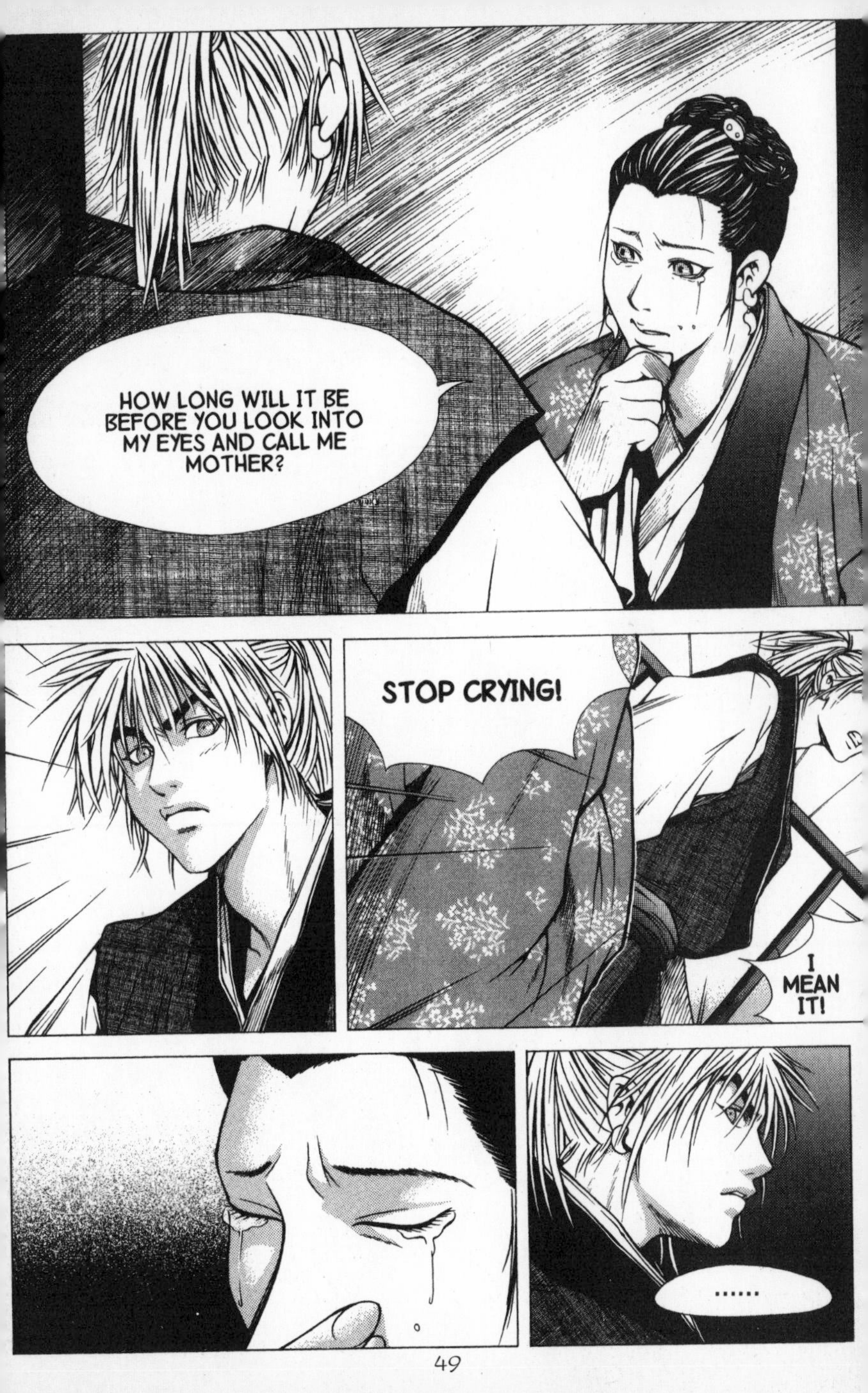
HOW LONG WILL IT BE BEFORE YOU LOOK INTO MY EYES AND CALL ME MOTHER?
STOP CRYING!
I MEAN IT!
......

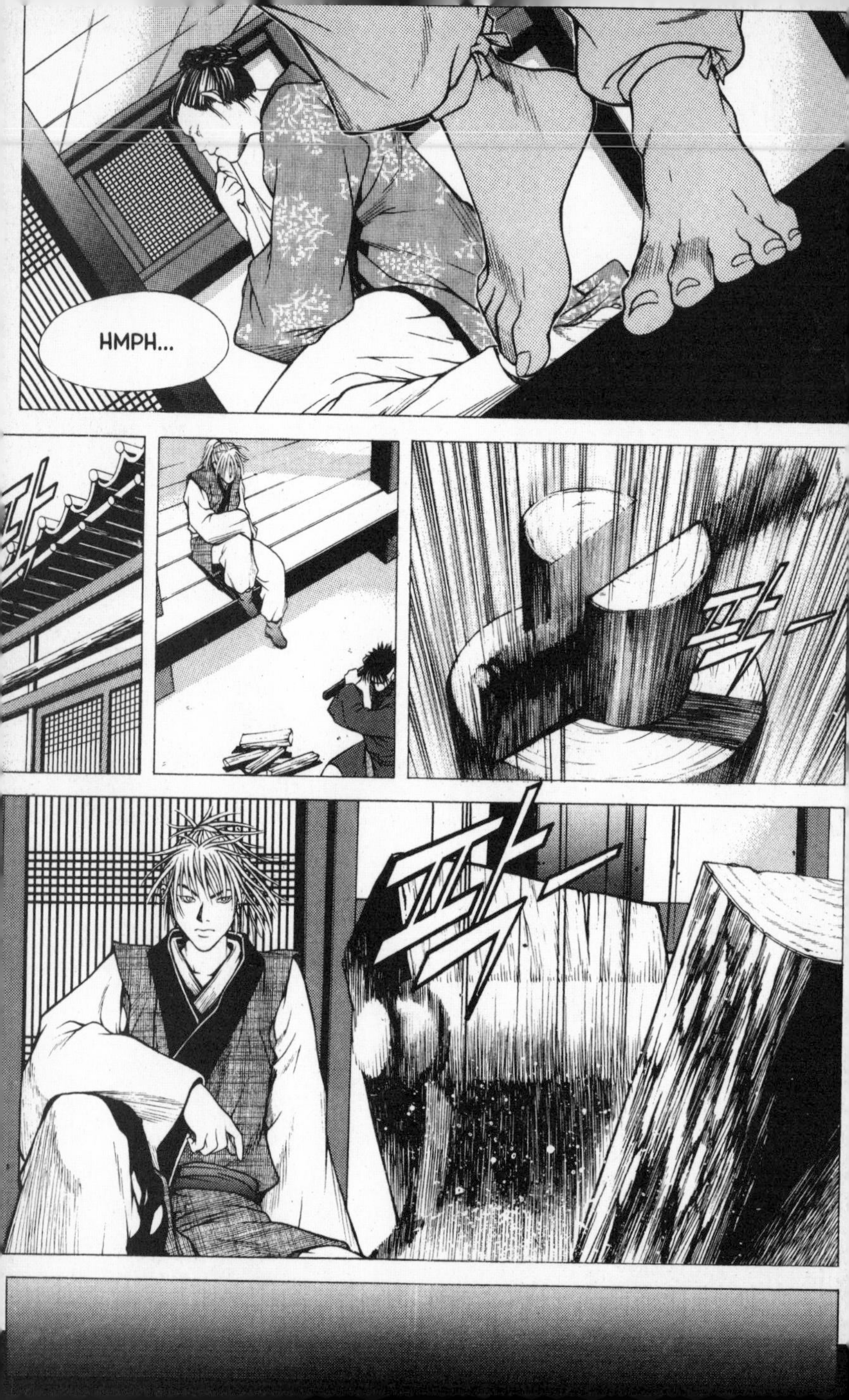
HMPH...

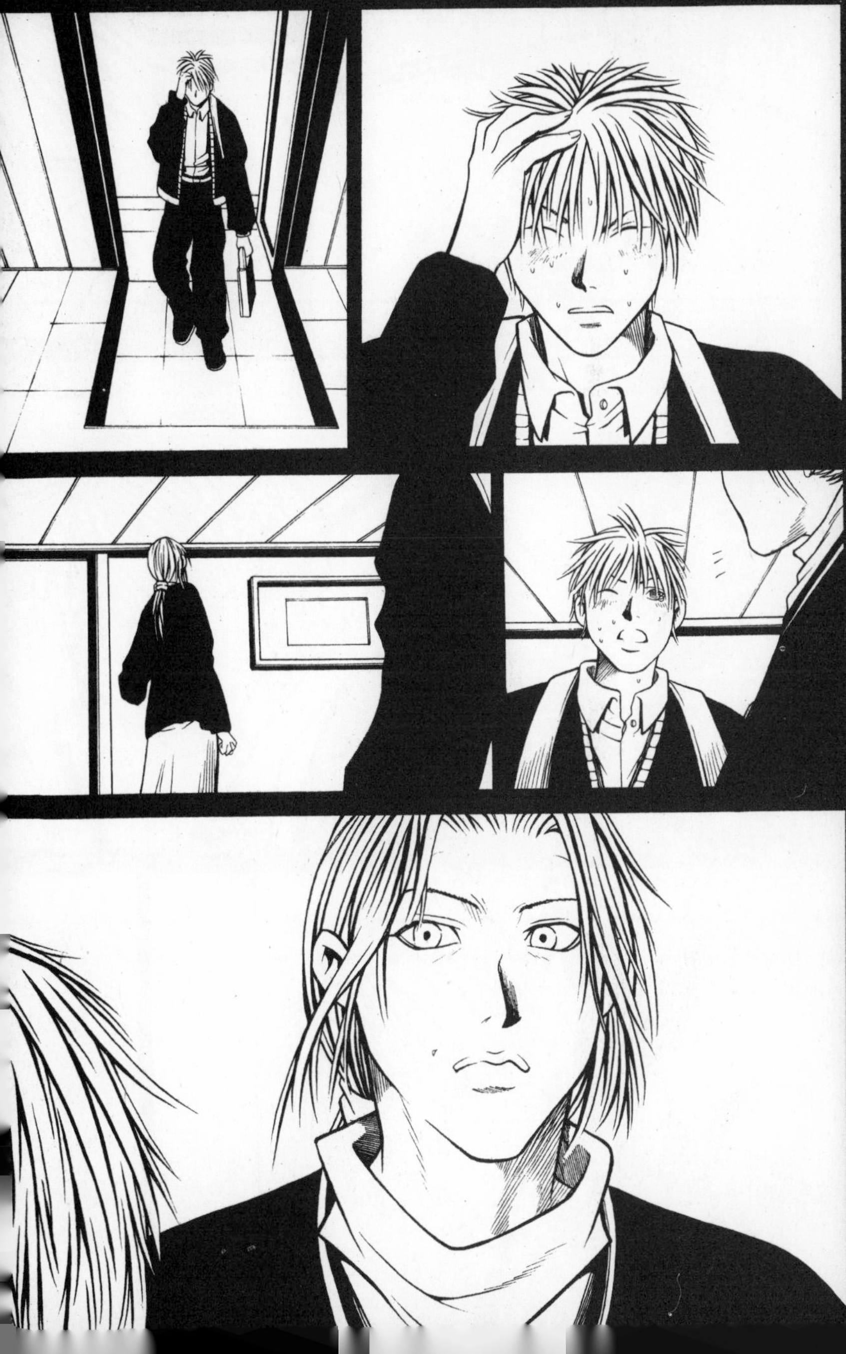

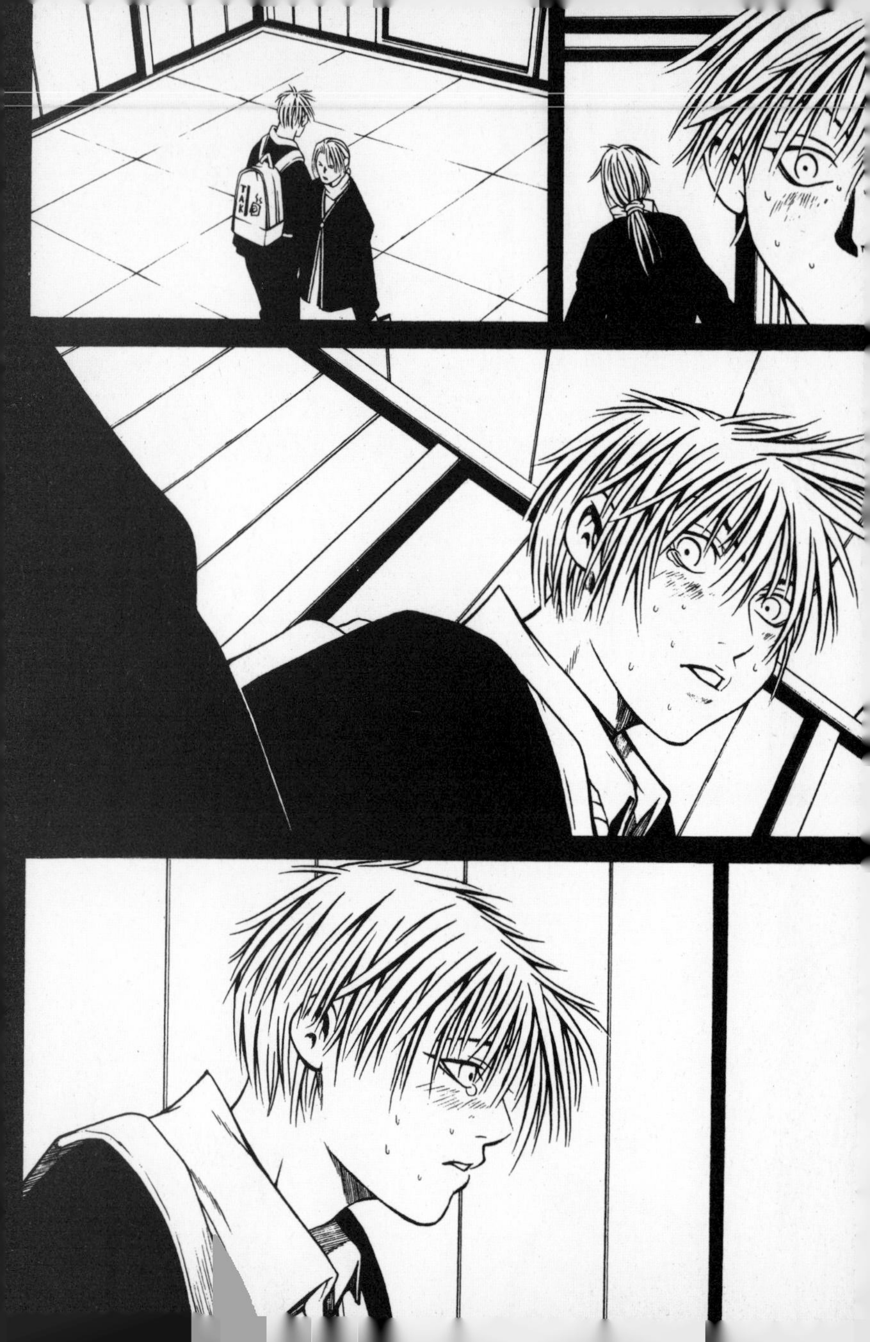

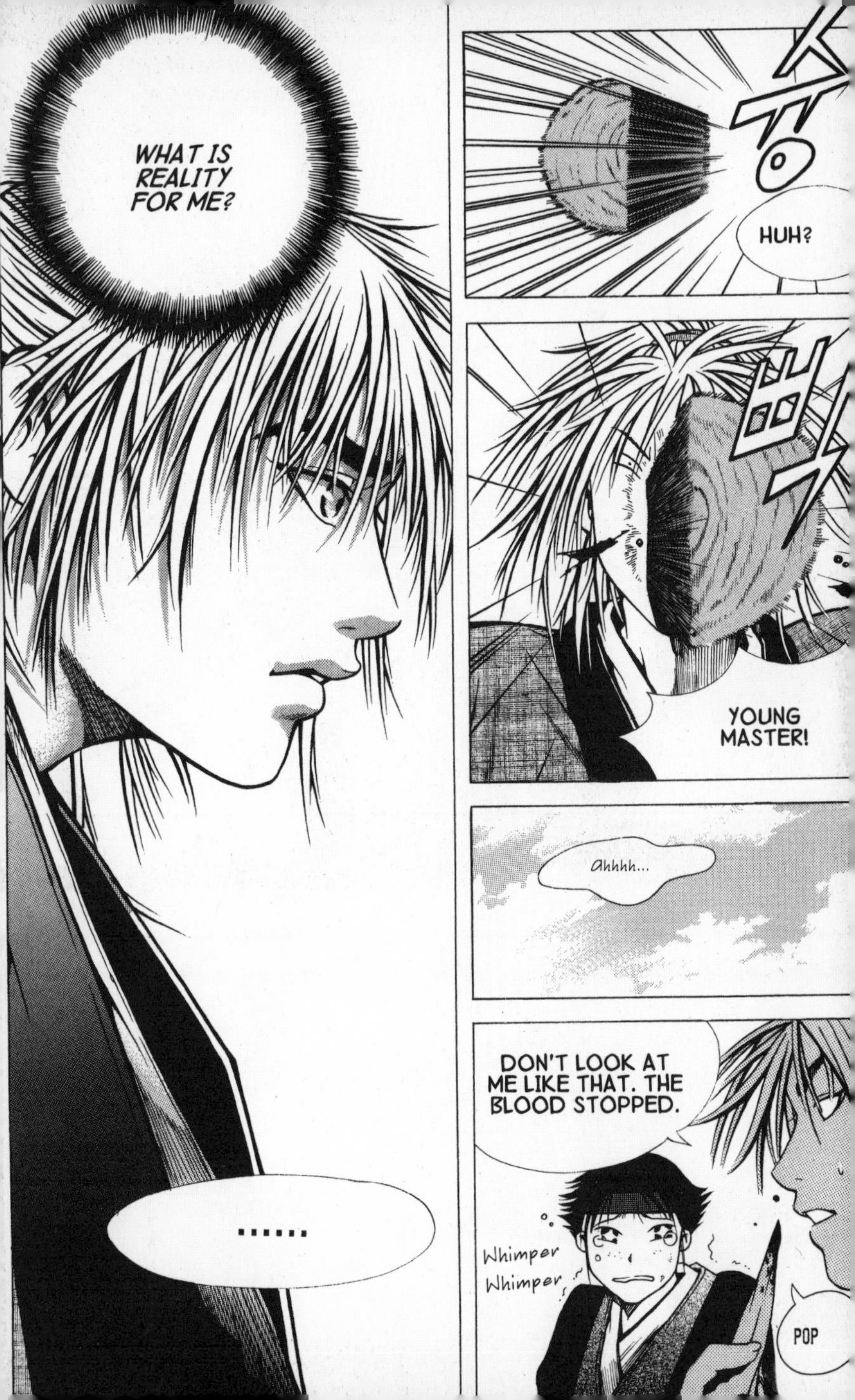
WHAT IS REALITY FOR ME?
......
HUH?
YOUNG MASTER!
Ahhhh...
DON'T LOOK AT ME LIKE THAT. THE BLOOD STOPPED.
Whimper Whimper
POP

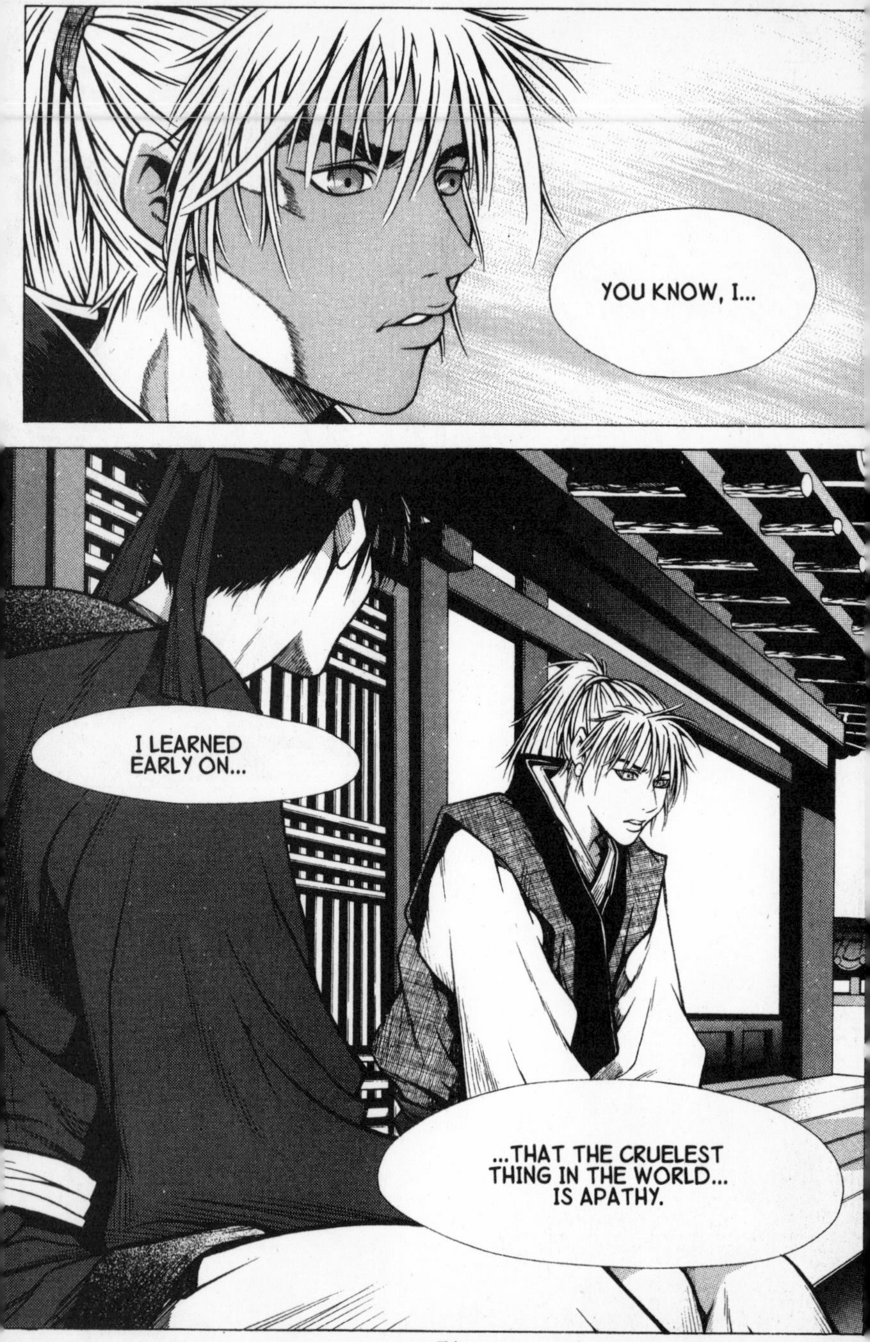
YOU KNOW, I...
I LEARNED EARLY ON...
...THAT THE CRUELEST THING IN THE WORLD... IS APATHY.

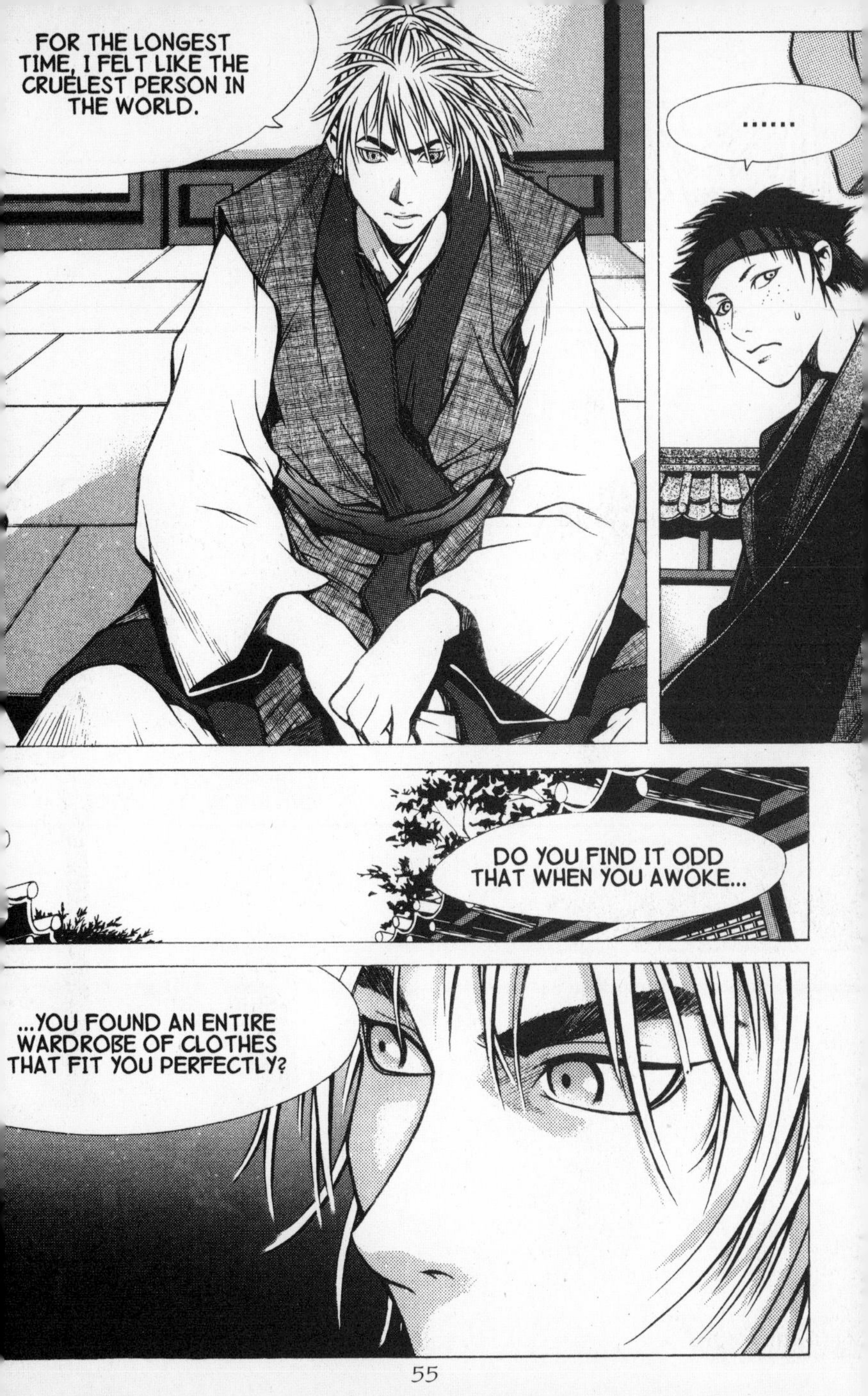
FOR THE LONGEST TIME, I FELT LIKE THE CRUELEST PERSON IN THE WORLD.
......
DO YOU FIND IT ODD THAT WHEN YOU AWOKE...
...YOU FOUND AN ENTIRE WARDROBE OF CLOTHES THAT FIT YOU PERFECTLY?

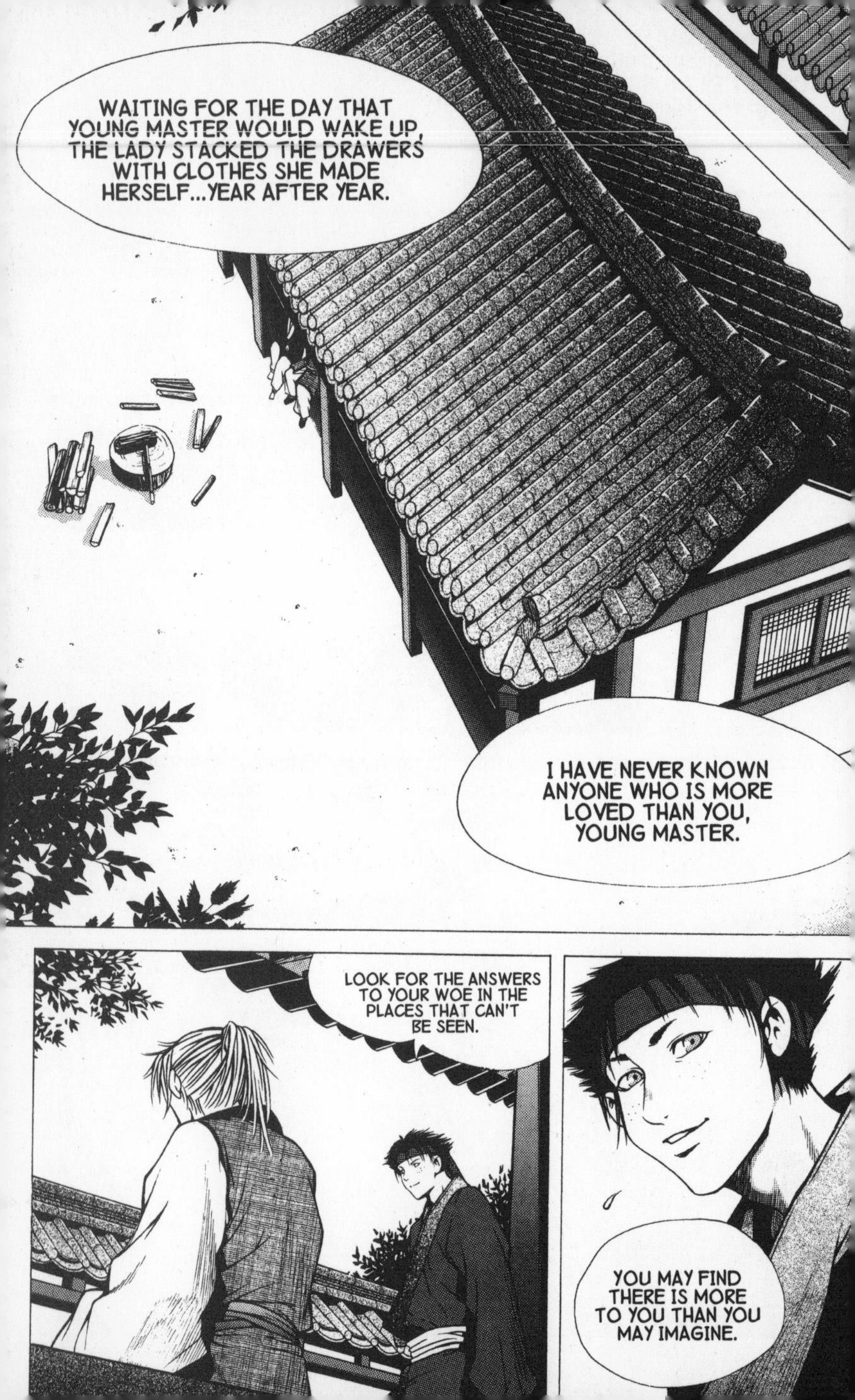
WAITING FOR THE DAY THAT YOUNG MASTER WOULD WAKE UP, THE LADY STACKED THE DRAWERS WITH CLOTHES SHE MADE HERSELF...YEAR AFTER YEAR.
I HAVE NEVER KNOWN ANYONE WHO IS MORE LOVED THAN YOU, YOUNG MASTER.
LOOK FOR THE ANSWERS TO YOUR WOE IN THE PLACES THAT CAN'T BE SEEN.
YOU MAY FIND THERE IS MORE TO YOU THAN YOU MAY IMAGINE.

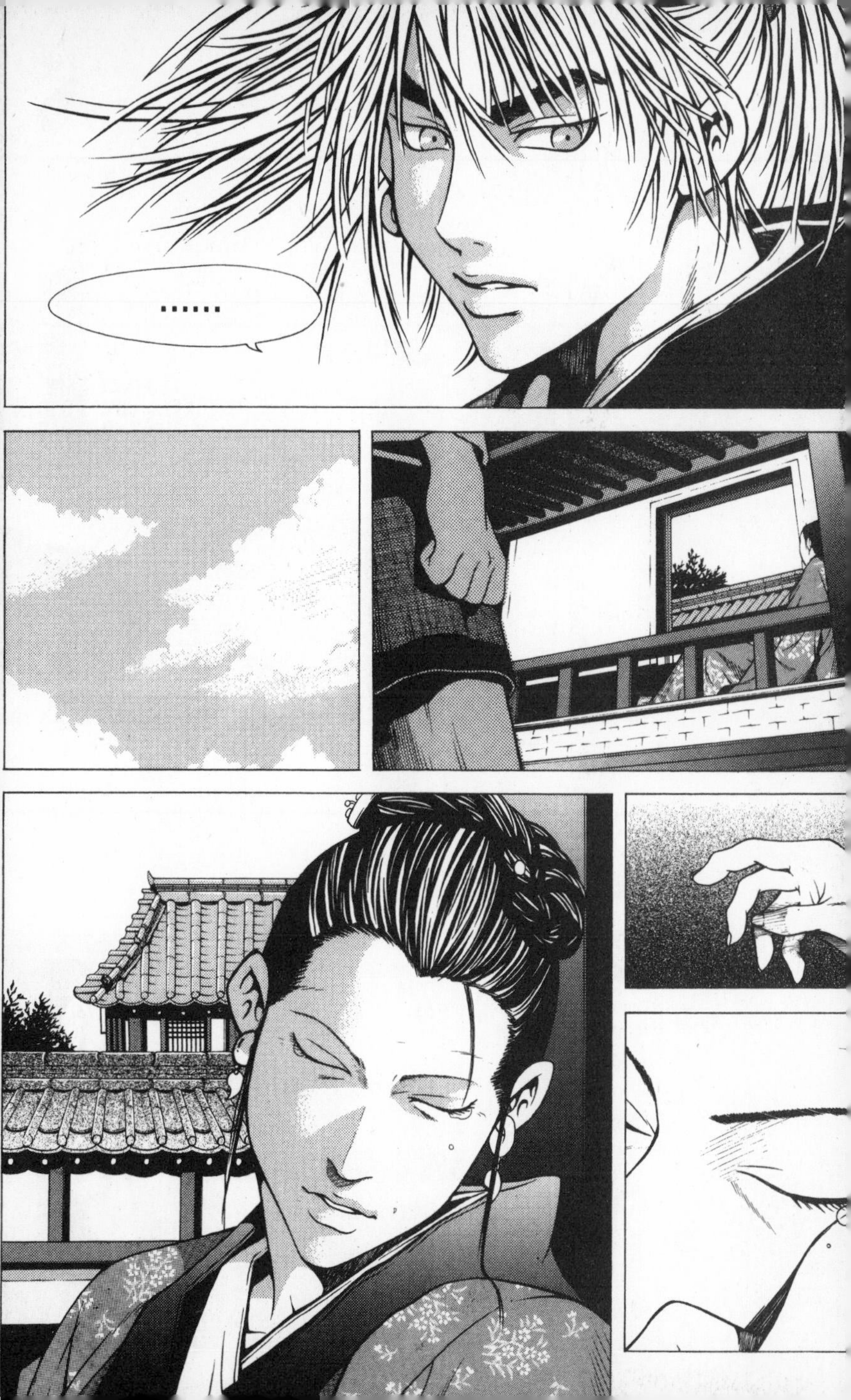
......

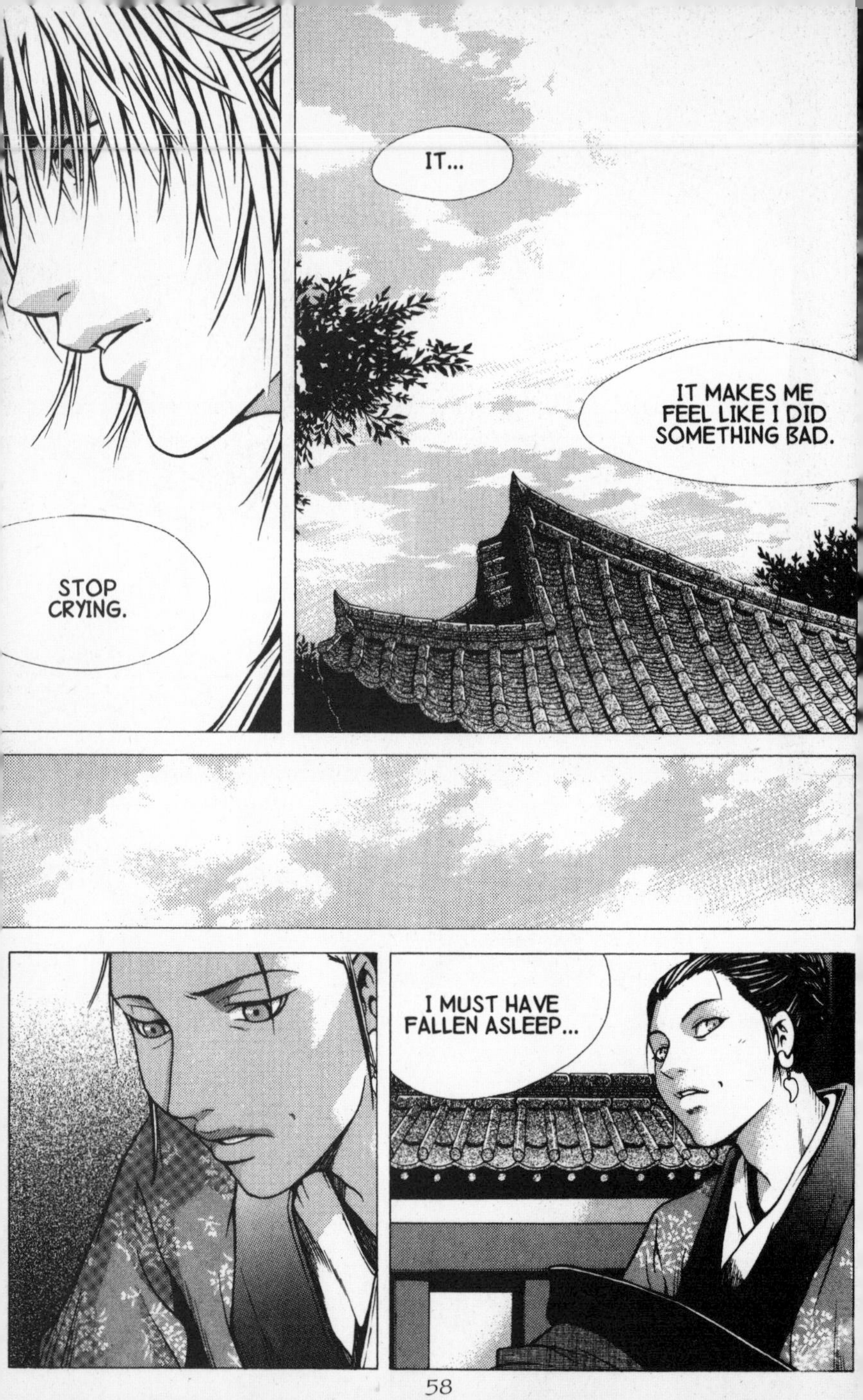
STOP CRYING.
IT...
IT MAKES ME FEEL LIKE I DID SOMETHING BAD.
I MUST HAVE FALLEN ASLEEP...

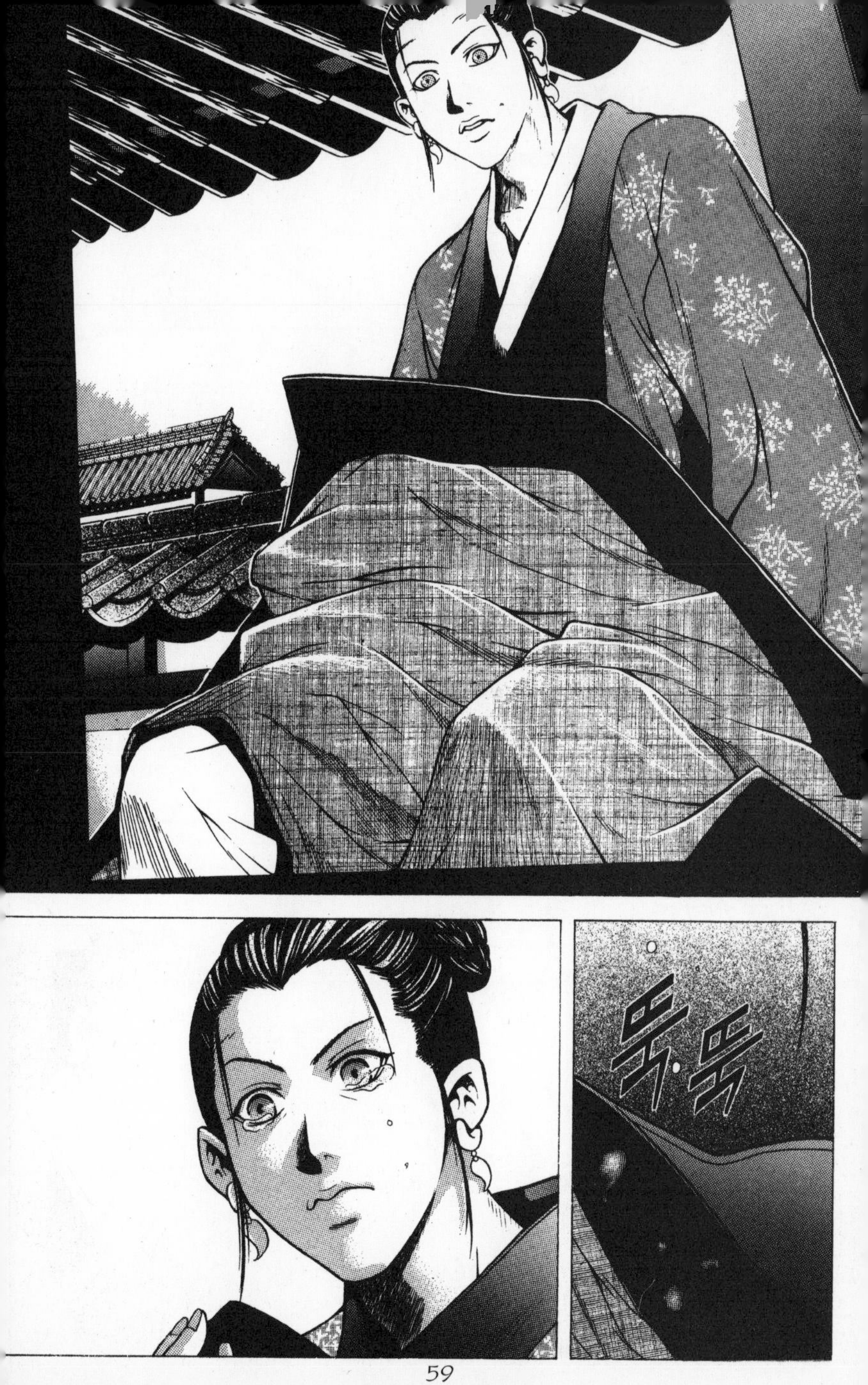
뚝·뚝

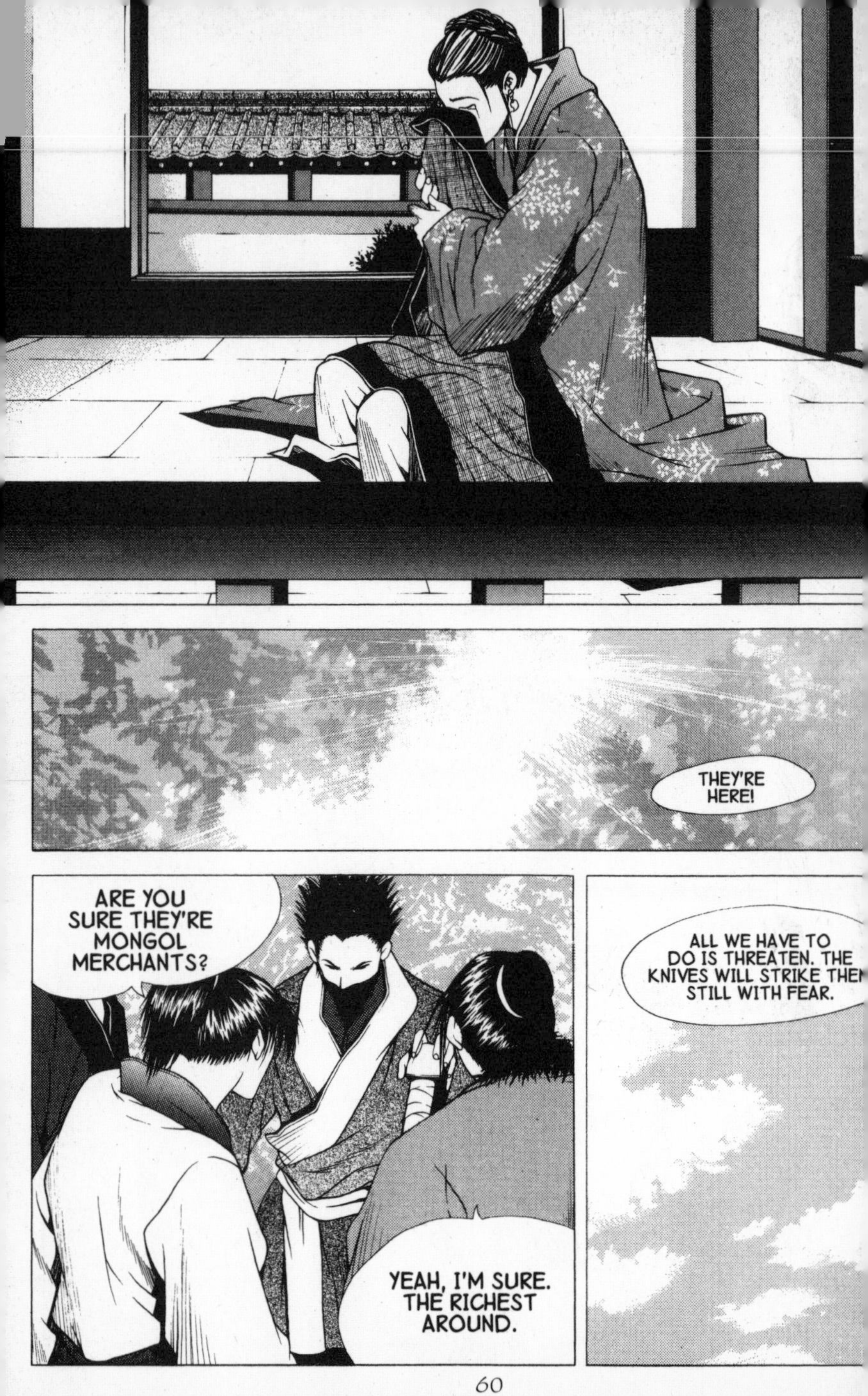
THEY'RE HERE!
ARE YOU SURE THEY'RE MONGOL MERCHANTS?
YEAH, I'M SURE. THE RICHEST AROUND.
ALL WE HAVE TO DO IS THREATEN. THE KNIVES WILL STRIKE THE
STILL WITH FEAR.

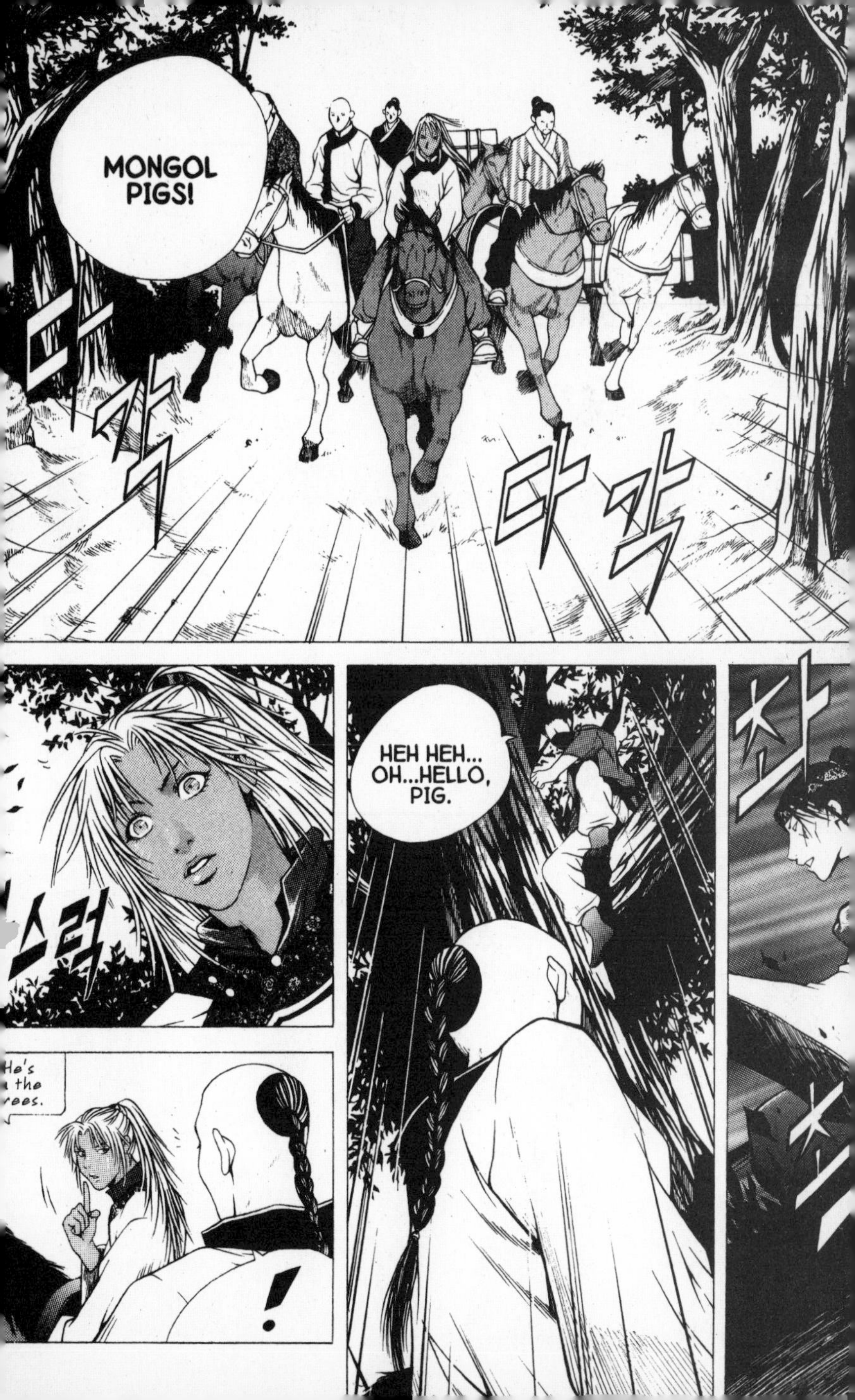
MONGOL PIGS!
다각
다각
스럭
He's
the
rees.
!
HEH HEH... OH...HELLO, PIG.

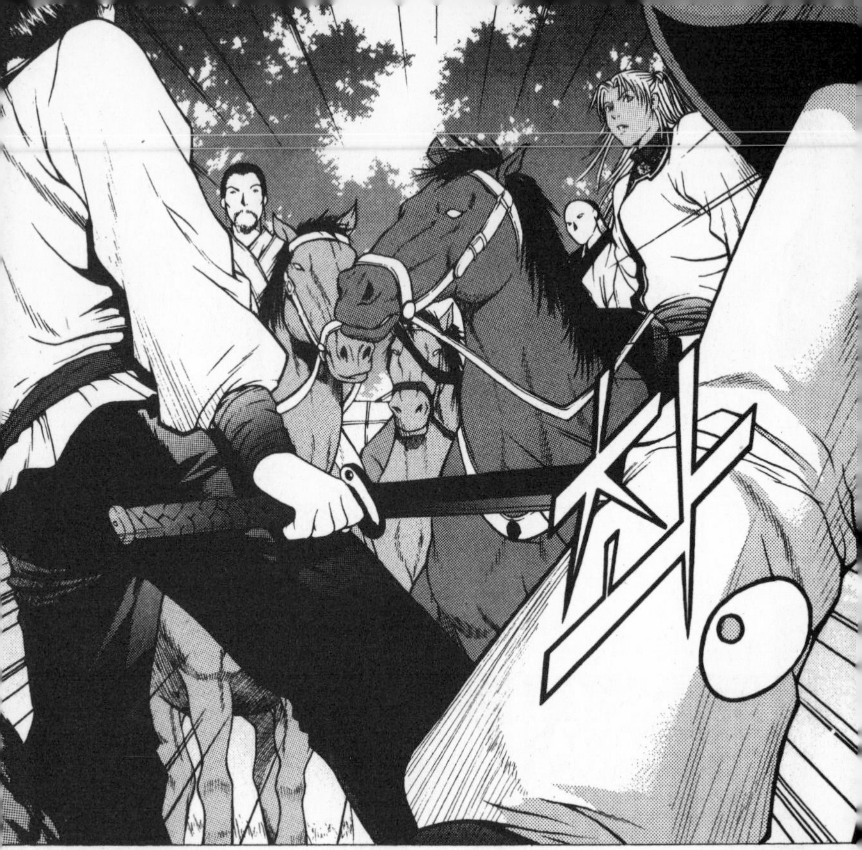

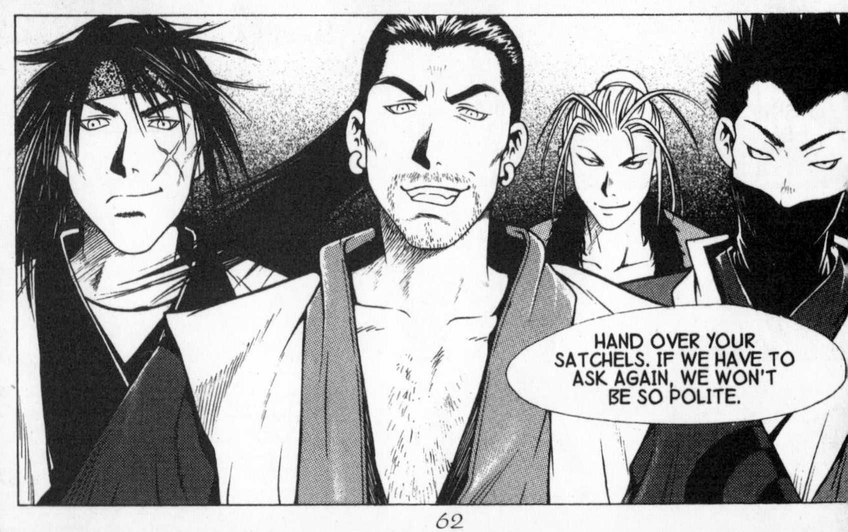
HAND OVER YOUR SATCHELS. IF WE HAVE TO ASK AGAIN, WE WON'T BE SO POLITE.

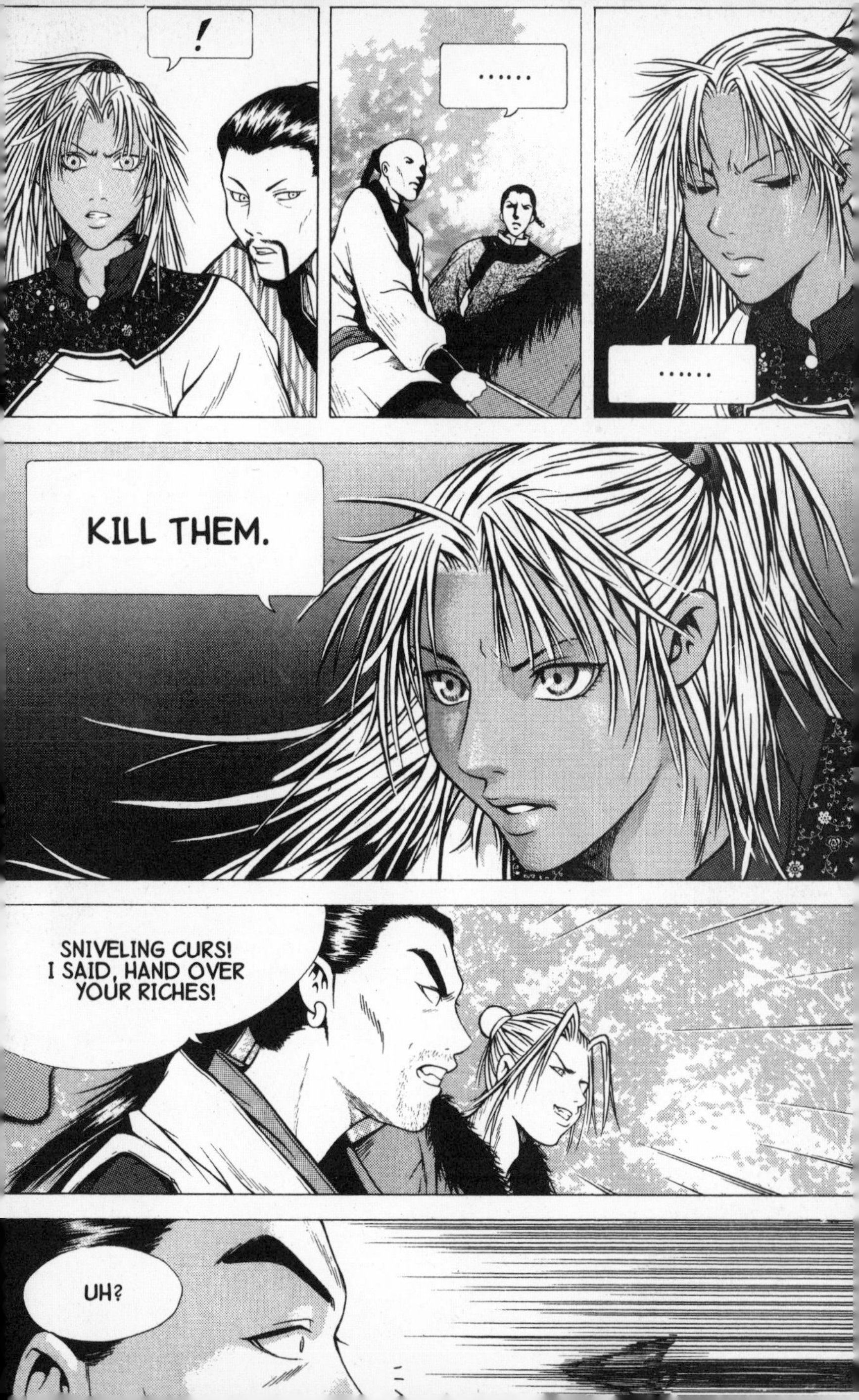
!
......
......
KILL THEM.
SNIVELING CURS! I SAID, HAND OVER YOUR RICHES!
UH?

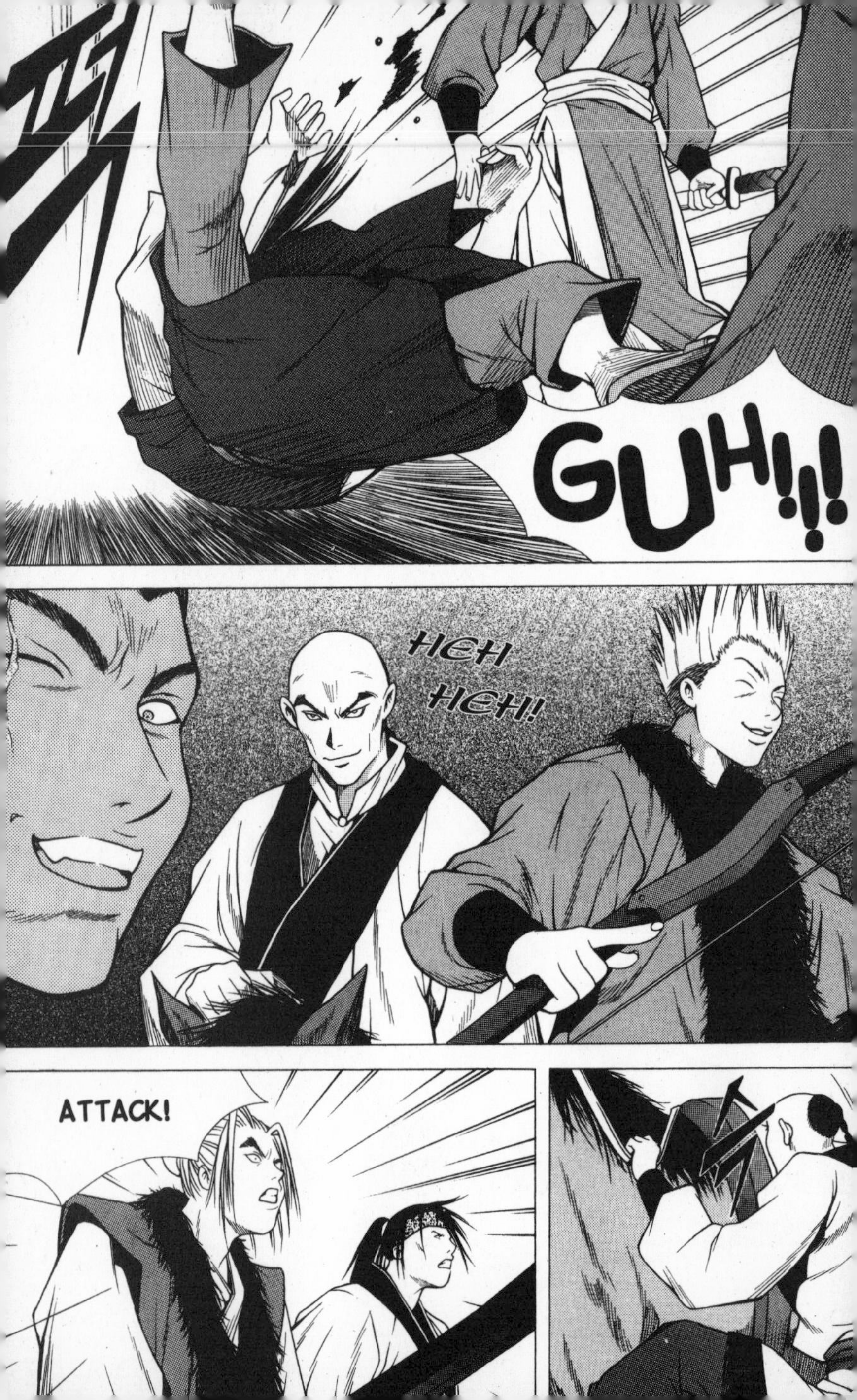
GUH!!!
HEH HEH!
ATTACK!

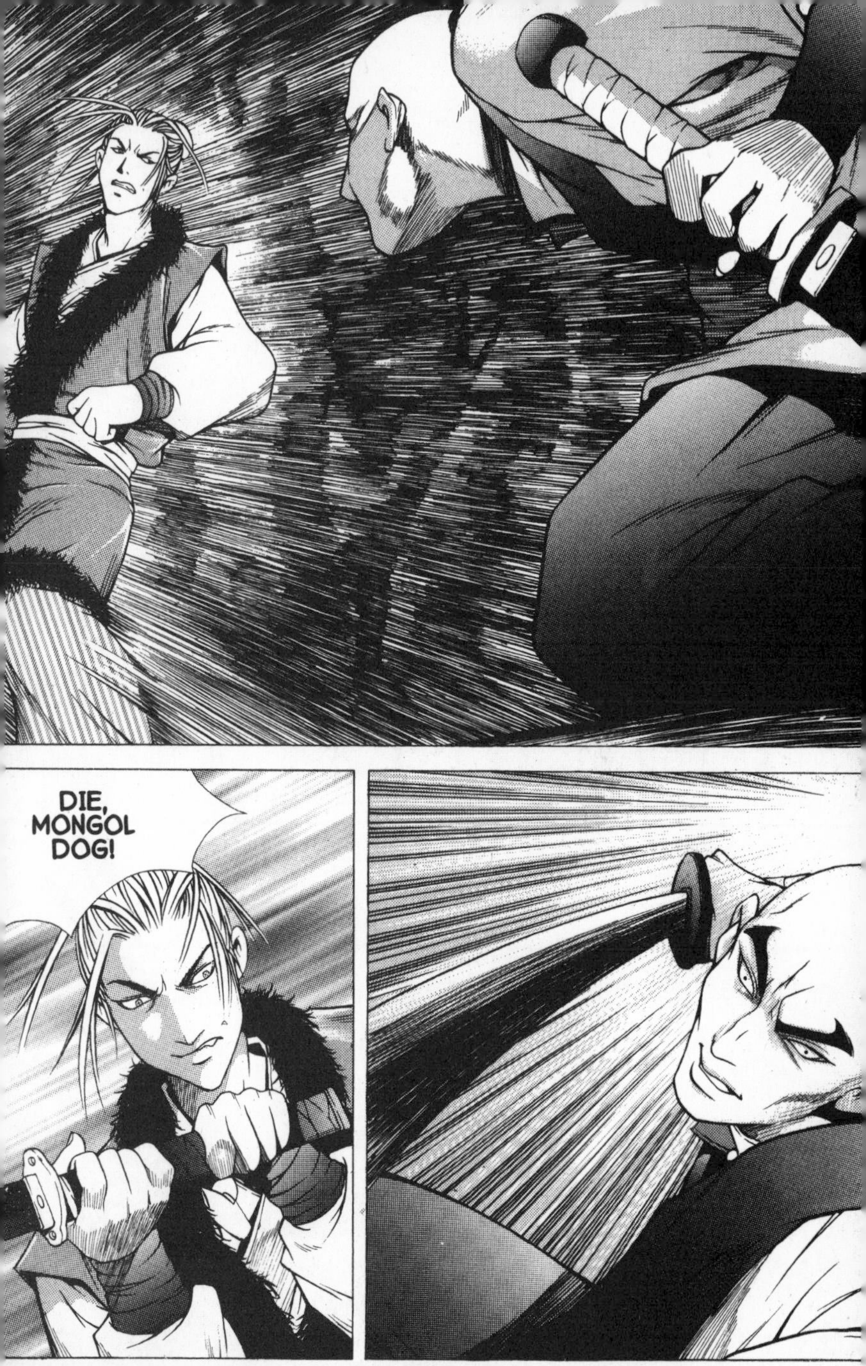
DIE, MONGOL DOG!

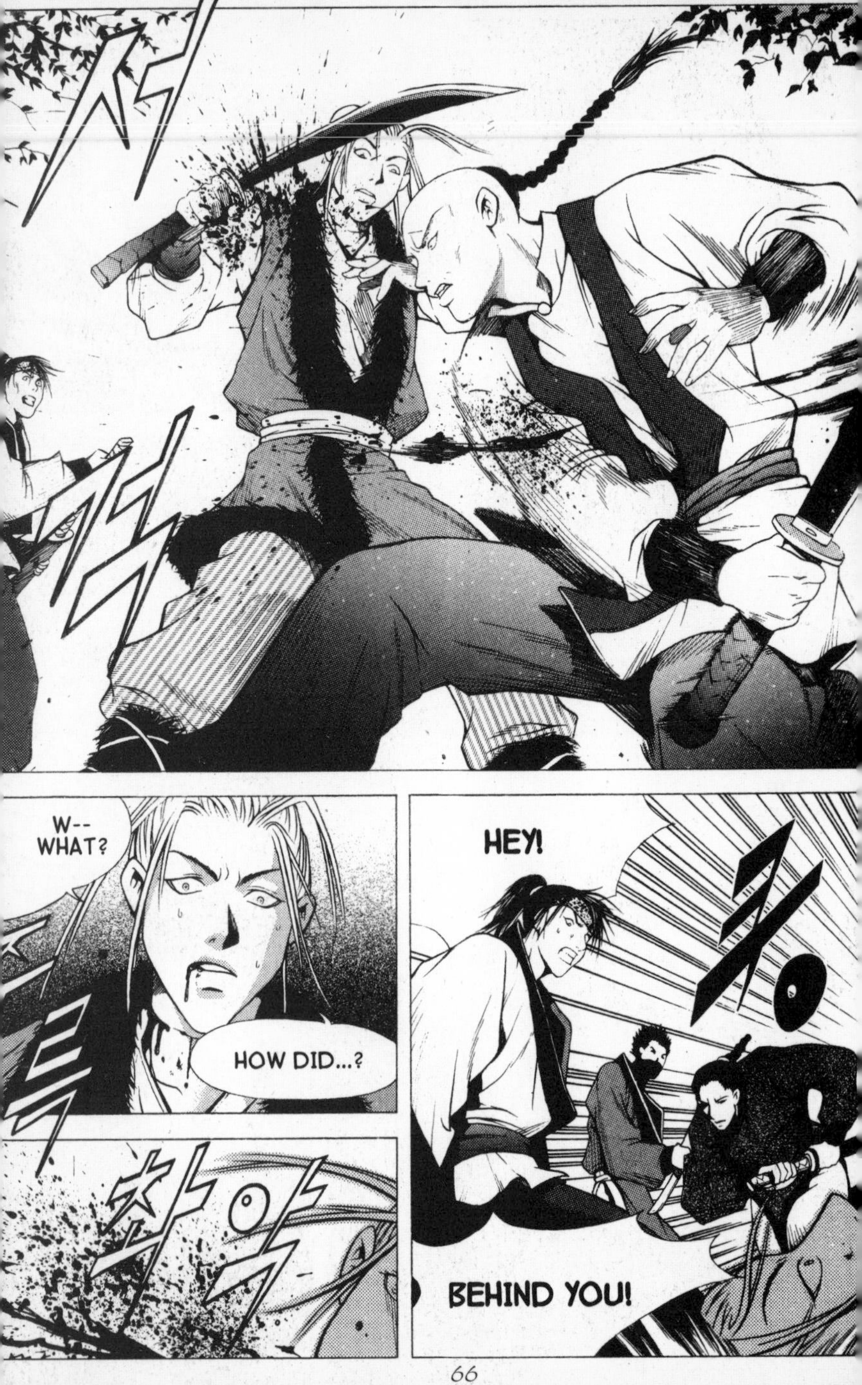
W--
WHAT?
HOW DID...?
HEY!
BEHIND YOU!

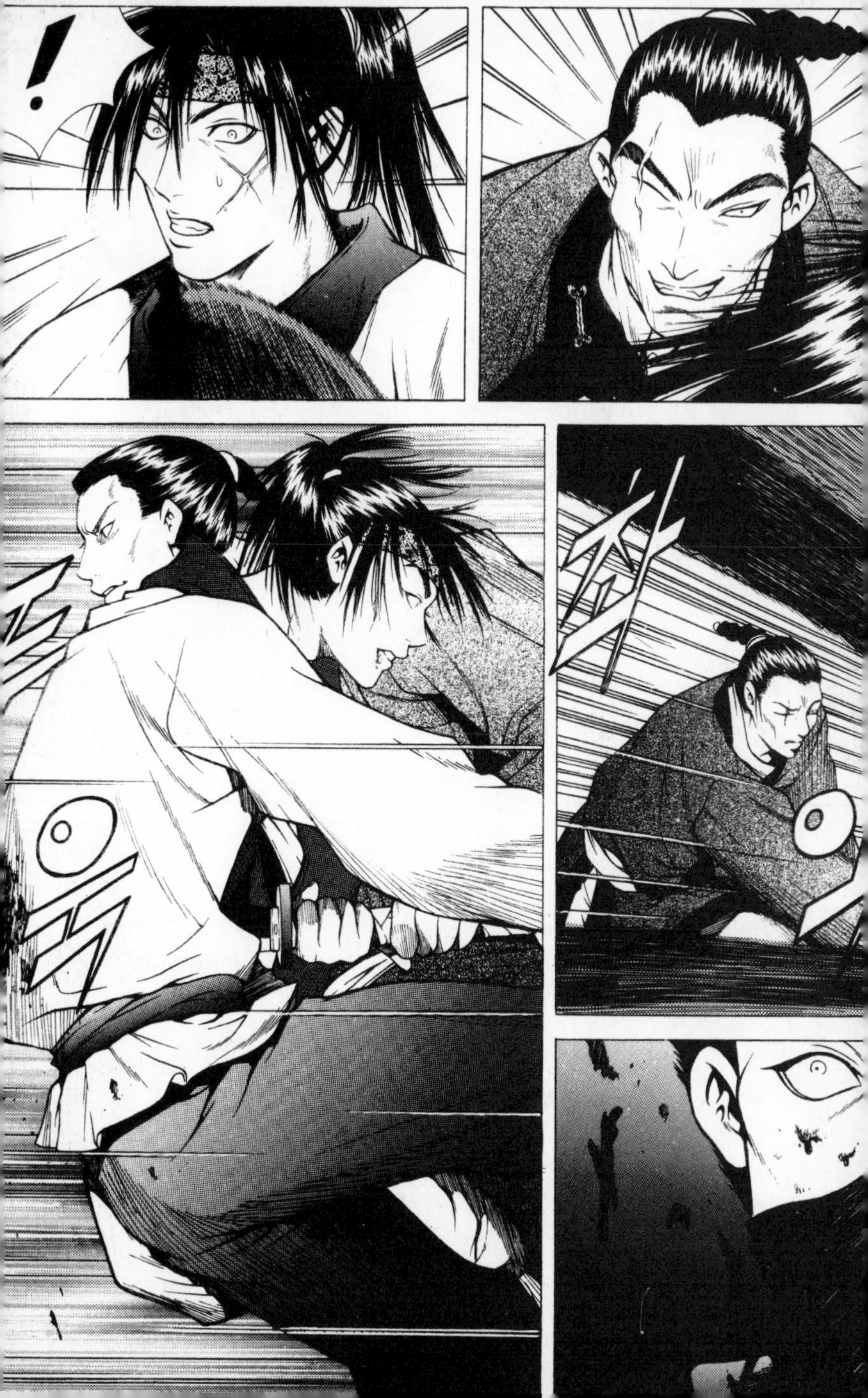
!

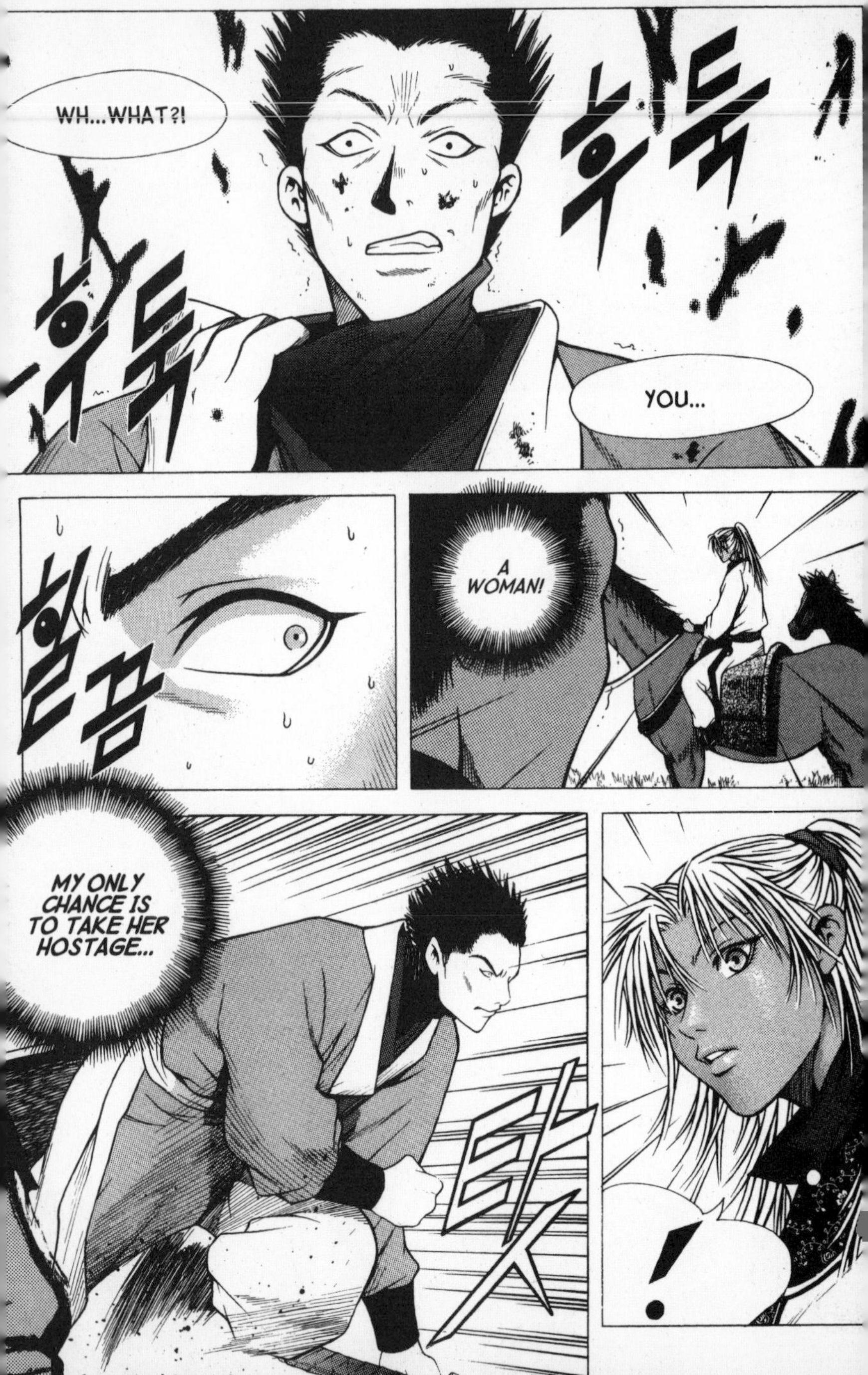
WH...WHAT?!
후둑
후둑
YOU...
힐끔
A WOMAN!
MY ONLY CHANCE IS TO TAKE HER HOSTAGE...
탓
!

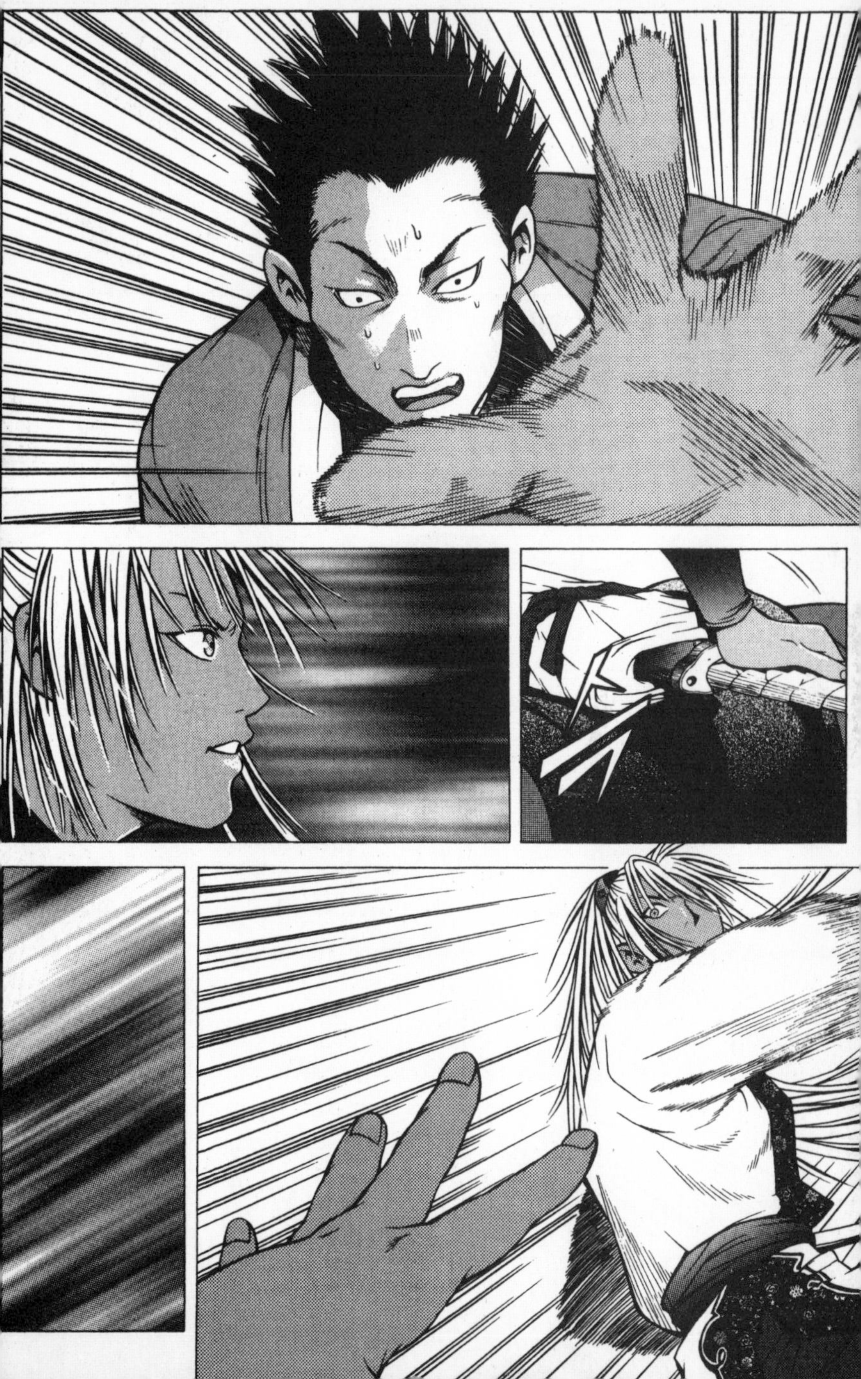

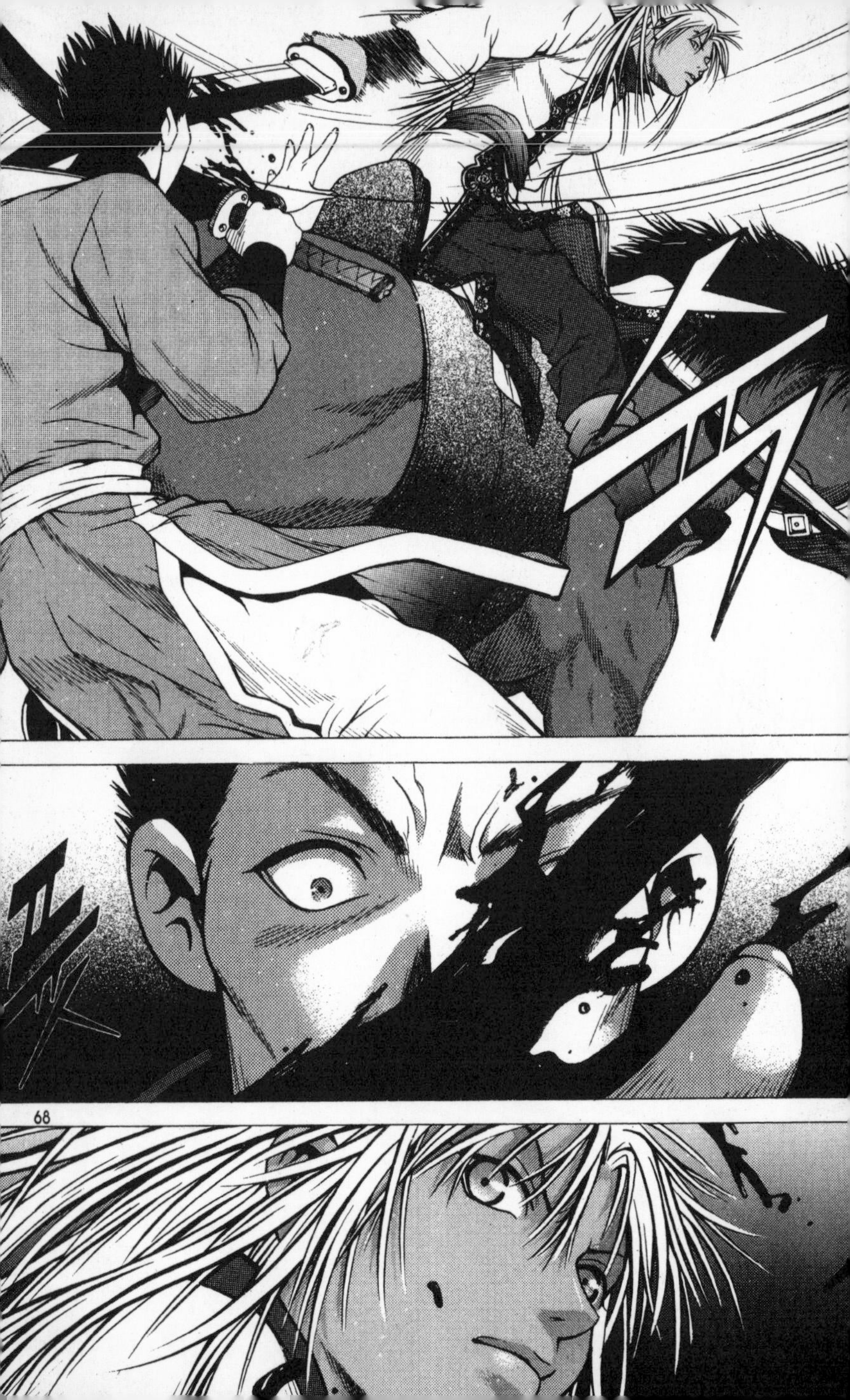

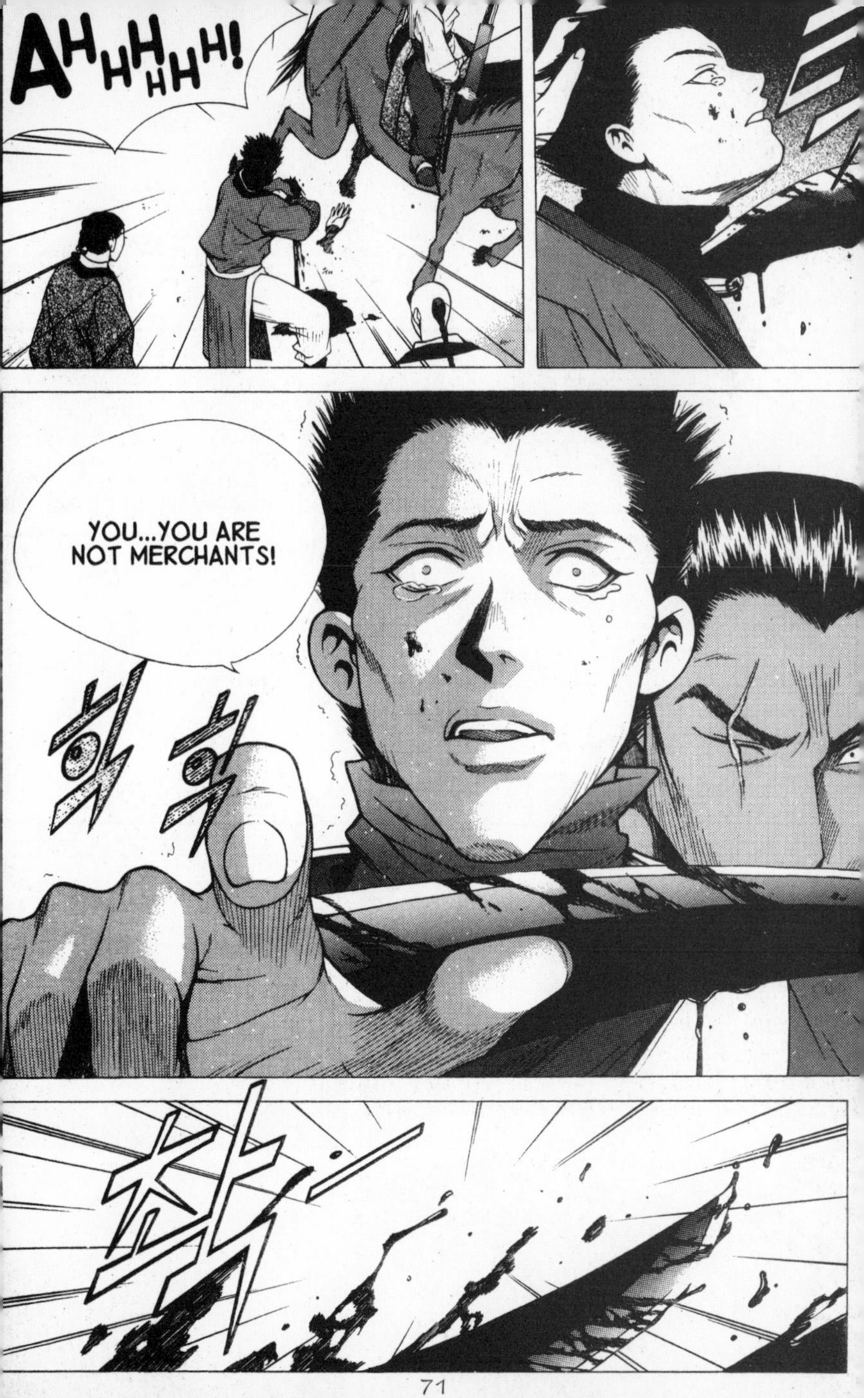
AHHHHHH!
YOU...YOU ARE NOT MERCHANTS!

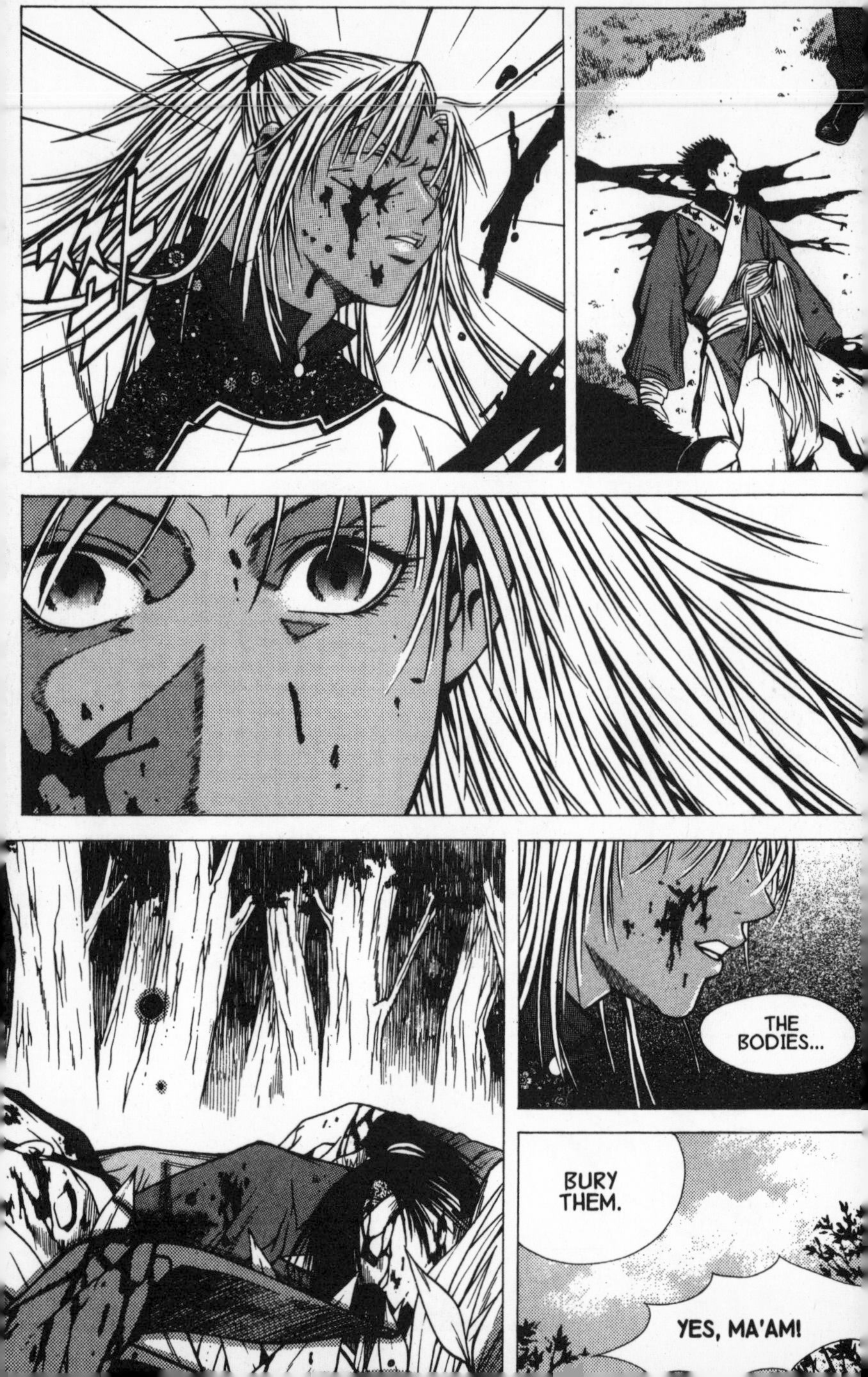
THE BODIES...
BURY THEM.
YES, MA'AM!

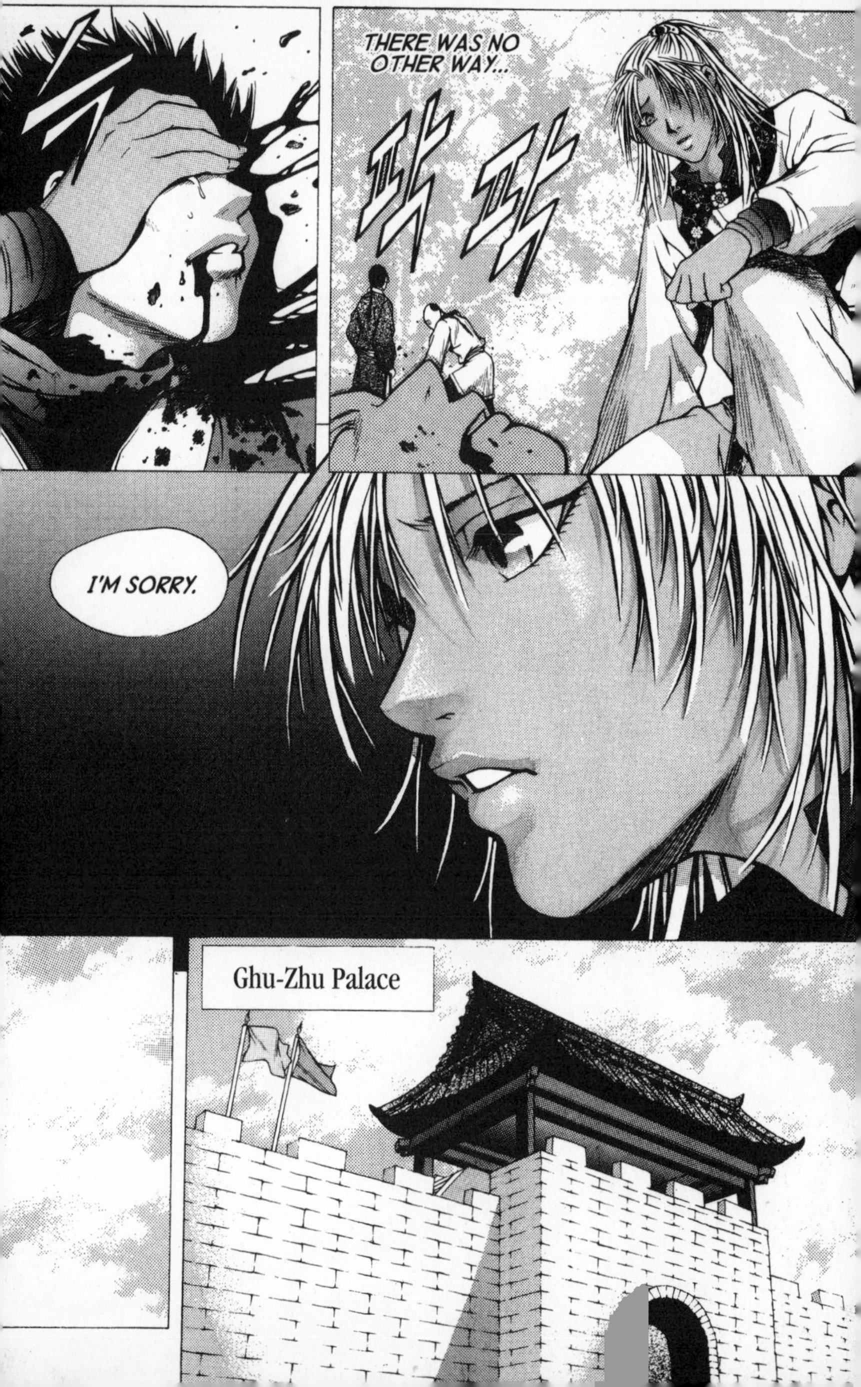
THERE WAS NO OTHER WAY...
파 팍
I'M SORRY.
Ghu-Zhu Palace

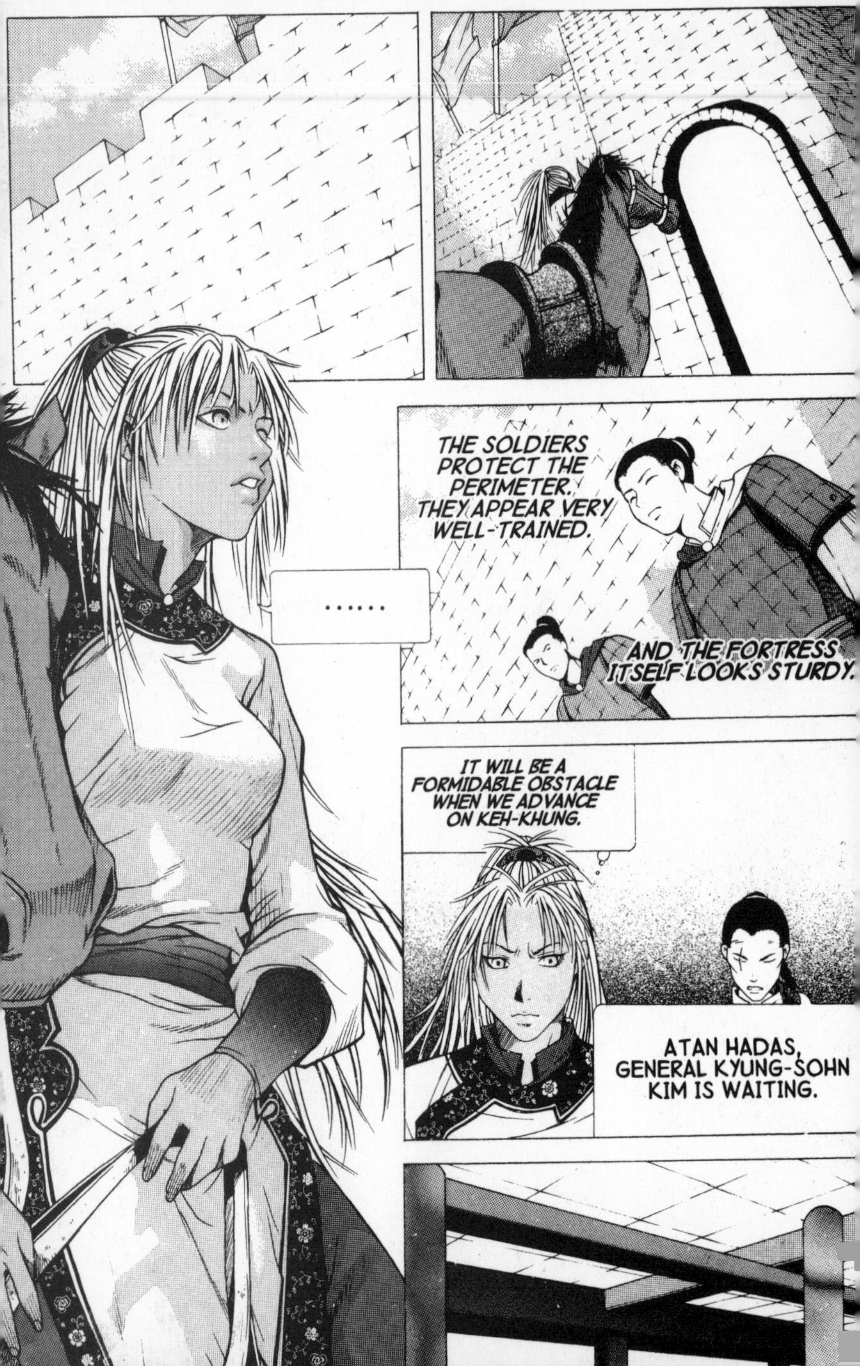
......
THE SOLDIERS PROTECT THE PERIMETER. THEY APPEAR VERY WELL-TRAINED.
AND THE FORTRESS ITSELF LOOKS STURDY.
IT WILL BE A FORMIDABLE OBSTACLE WHEN WE ADVANCE ON KEH-KHUNG.
ATAN HADAS, GENERAL KYUNG-SOHN KIM IS WAITING.

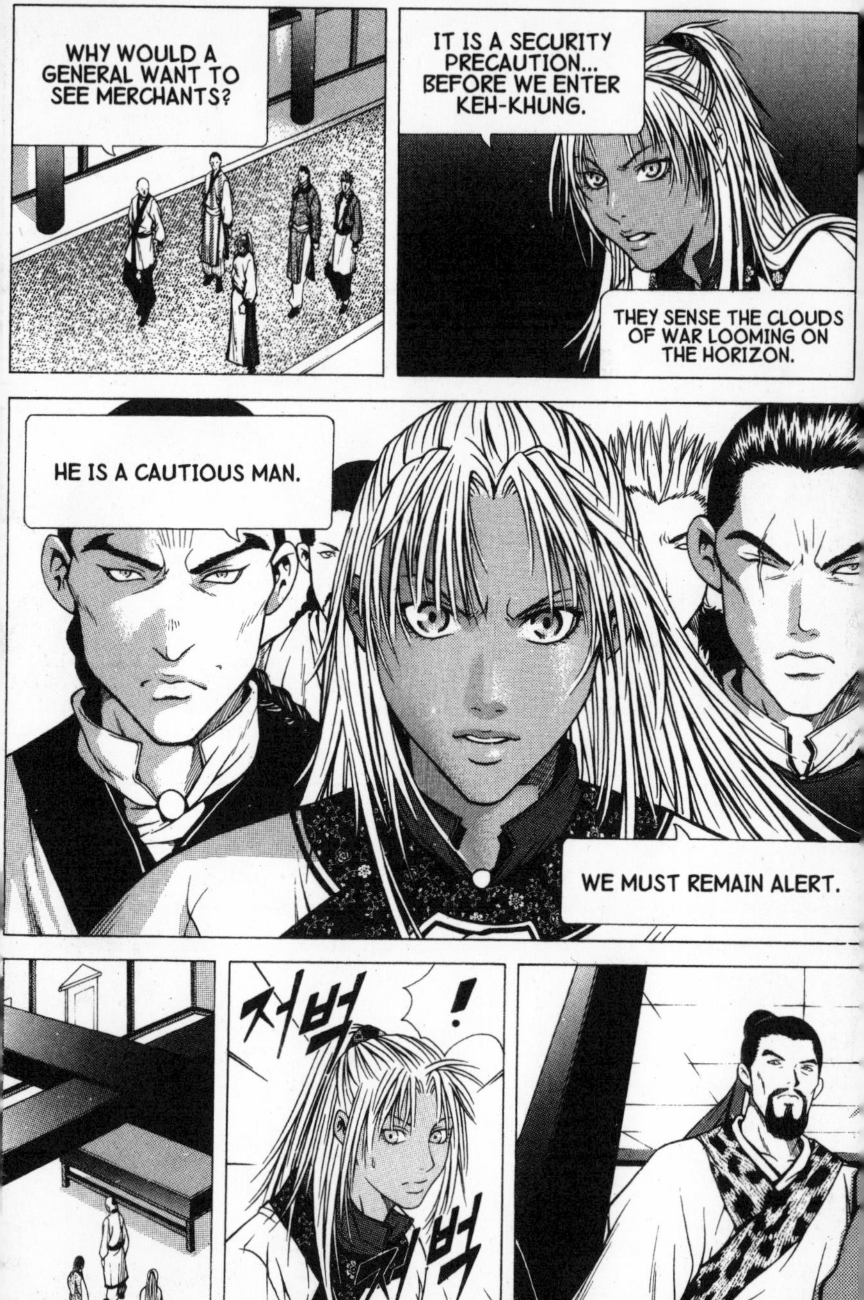
WHY WOULD A GENERAL WANT TO SEE MERCHANTS?
IT IS A SECURITY PRECAUTION... BEFORE WE ENTER KEH-KHUNG.
THEY SENSE THE CLOUDS OF WAR LOOMING ON THE HORIZON.
HE IS A CAUTIOUS MAN.
WE MUST REMAIN ALERT.
저벅
!
저벅

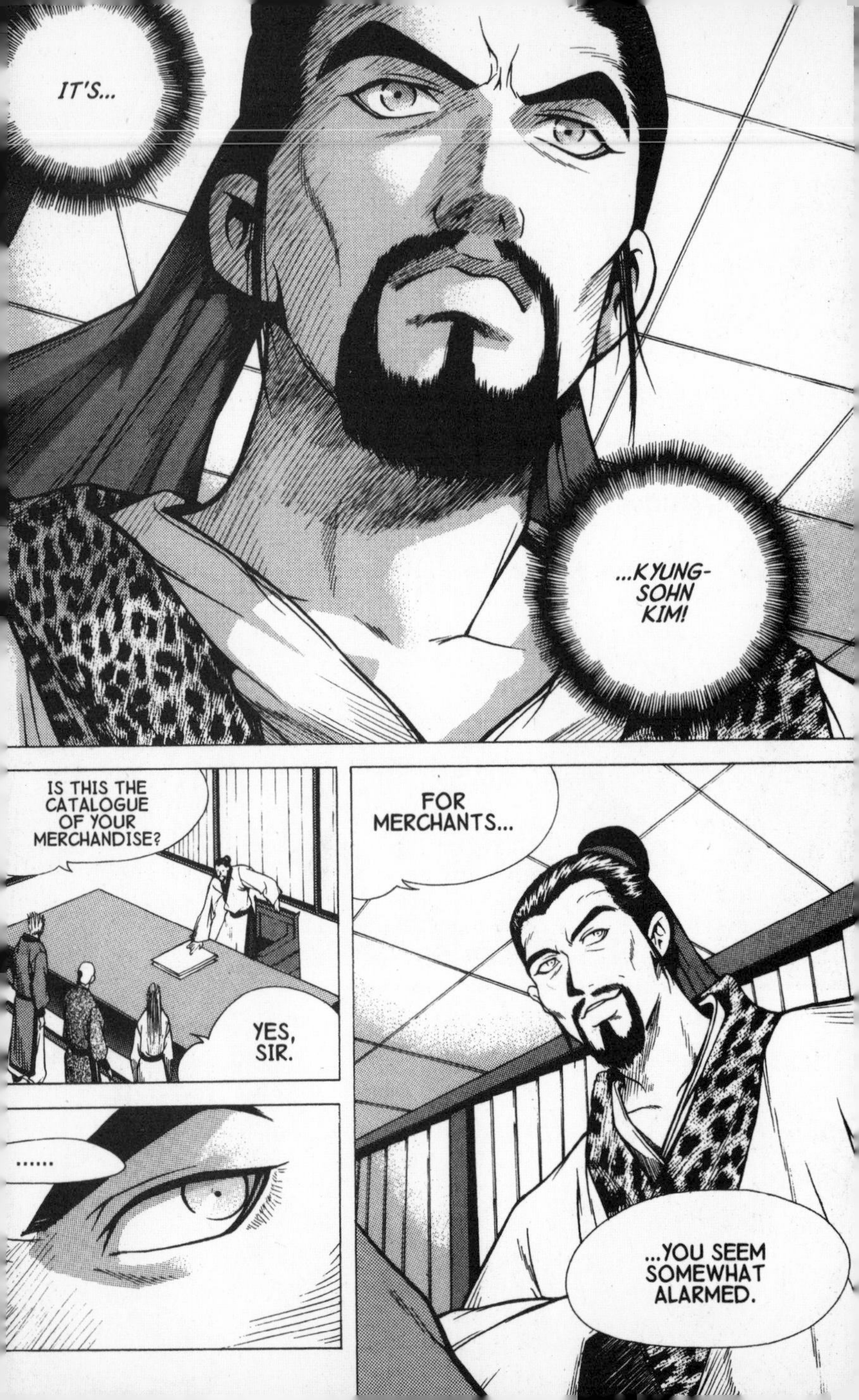
IT'S...
...KYUNG-SOHN KIM!
IS THIS THE CATALOGUE OF YOUR MERCHANDISE?
YES, SIR.
......
FOR MERCHANTS...
...YOU SEEM SOMEWHAT ALARMED.

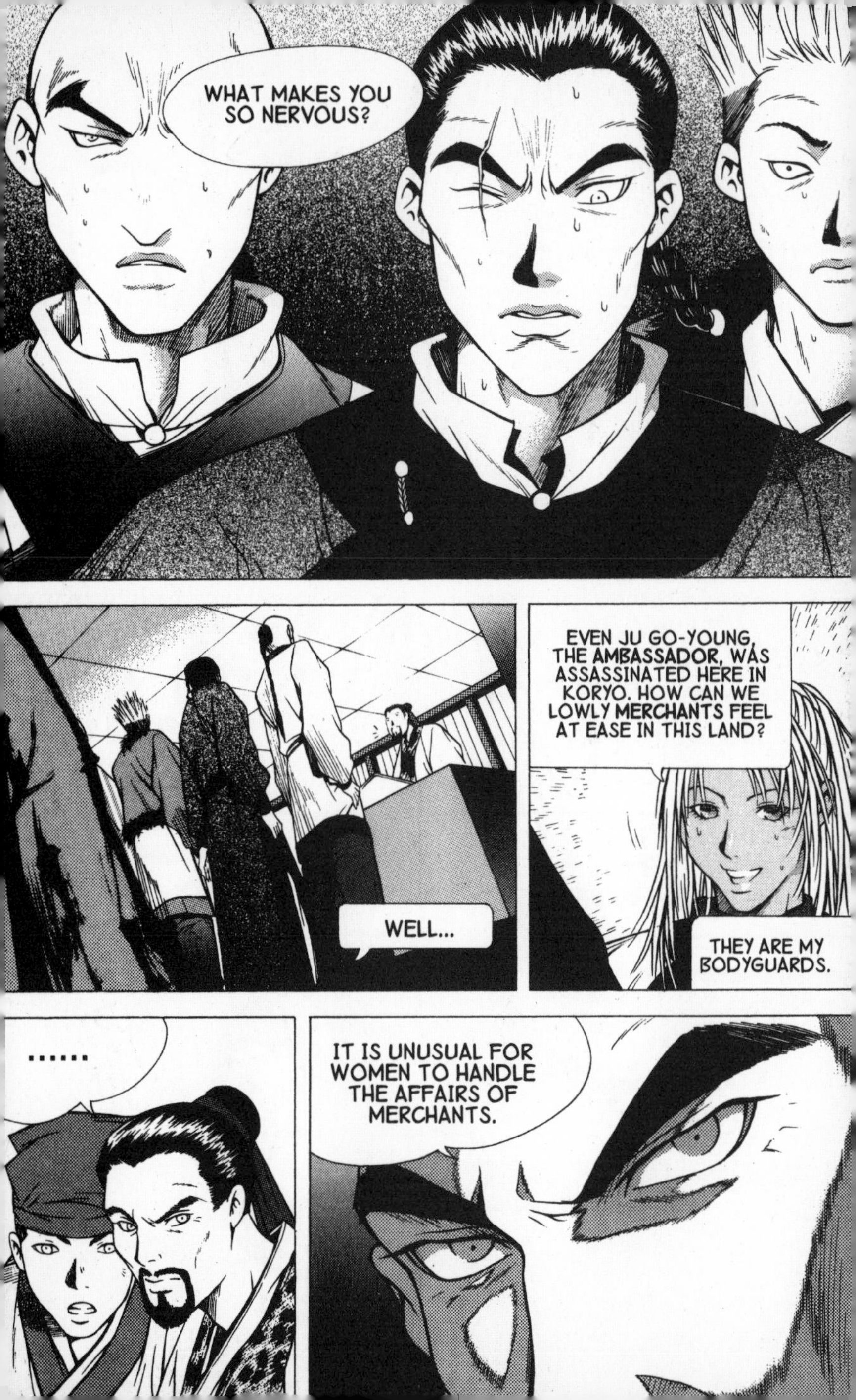
WHAT MAKES YOU SO NERVOUS?
WELL...
EVEN JU GO-YOUNG, THE AMBASSADOR, WAS ASSASSINATED HERE IN KORYO. HOW CAN WE LOWLY MERCHANTS FEEL AT EASE IN THIS LAND?
THEY ARE MY BODYGUARDS.
......
IT IS UNUSUAL FOR WOMEN TO HANDLE THE AFFAIRS OF MERCHANTS.

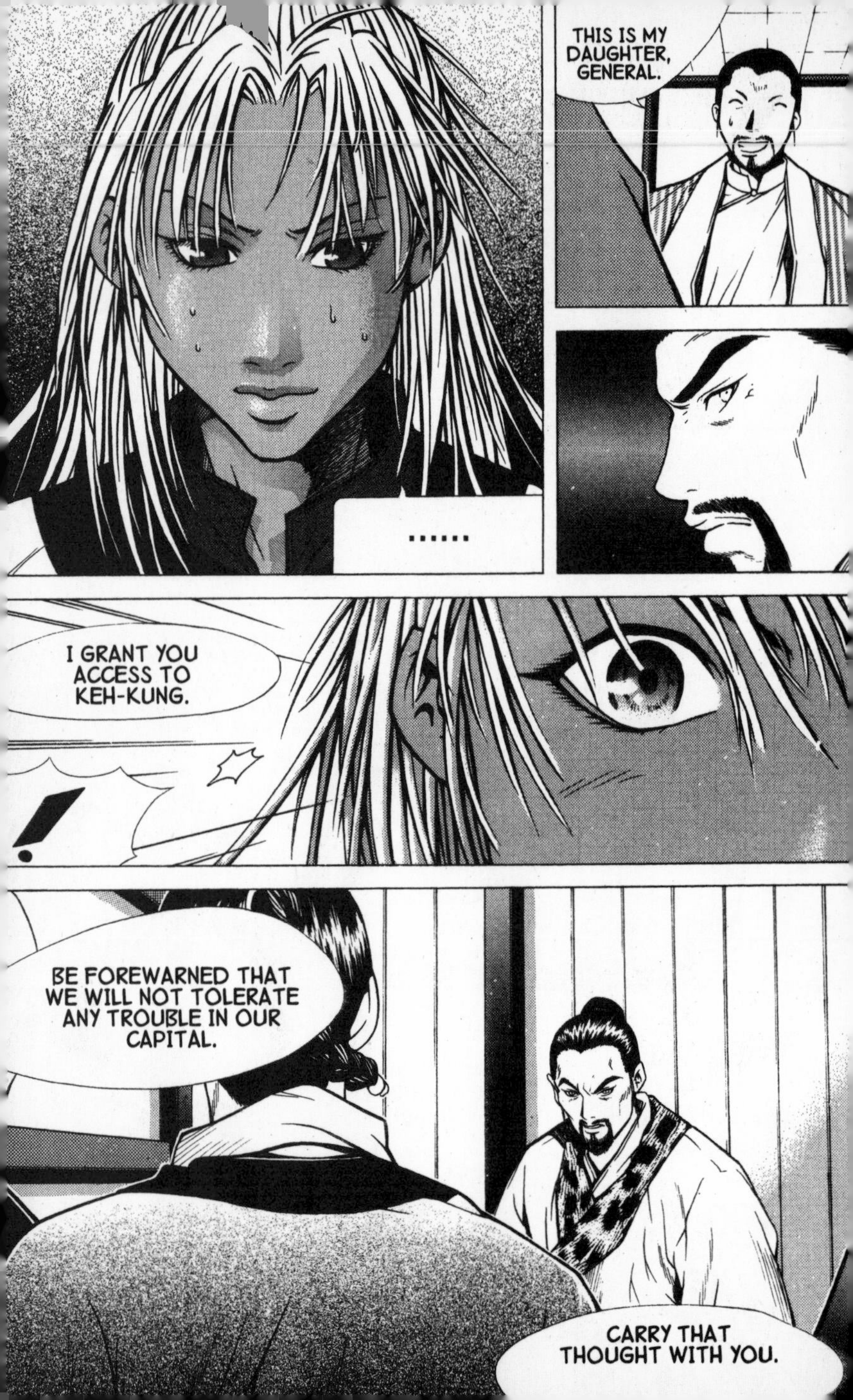

......
THIS IS MY DAUGHTER, GENERAL.
I GRANT YOU ACCESS TO KEH-KUNG.
!
BE FOREWARNED THAT WE WILL NOT TOLERATE ANY TROUBLE IN OUR CAPITAL.
CARRY THAT THOUGHT WITH YOU.

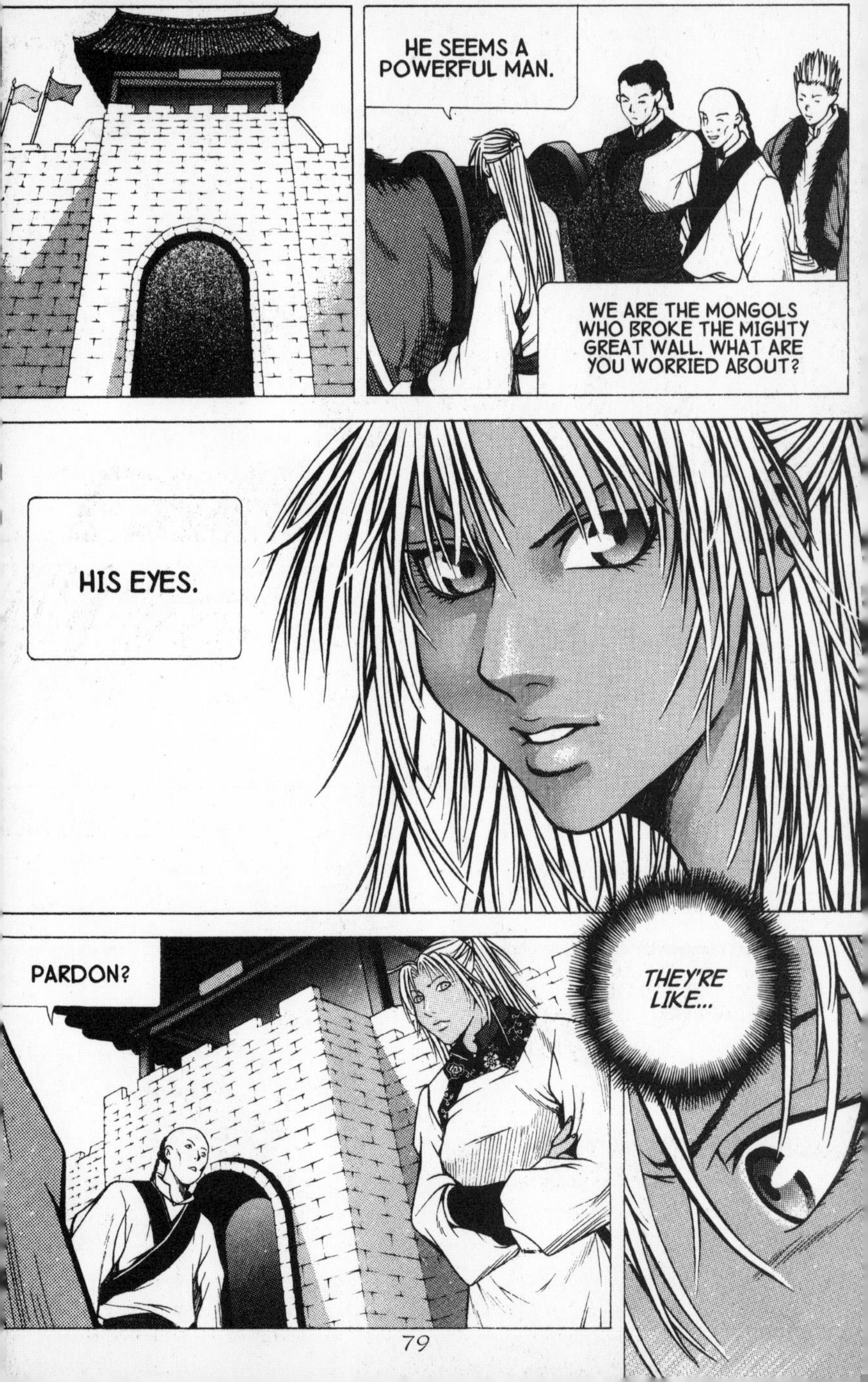
HE SEEMS A POWERFUL MAN.
WE ARE THE MONGOLS WHO BROKE THE MIGHTY GREAT WALL. WHAT ARE YOU WORRIED ABOUT?
HIS EYES.
PARDON?
THEY'RE LIKE...

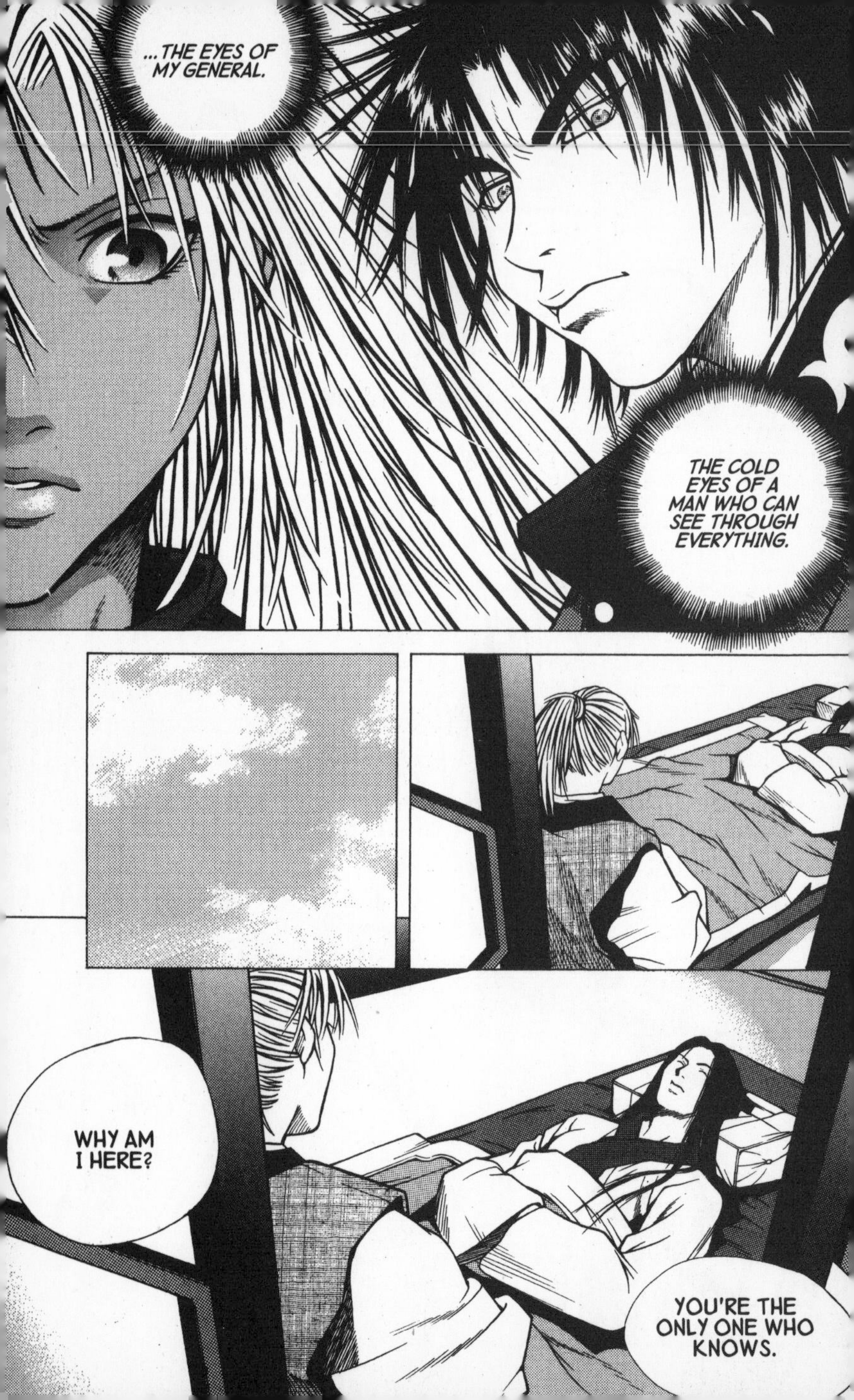
...THE EYES OF MY GENERAL.
THE COLD EYES OF A MAN WHO CAN SEE THROUGH EVERYTHING.
WHY AM I HERE?
YOU'RE THE ONLY ONE WHO KNOWS.

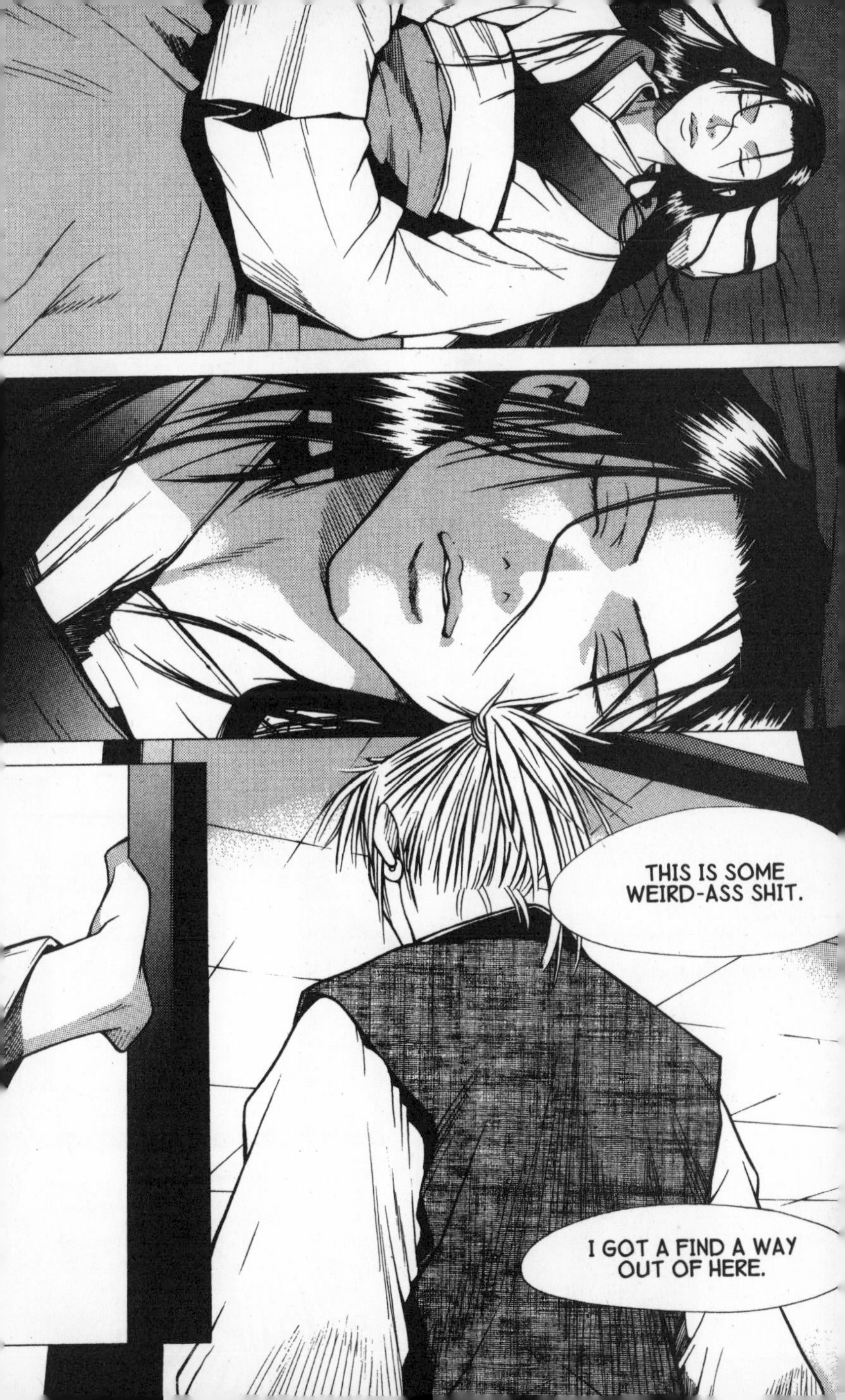
THIS IS SOME WEIRD-ASS SHIT.
I GOT A FIND A WAY OUT OF HERE.

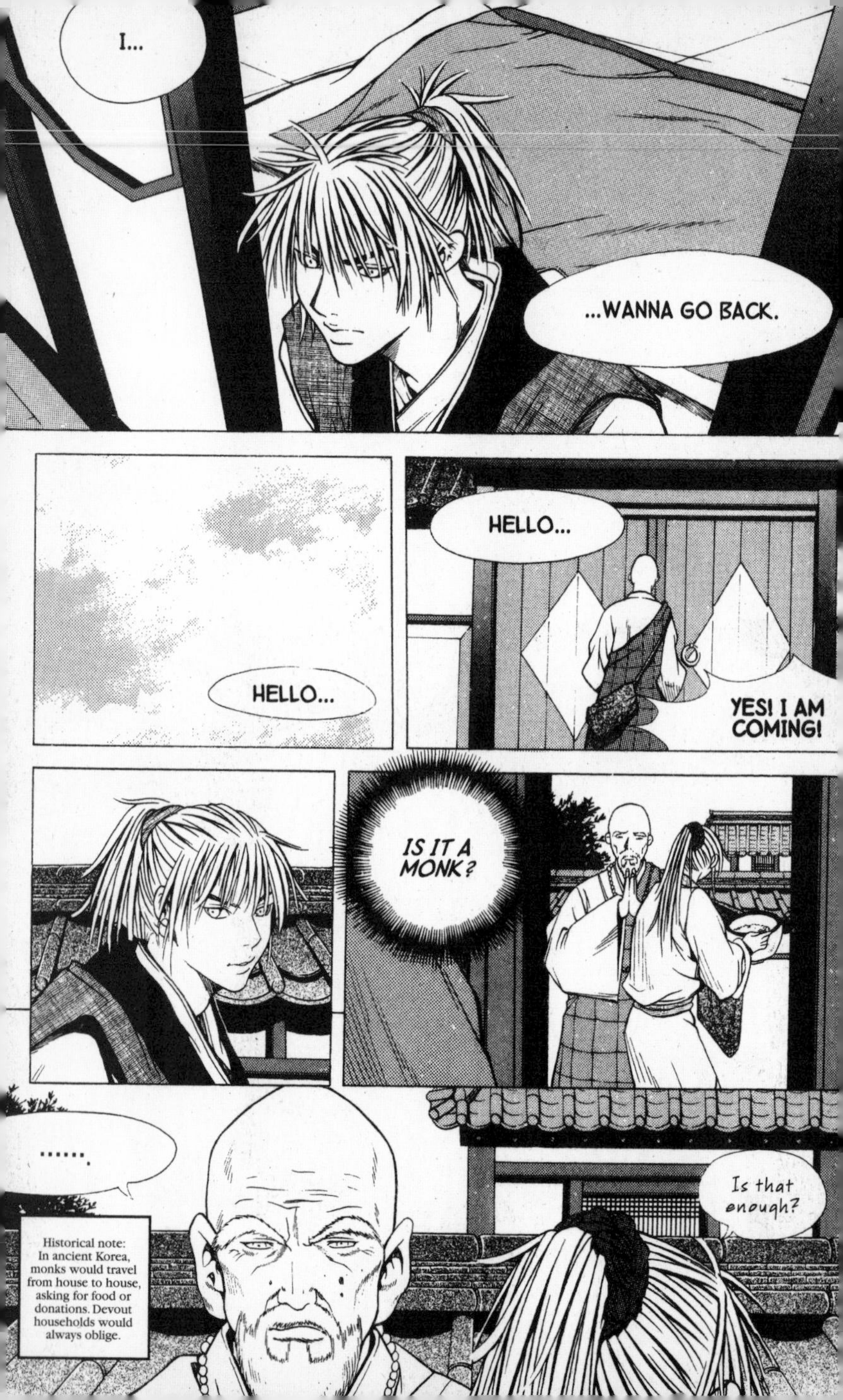
I...
...WANNA GO BACK.
HELLO...
HELLO...
YES! I AM COMING!
IS IT A MONK?
......
Historical note: In ancient Korea, monks would travel from house to house, asking for food or donations. Devout households would always oblige.
Is that enough?

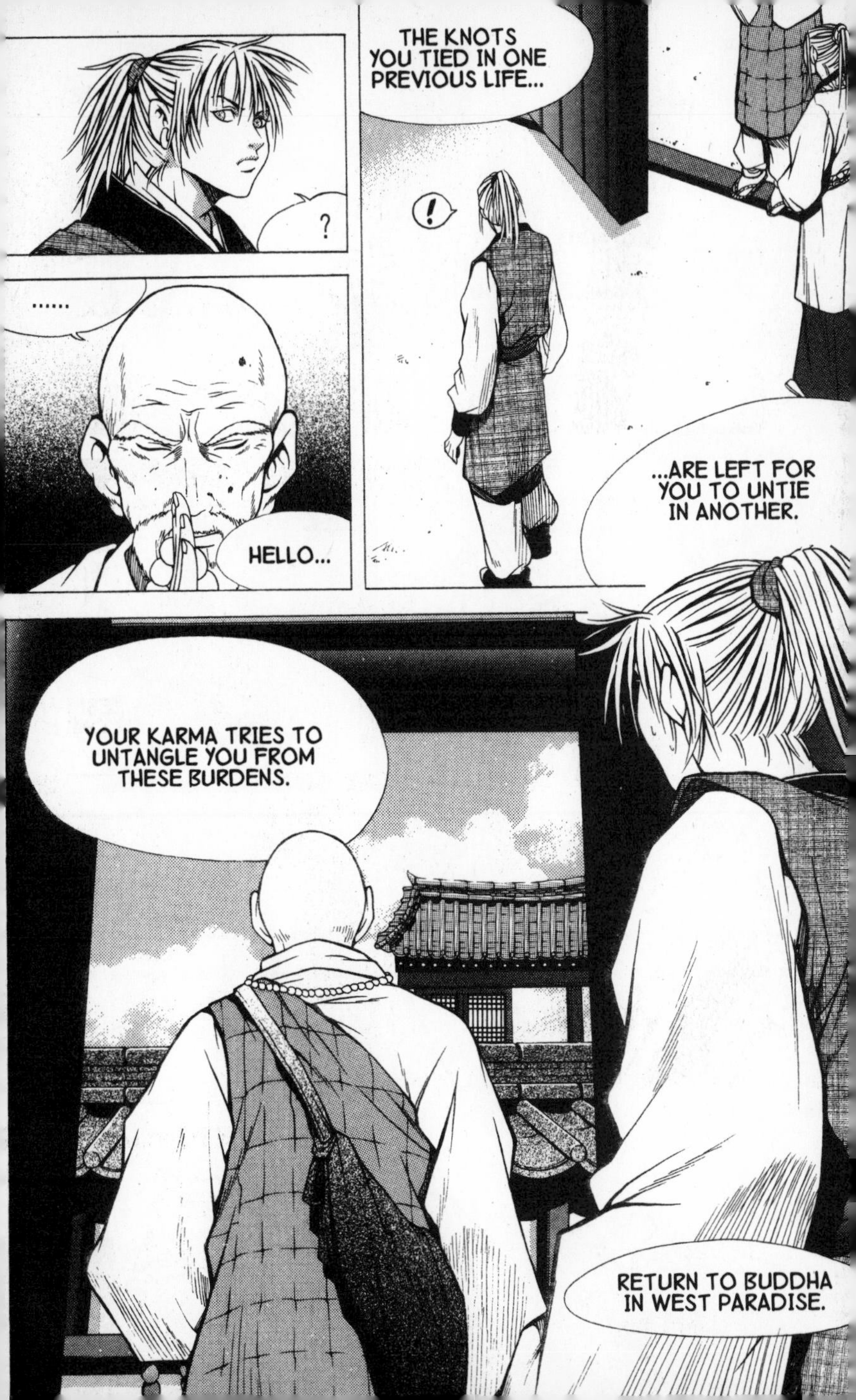
?
......
HELLO...
THE KNOTS YOU TIED IN ONE PREVIOUS LIFE...
!
...ARE LEFT FOR YOU TO UNTIE IN ANOTHER.
YOUR KARMA TRIES TO UNTANGLE YOU FROM THESE BURDENS.
RETURN TO BUDDHA IN WEST PARADISE.

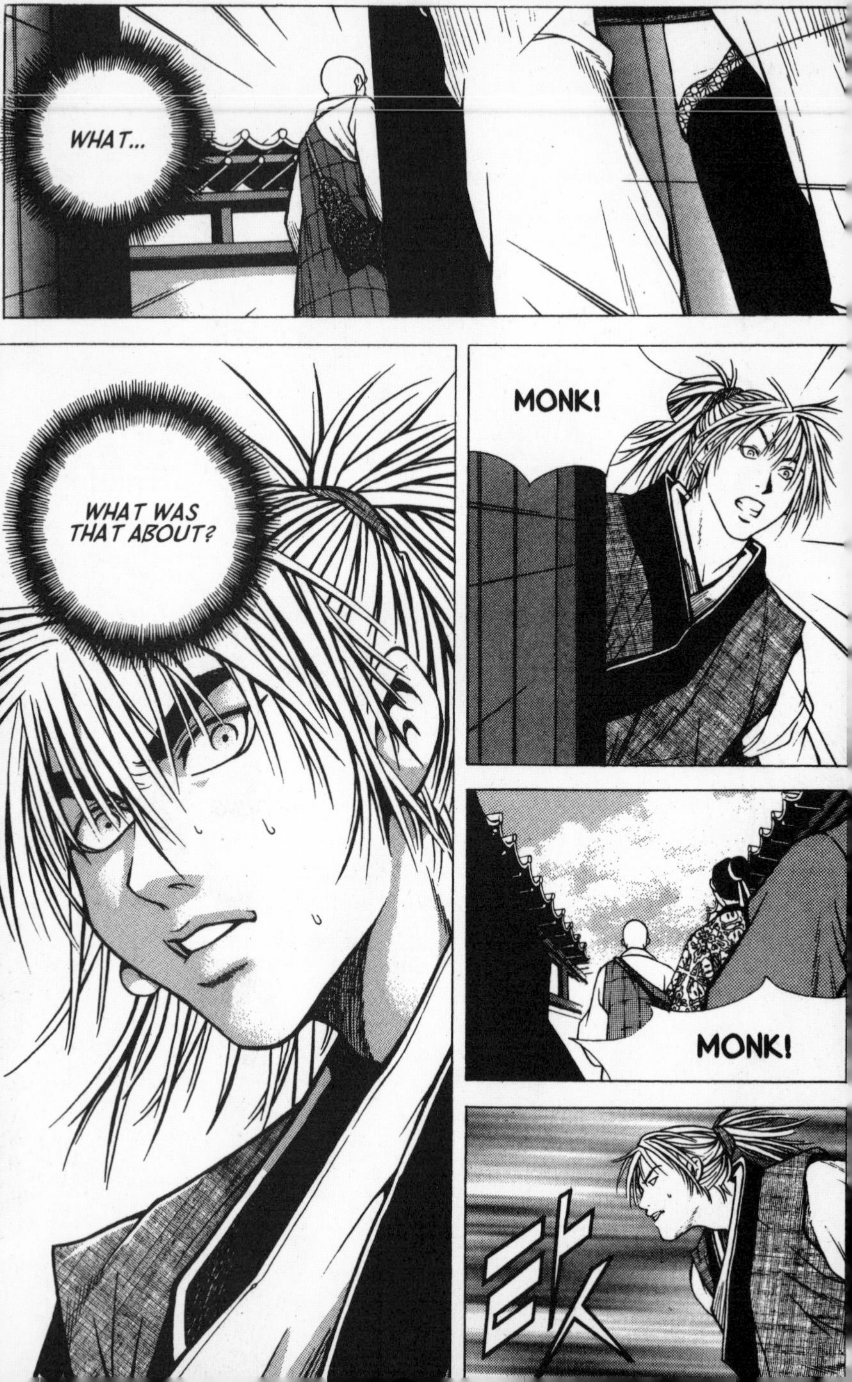
WHAT...
WHAT WAS THAT ABOUT?
MONK!
MONK!

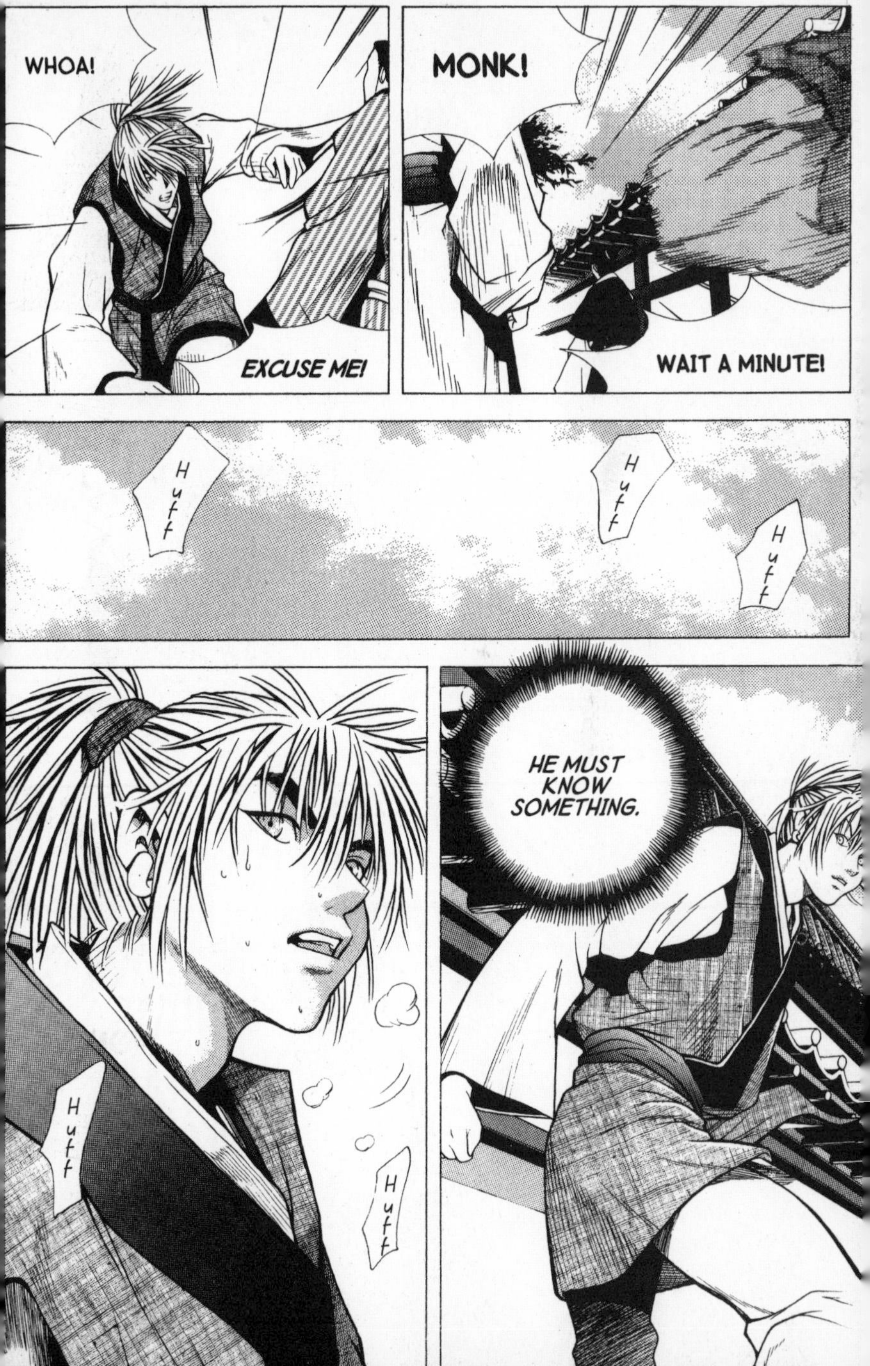
WHOA!
EXCUSE ME!
MONK!
WAIT A MINUTE!
Huff
Huff
Huff
Huff
Huff
HE MUST KNOW SOMETHING.

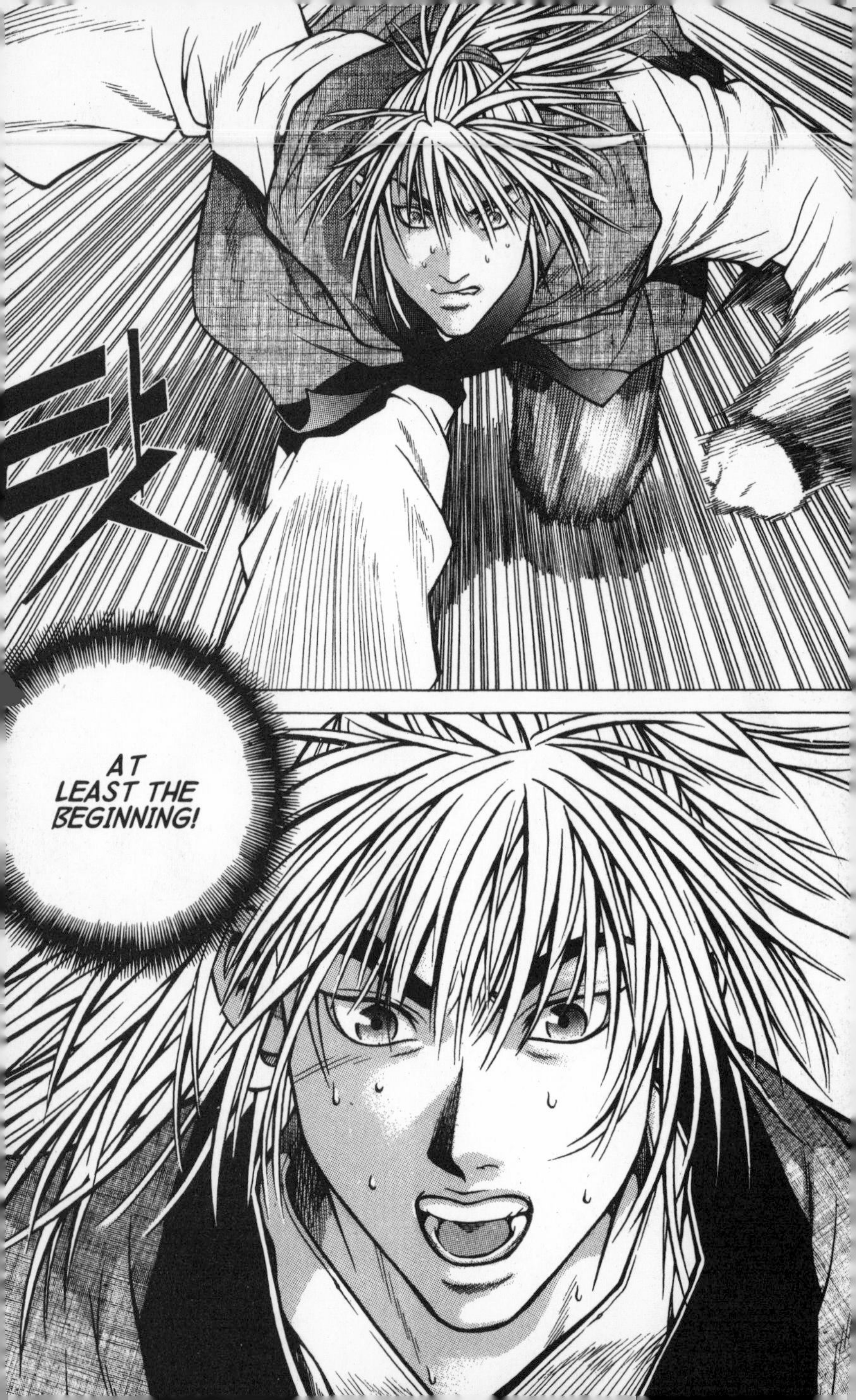
AT LEAST THE BEGINNING!

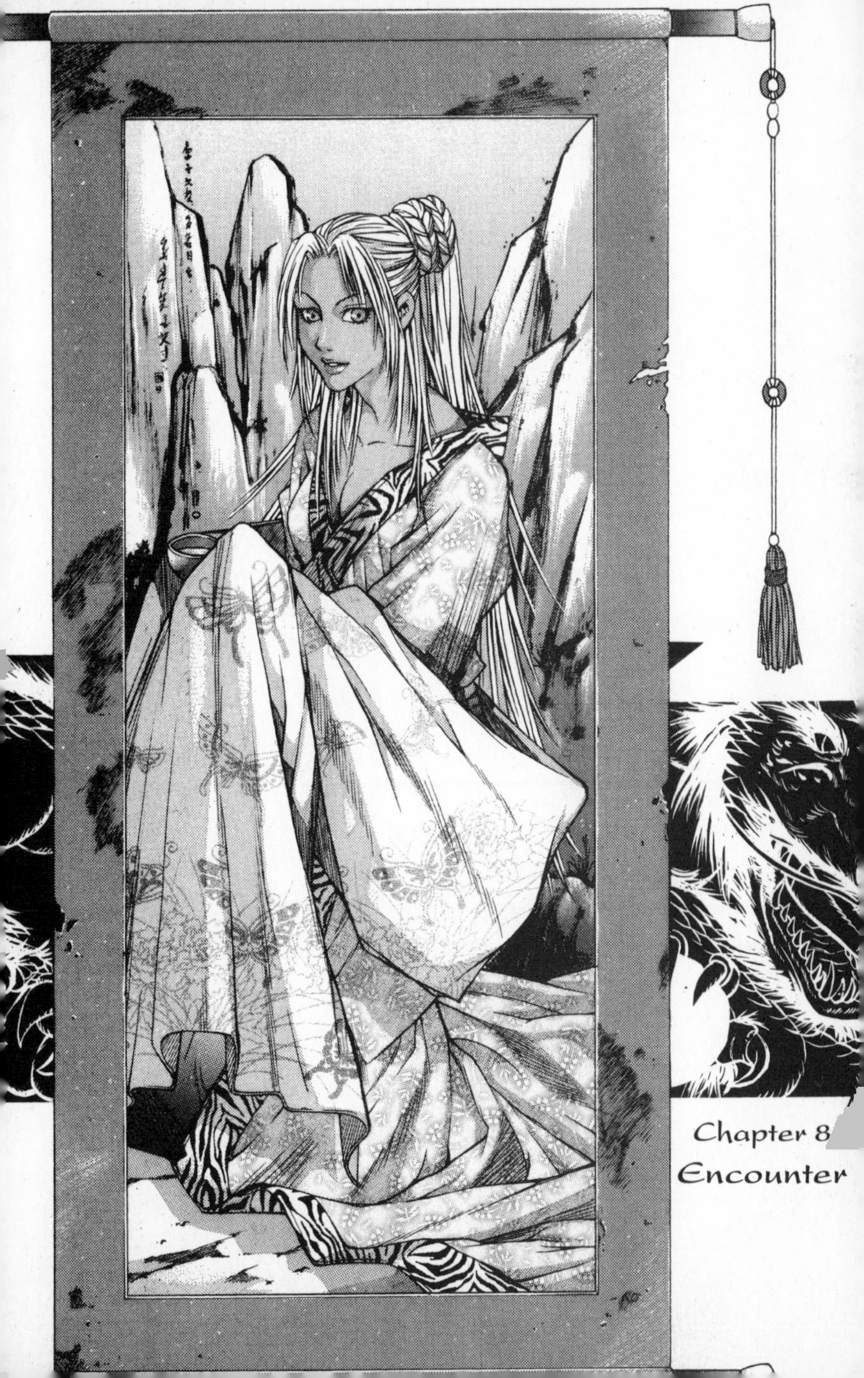

Chapter 8
Encounter

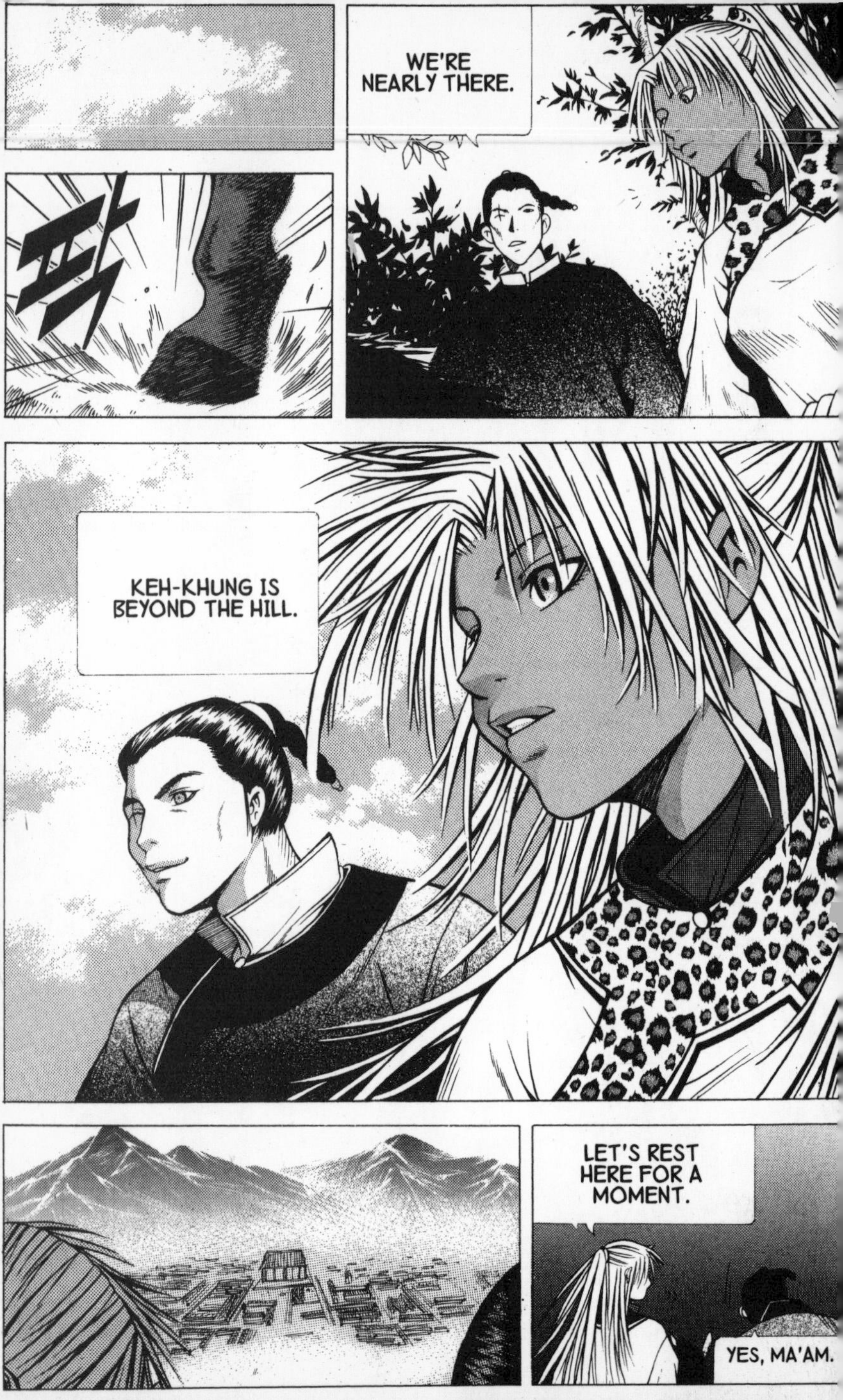
WE'RE NEARLY THERE.
KEH-KHUNG IS BEYOND THE HILL.
LET'S REST HERE FOR A MOMENT.
YES, MA'AM.

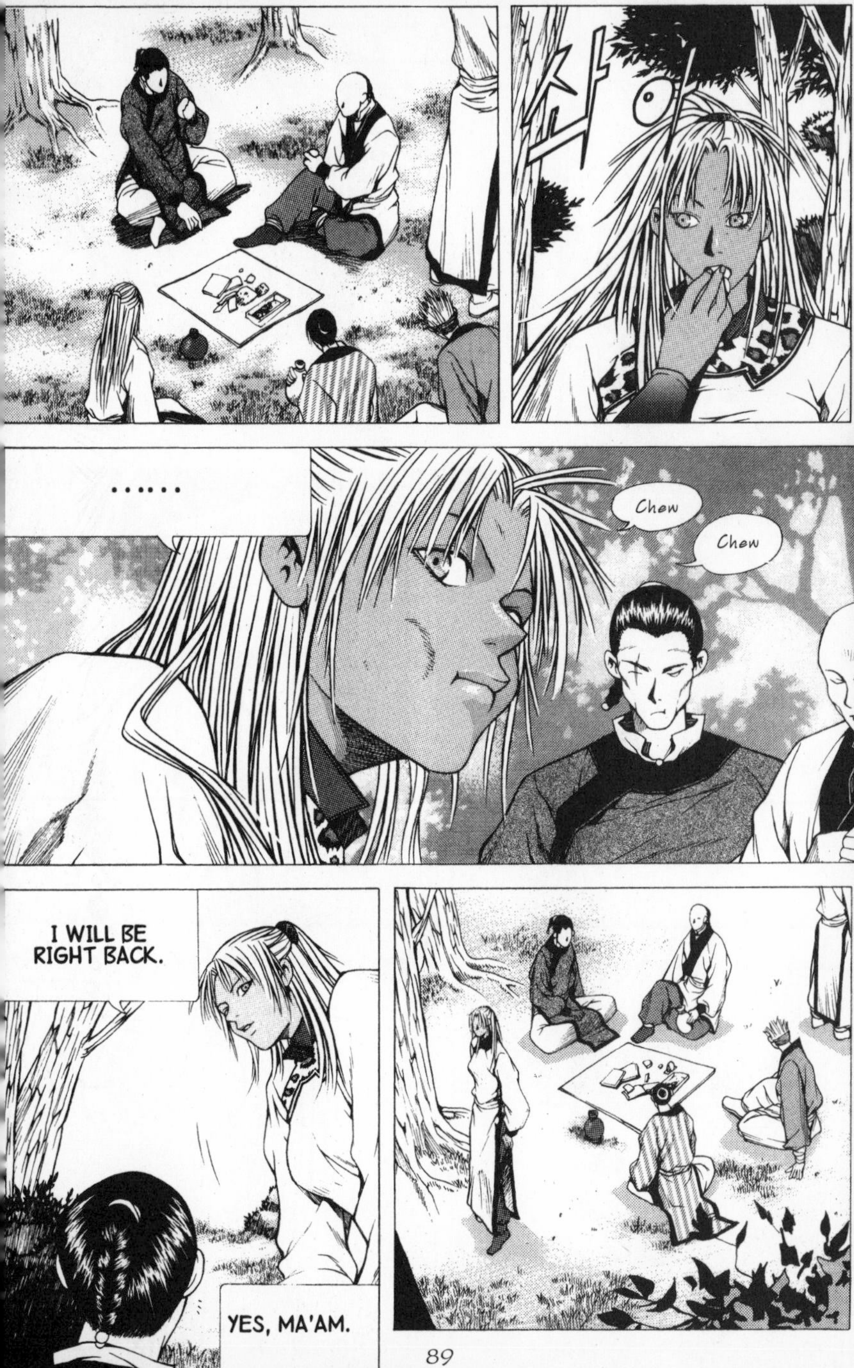
......
Chew
Chew
I WILL BE RIGHT BACK.
YES, MA'AM.

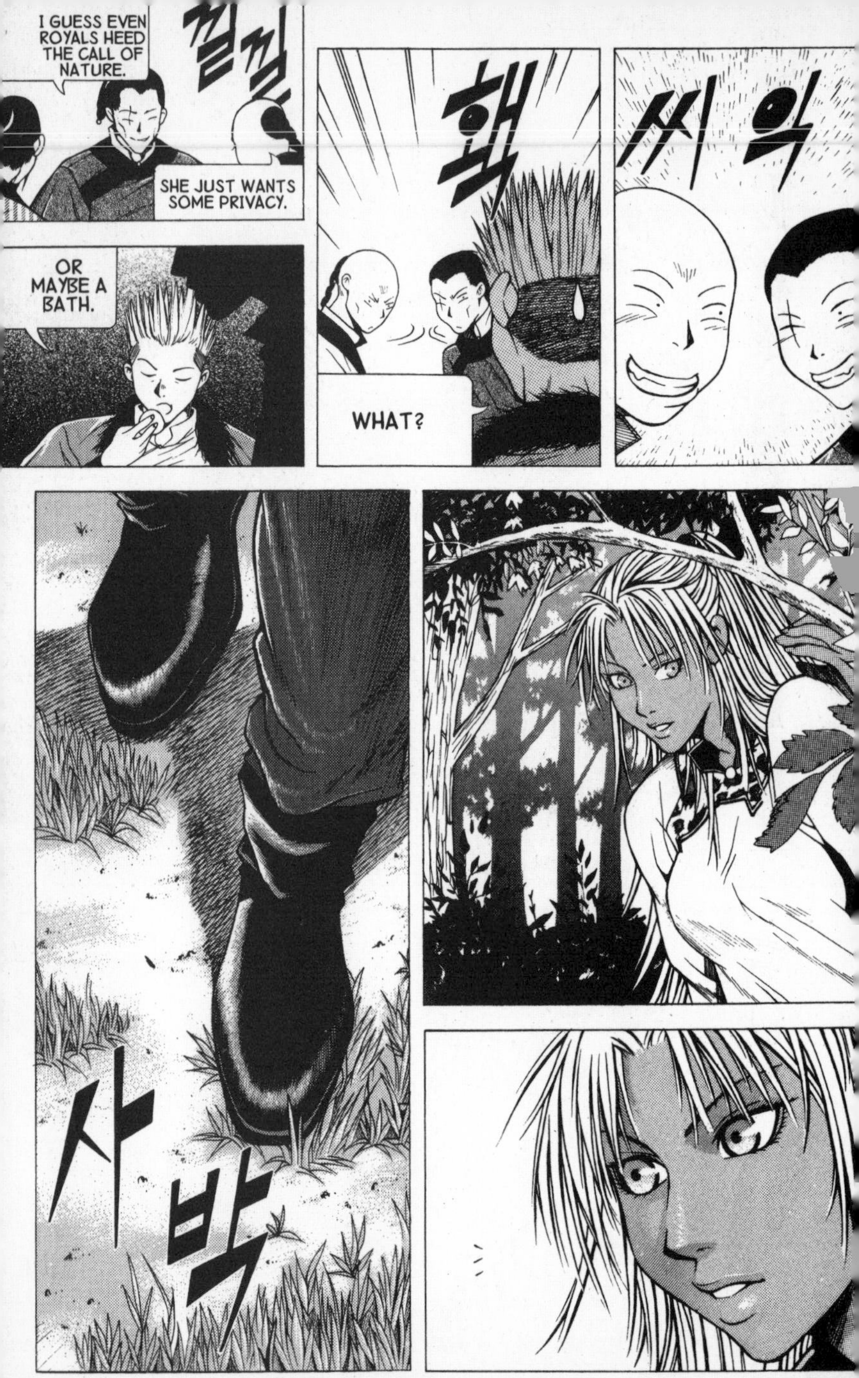
I GUESS EVEN ROYALS HEED THE CALL OF NATURE.
낄낄
SHE JUST WANTS SOME PRIVACY.
OR MAYBE A BATH.
홱
WHAT?
씨익
사박

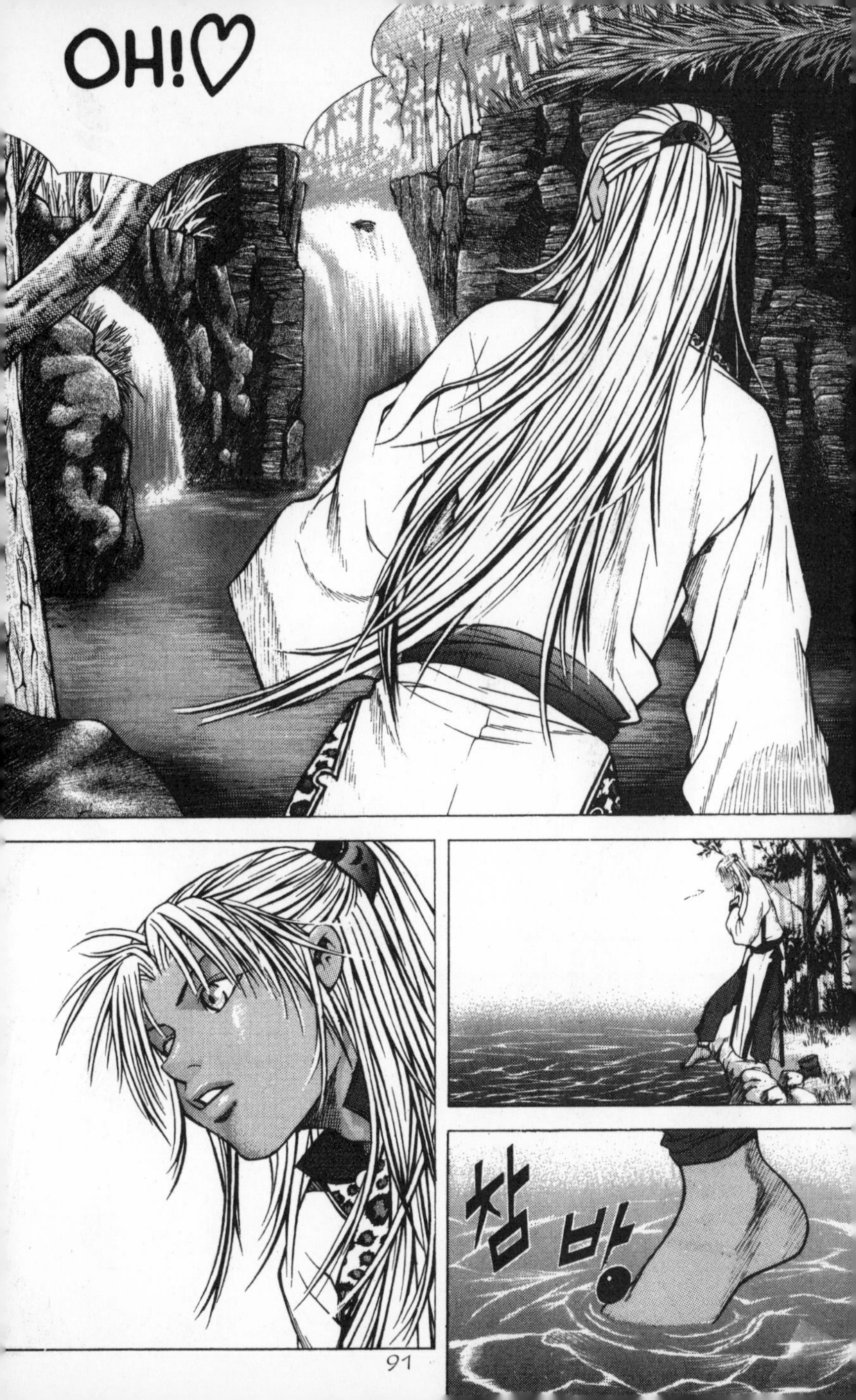
OH!♡
참방!

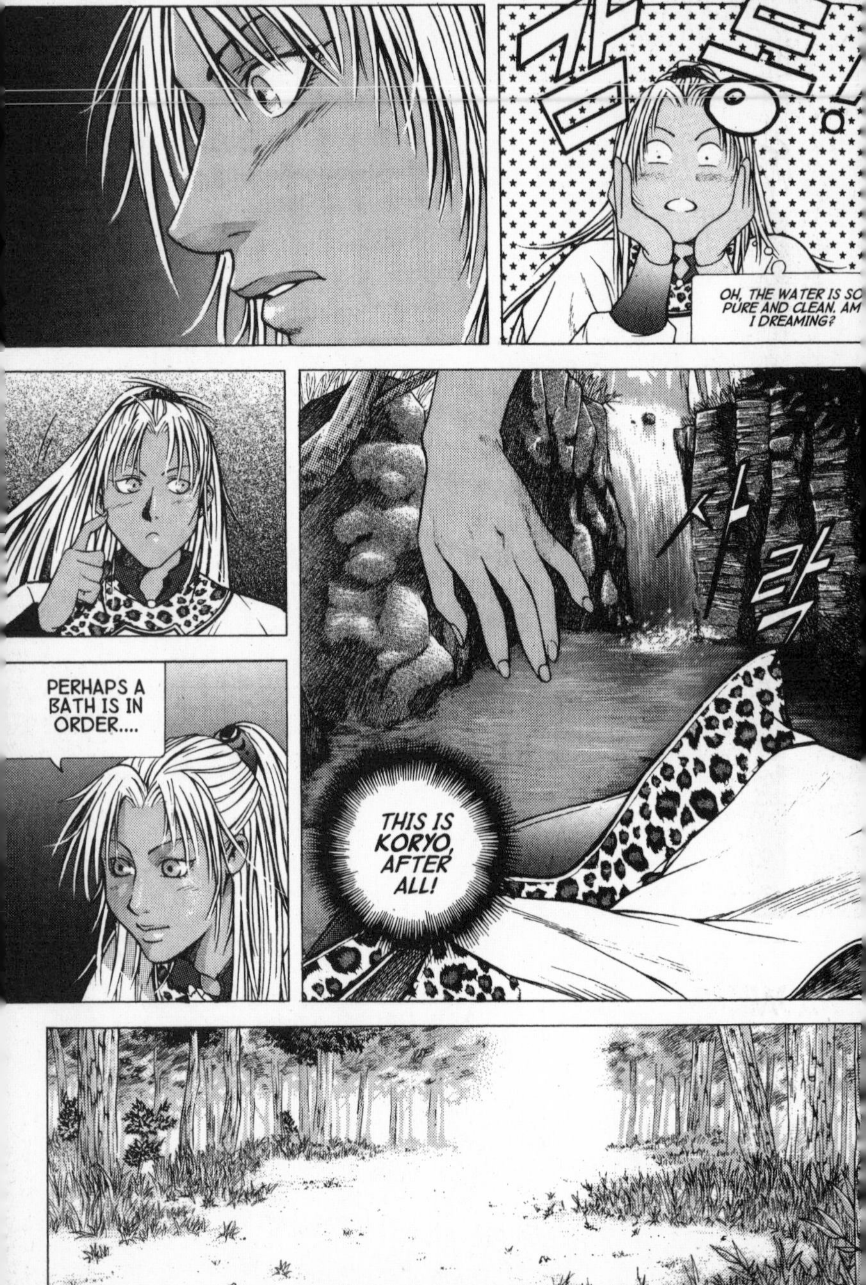
OH, THE WATER IS SO PURE AND CLEAN. AM I DREAMING?
PERHAPS A BATH IS IN ORDER....
THIS IS KORYO, AFTER ALL!

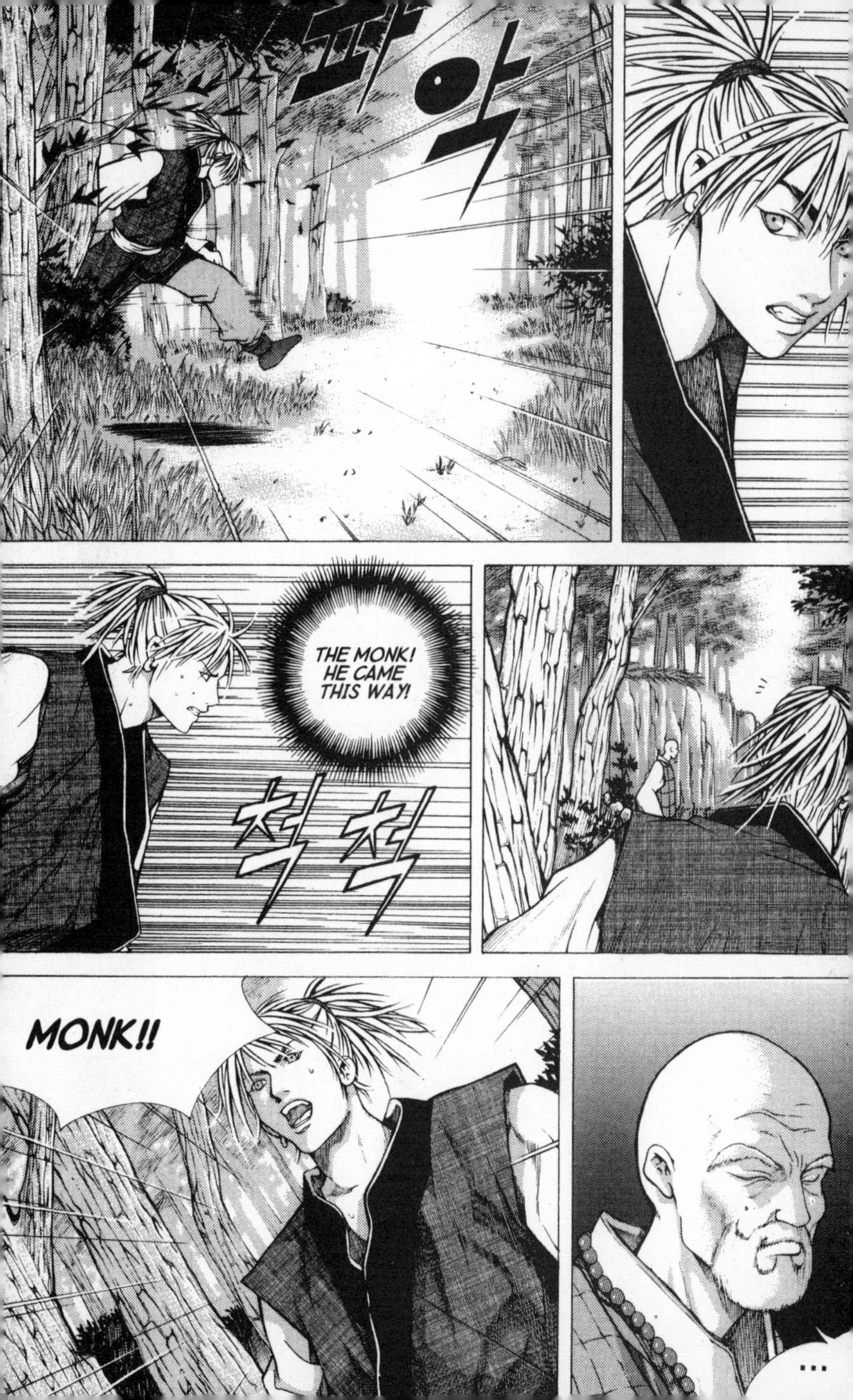
THE MONK! HE CAME THIS WAY!
MONK!!
...

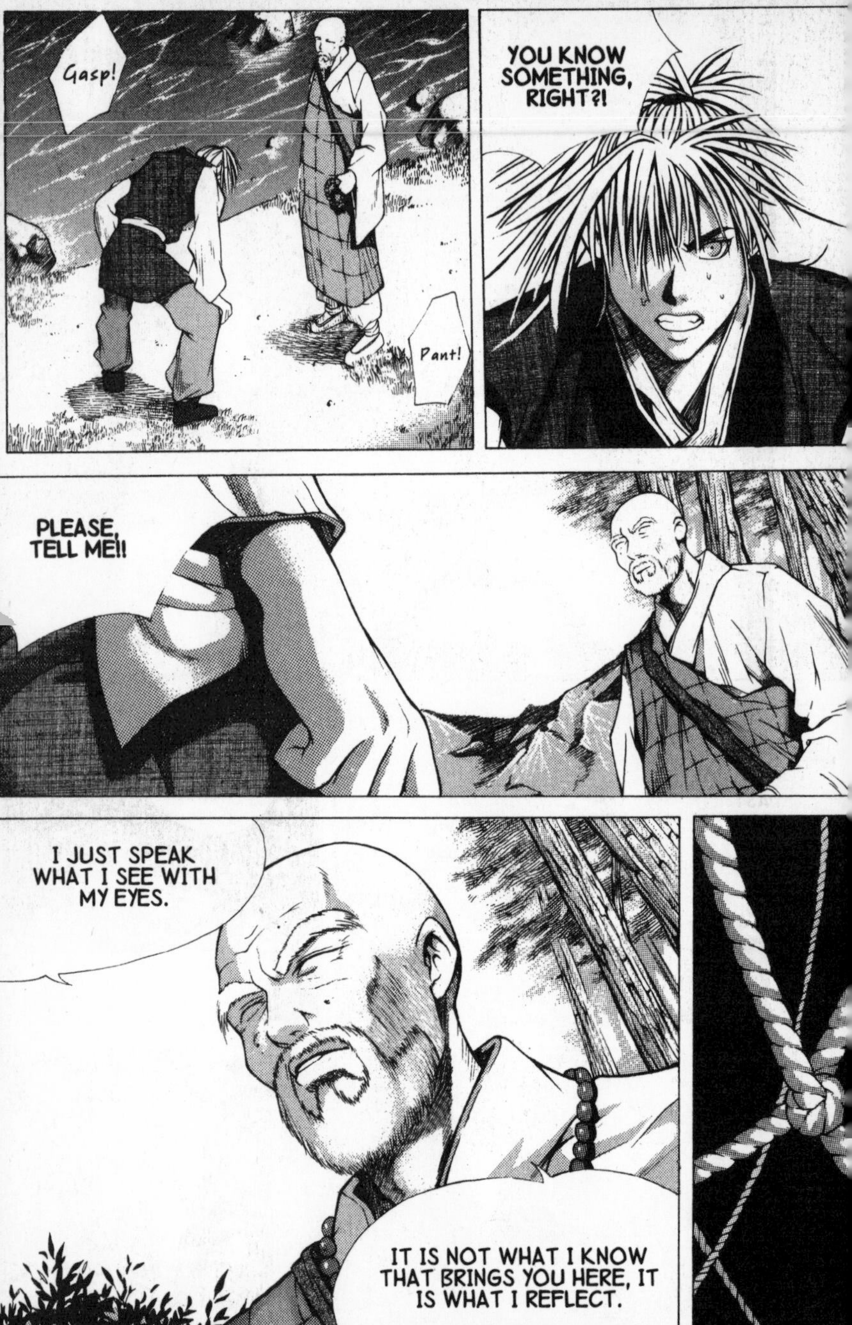
Gasp!
Pant!
YOU KNOW SOMETHING, RIGHT?!
PLEASE, TELL ME!!
I JUST SPEAK WHAT I SEE WITH MY EYES.
IT IS NOT WHAT I KNOW THAT BRINGS YOU HERE, IT IS WHAT I REFLECT.

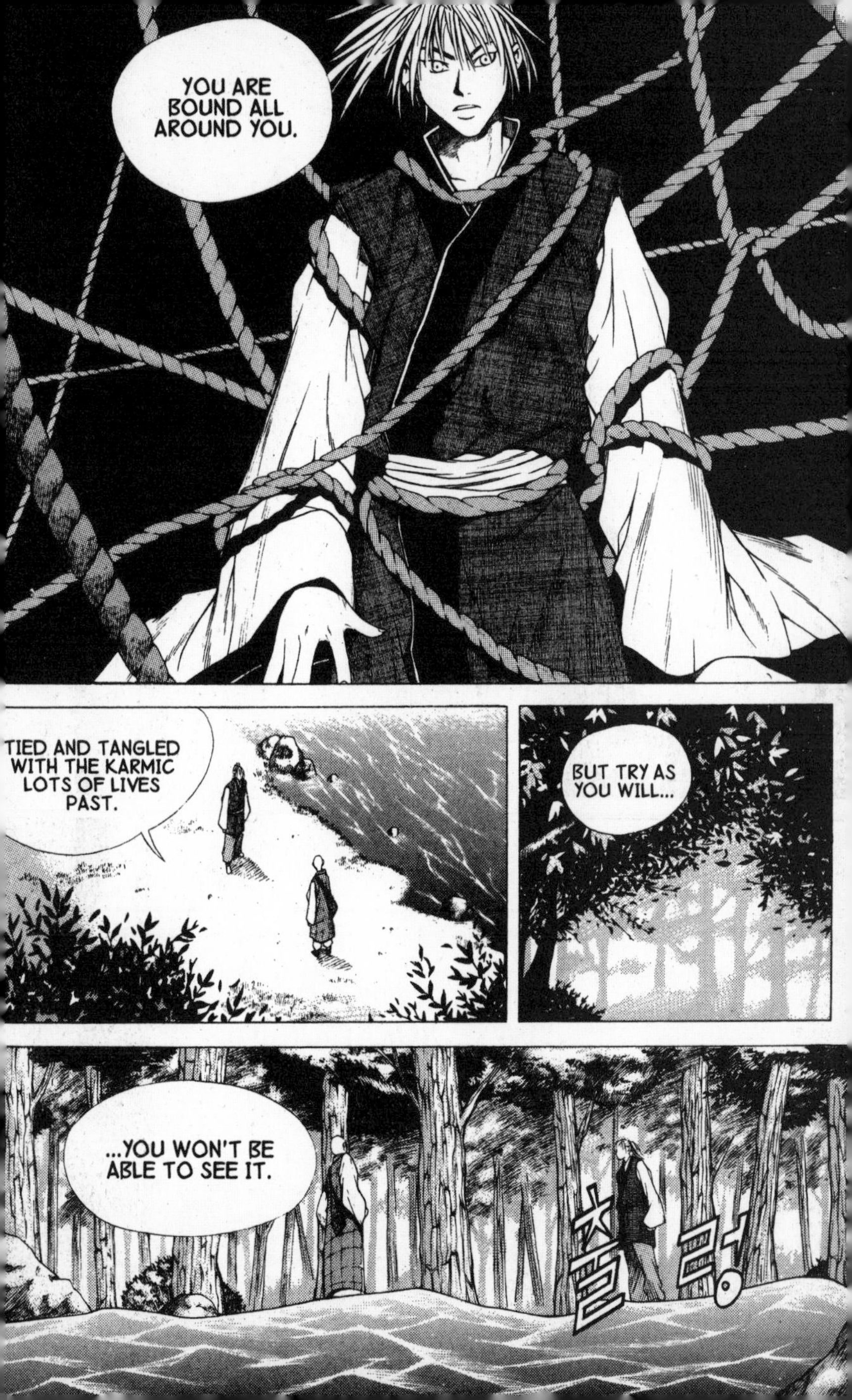
YOU ARE BOUND ALL AROUND YOU.
TIED AND TANGLED WITH THE KARMIC LOTS OF LIVES PAST.
BUT TRY AS YOU WILL...
...YOU WON'T BE ABLE TO SEE IT.

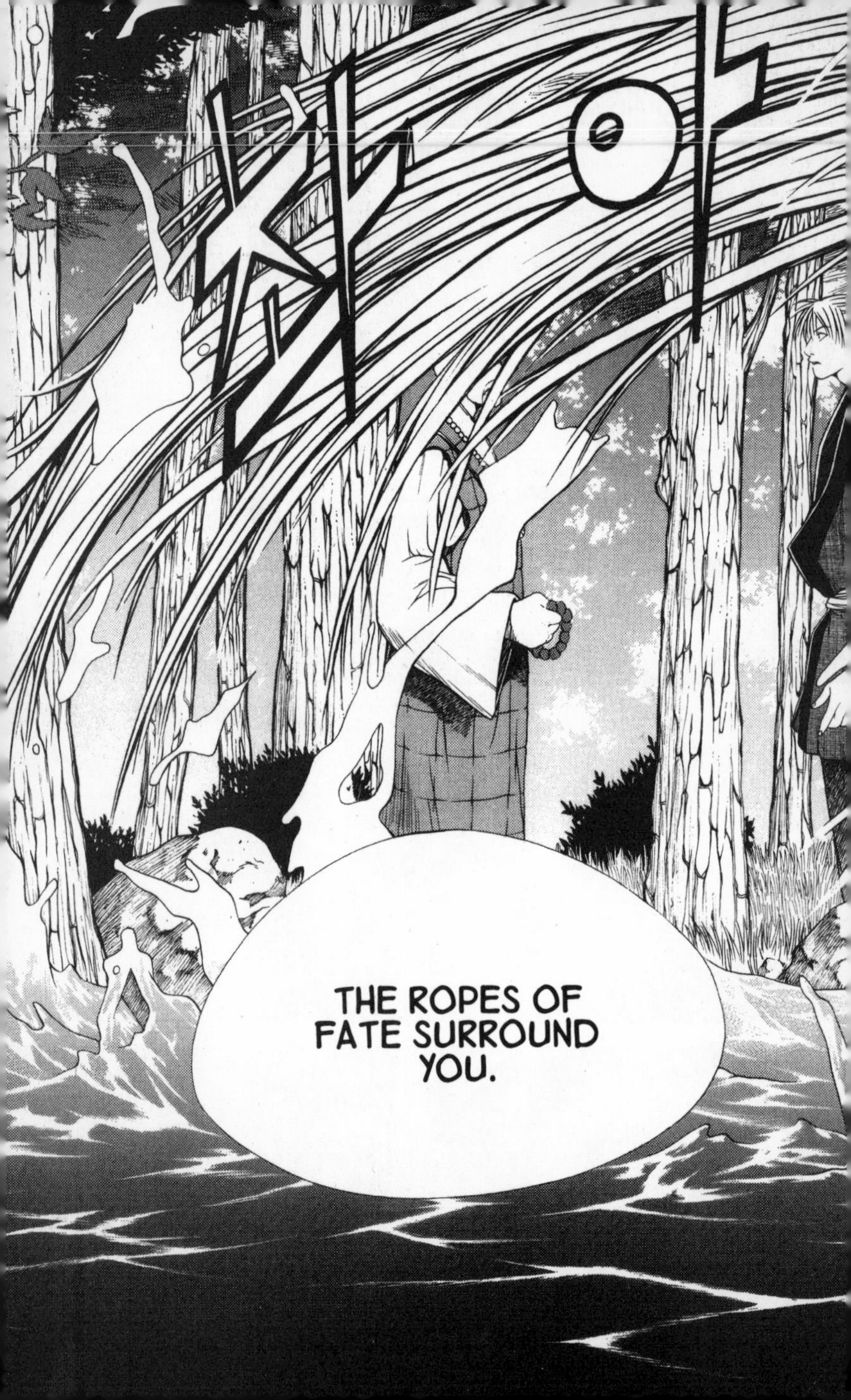
ドシュッ
THE ROPES OF FATE SURROUND YOU.

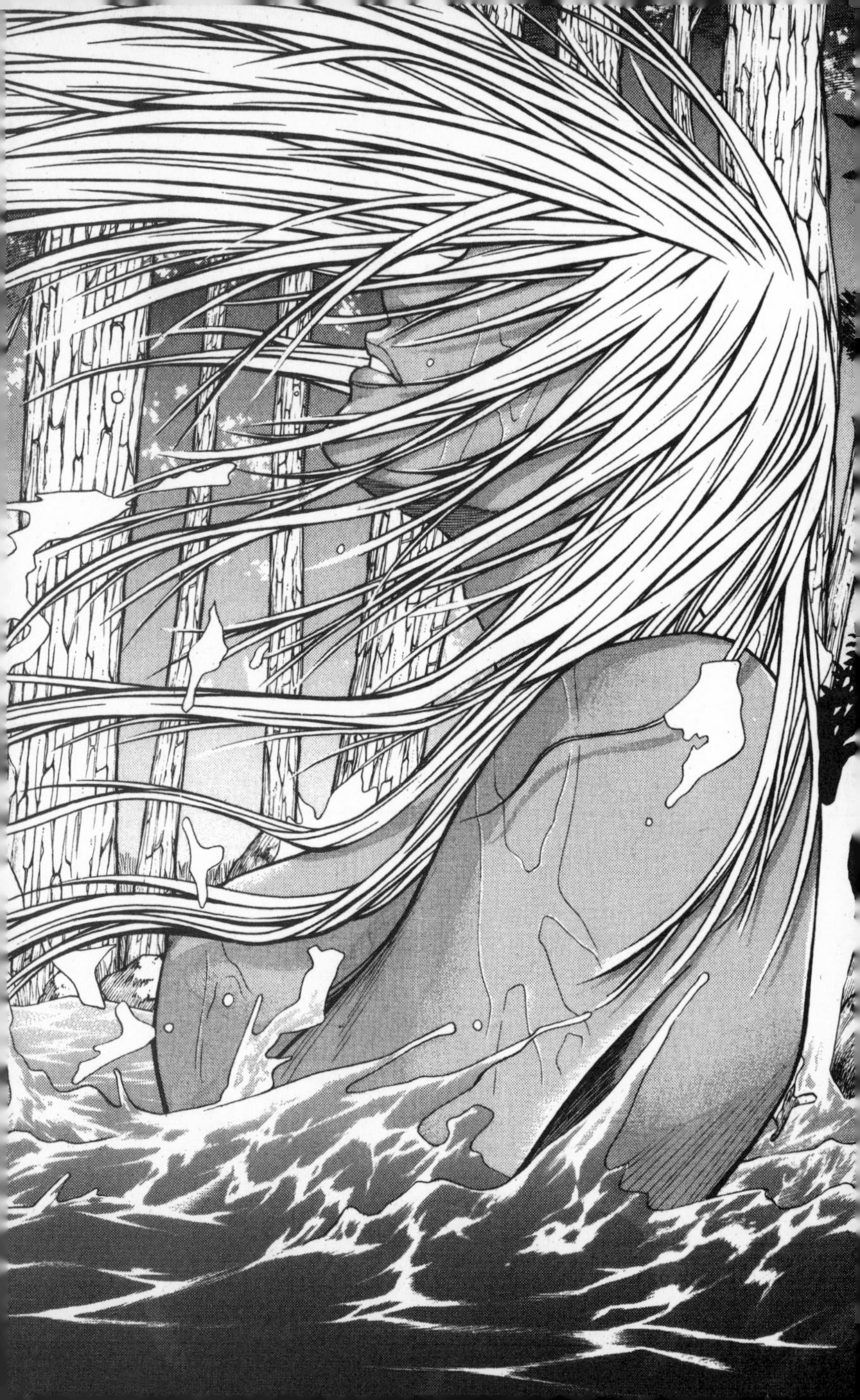

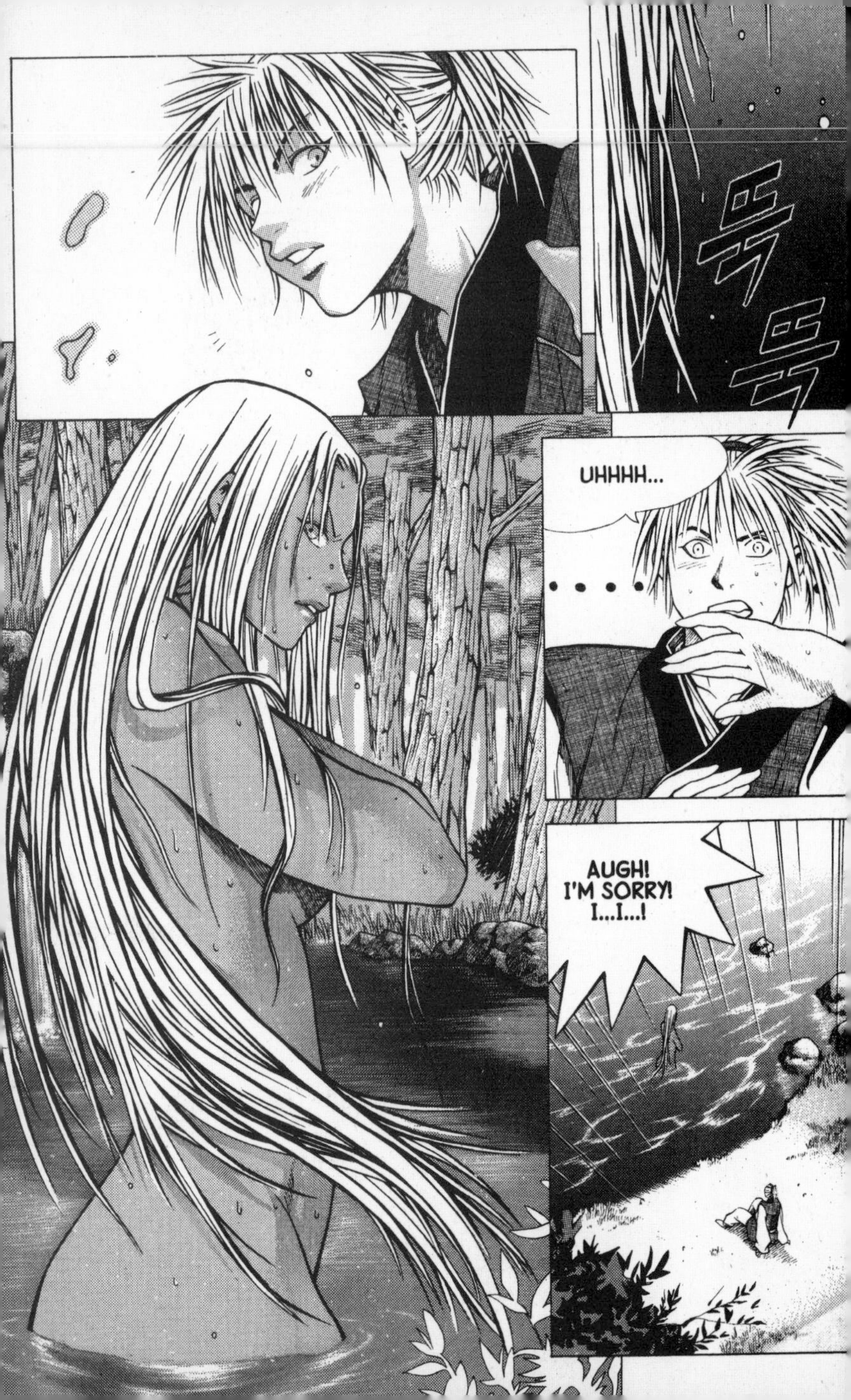
뚝
뚝
UHHHH...
• • • •
AUGH! I'M SORRY! I...I...!

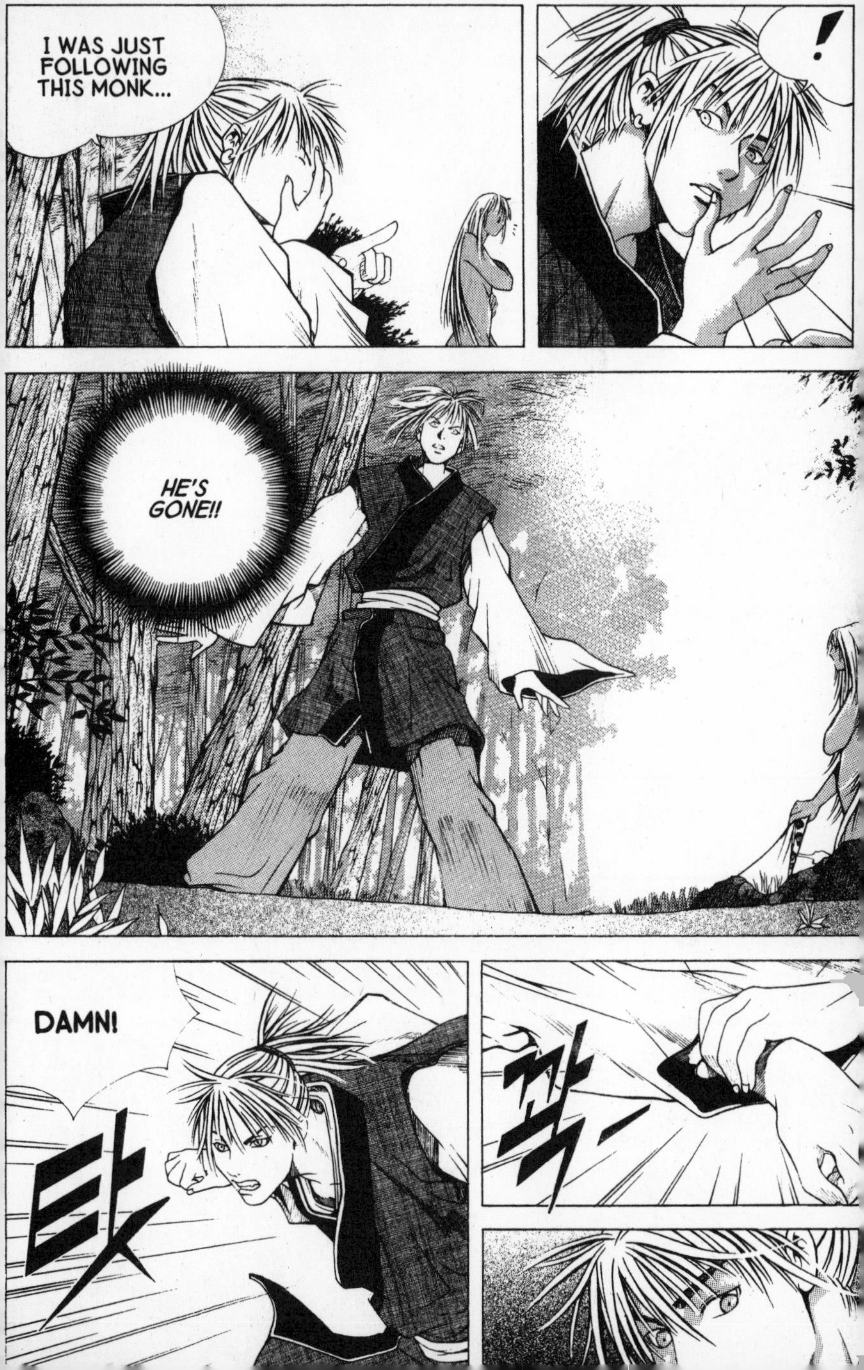
I WAS JUST FOLLOWING THIS MONK...
!
HE'S GONE!!
DAMN!

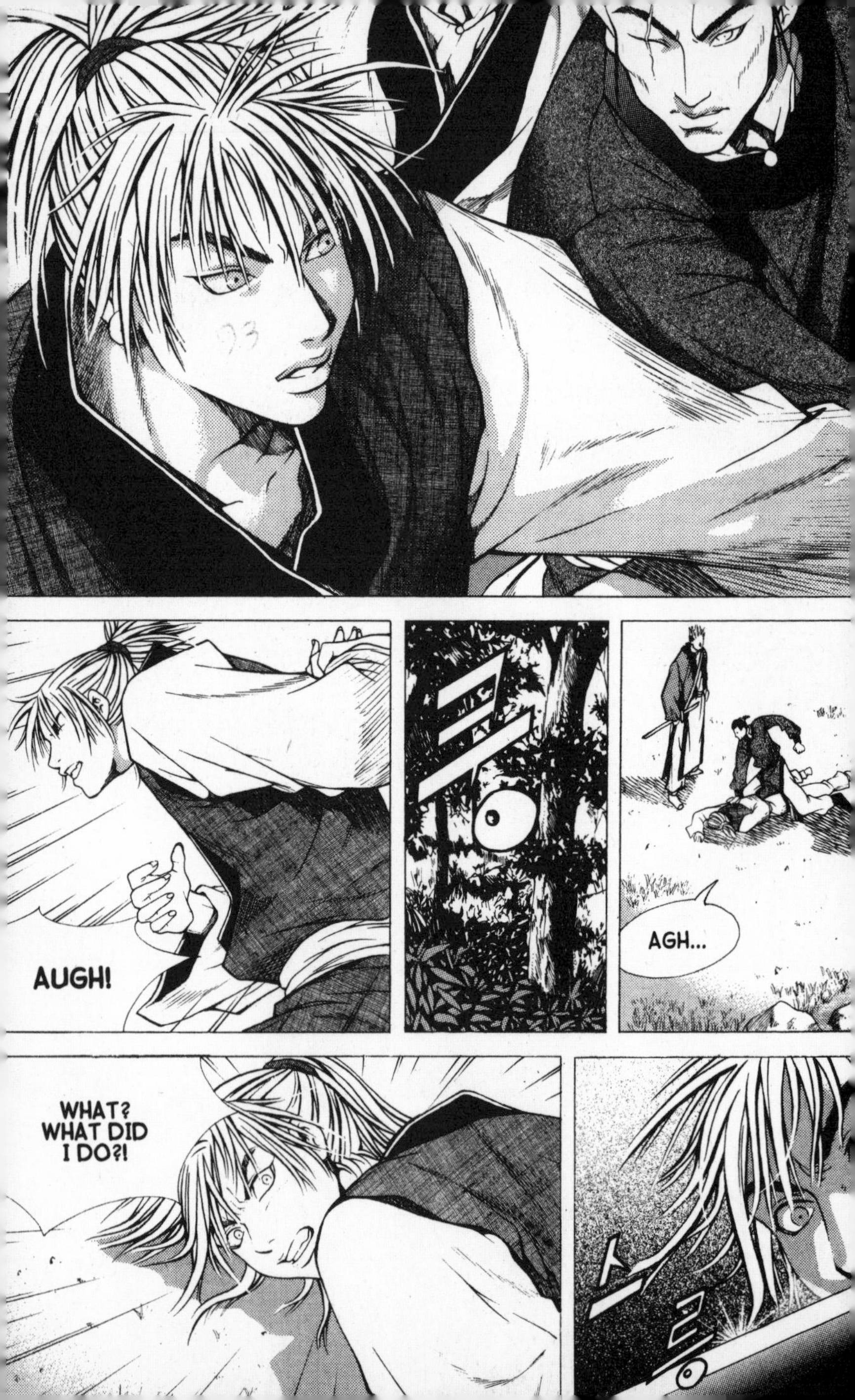
AUGH!
AGH...
WHAT? WHAT DID I DO?!

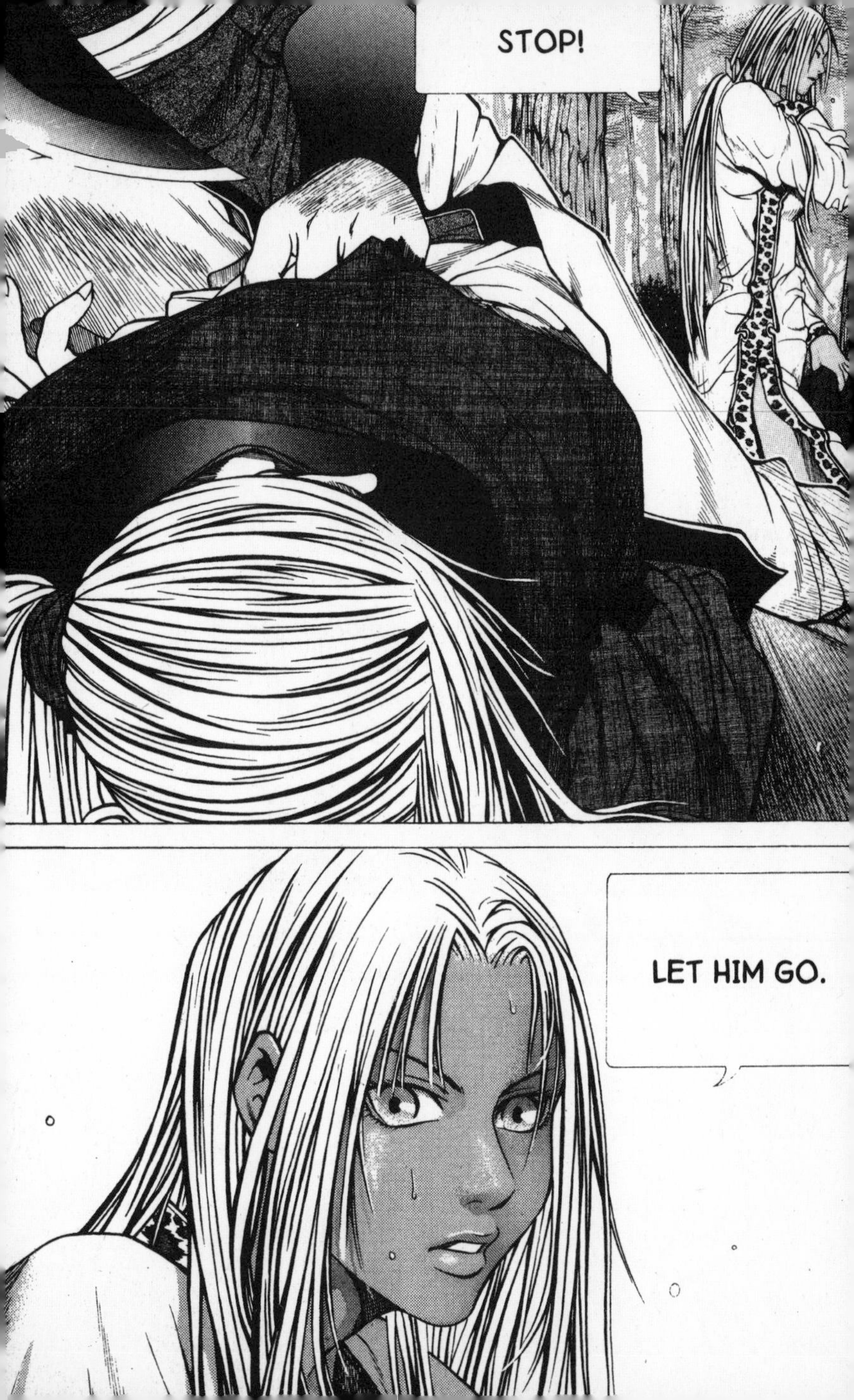
STOP!
LET HIM GO.

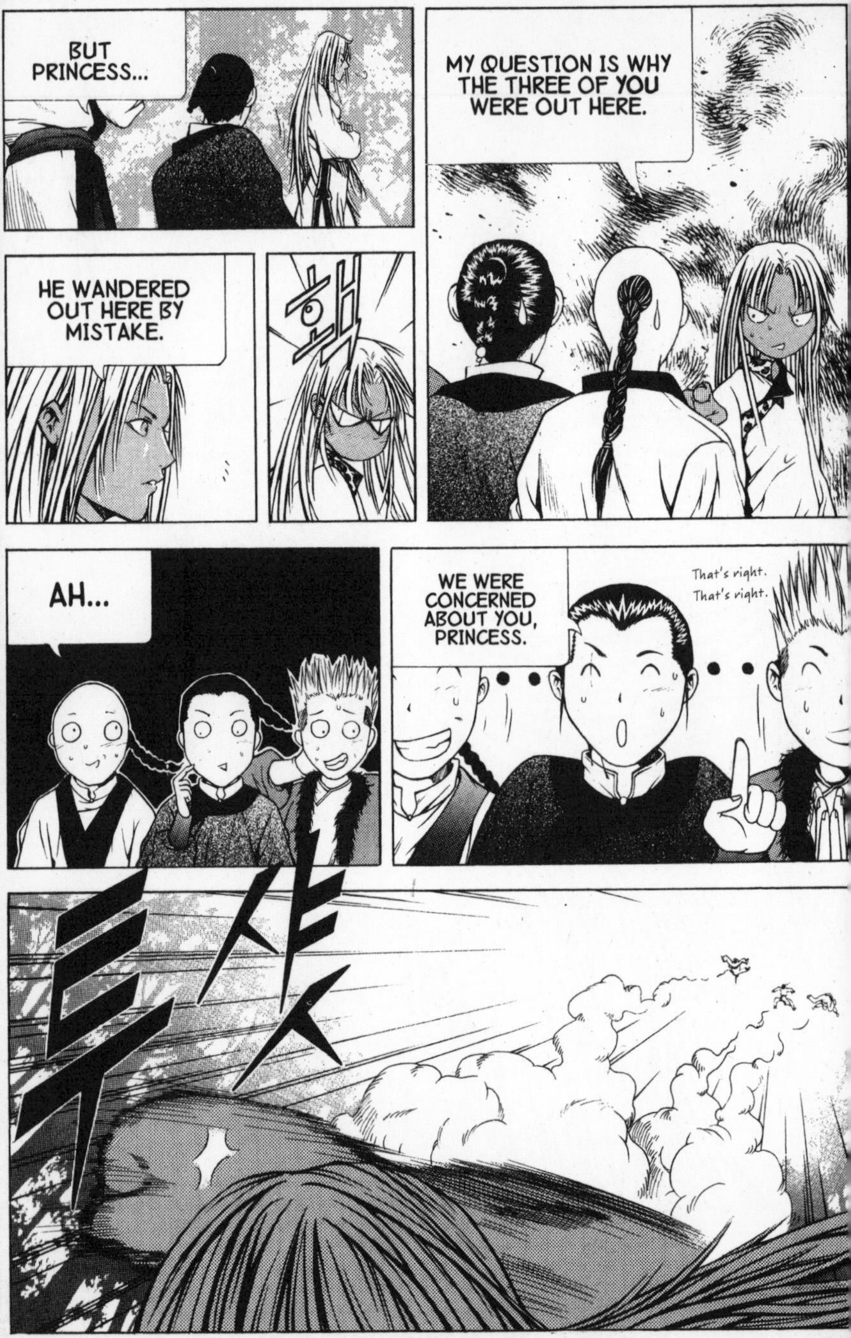
BUT PRINCESS...
HE WANDERED OUT HERE BY MISTAKE.
홱
MY QUESTION IS WHY THE THREE OF YOU WERE OUT HERE.
AH...
WE WERE CONCERNED ABOUT YOU, PRINCESS.
That's right. That's right.

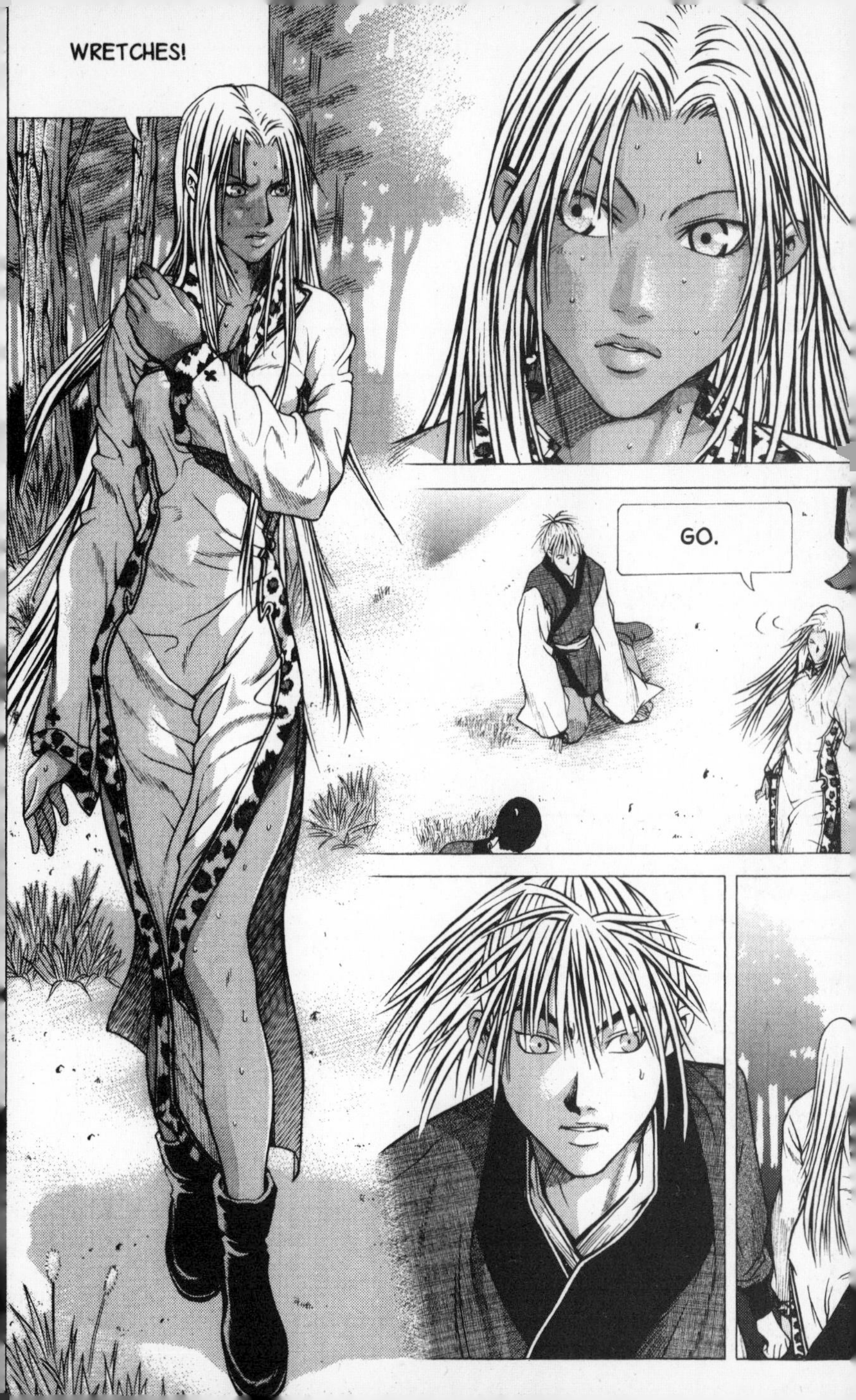
WRETCHES!
GO.

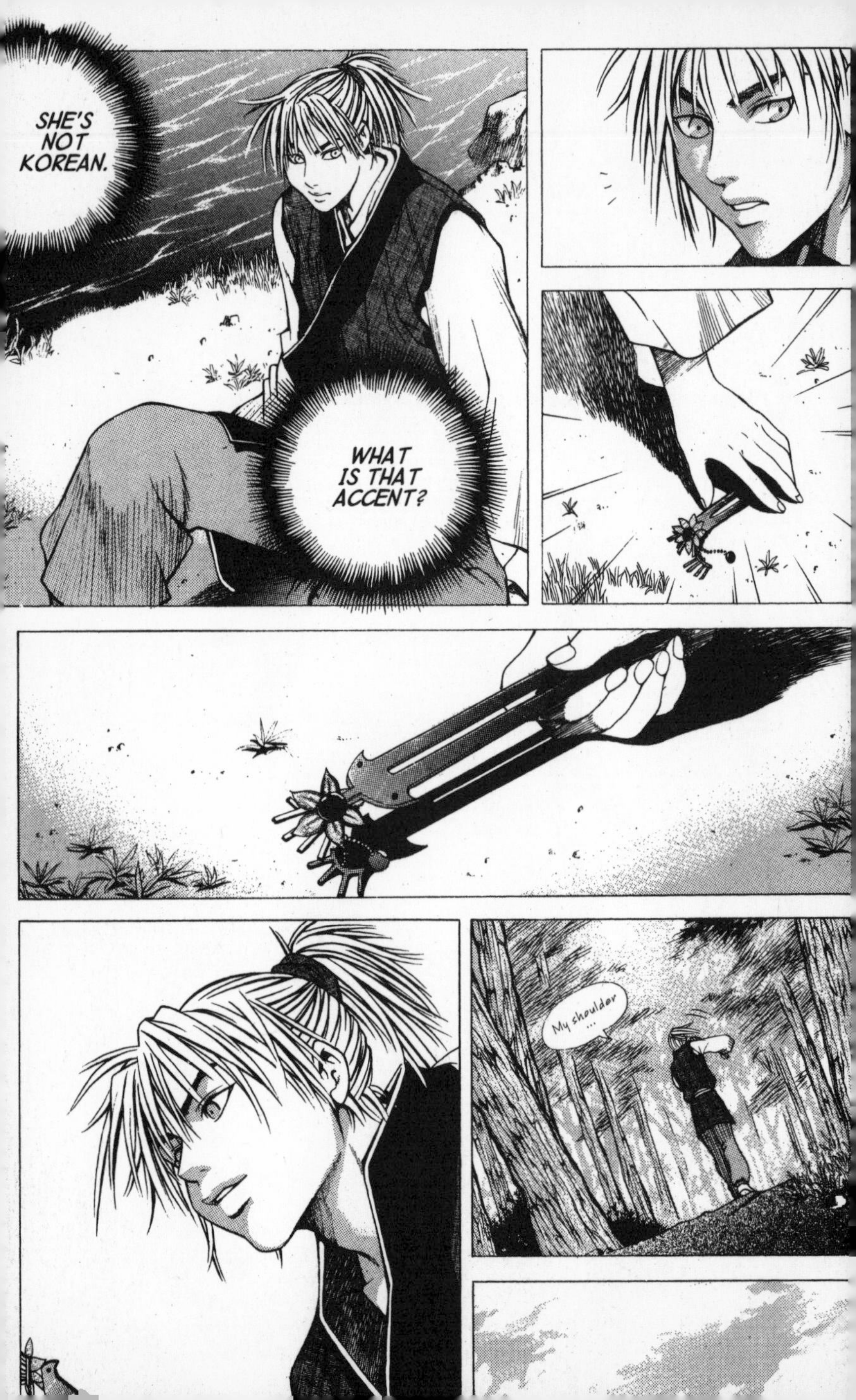
SHE'S NOT KOREAN.
WHAT IS THAT ACCENT?
My shoulder ...

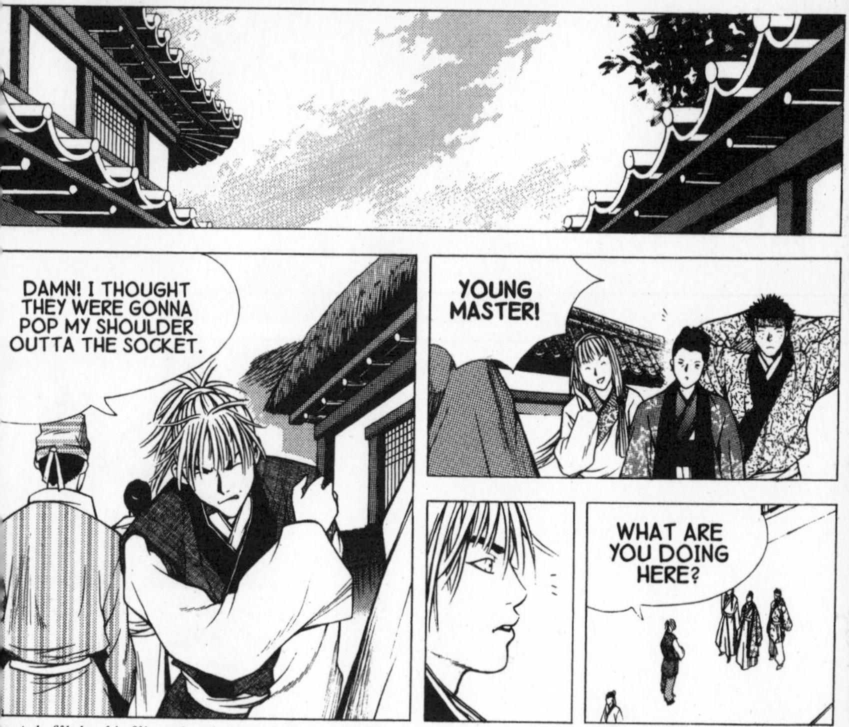
DAMN! I THOUGHT THEY WERE GONNA POP MY SHOULDER OUTTA THE SOCKET.
YOUNG MASTER!
WHAT ARE YOU DOING HERE?

ano is the fifth day of the fifth month on the lunar calendar. It is a day of festivities.

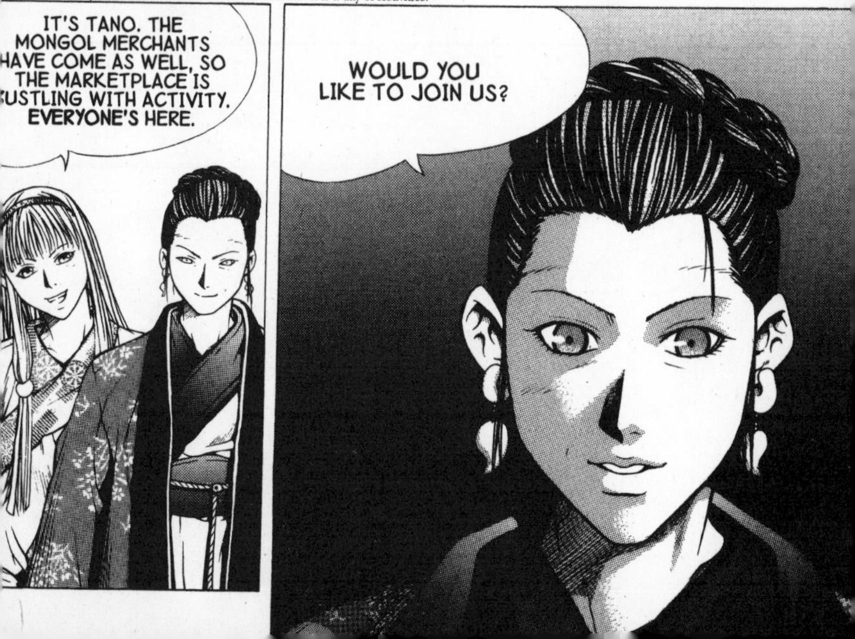
IT'S TANO. THE MONGOL MERCHANTS HAVE COME AS WELL, SO THE MARKETPLACE IS BUSTLING WITH ACTIVITY. EVERYONE'S HERE.
WOULD YOU LIKE TO JOIN US?

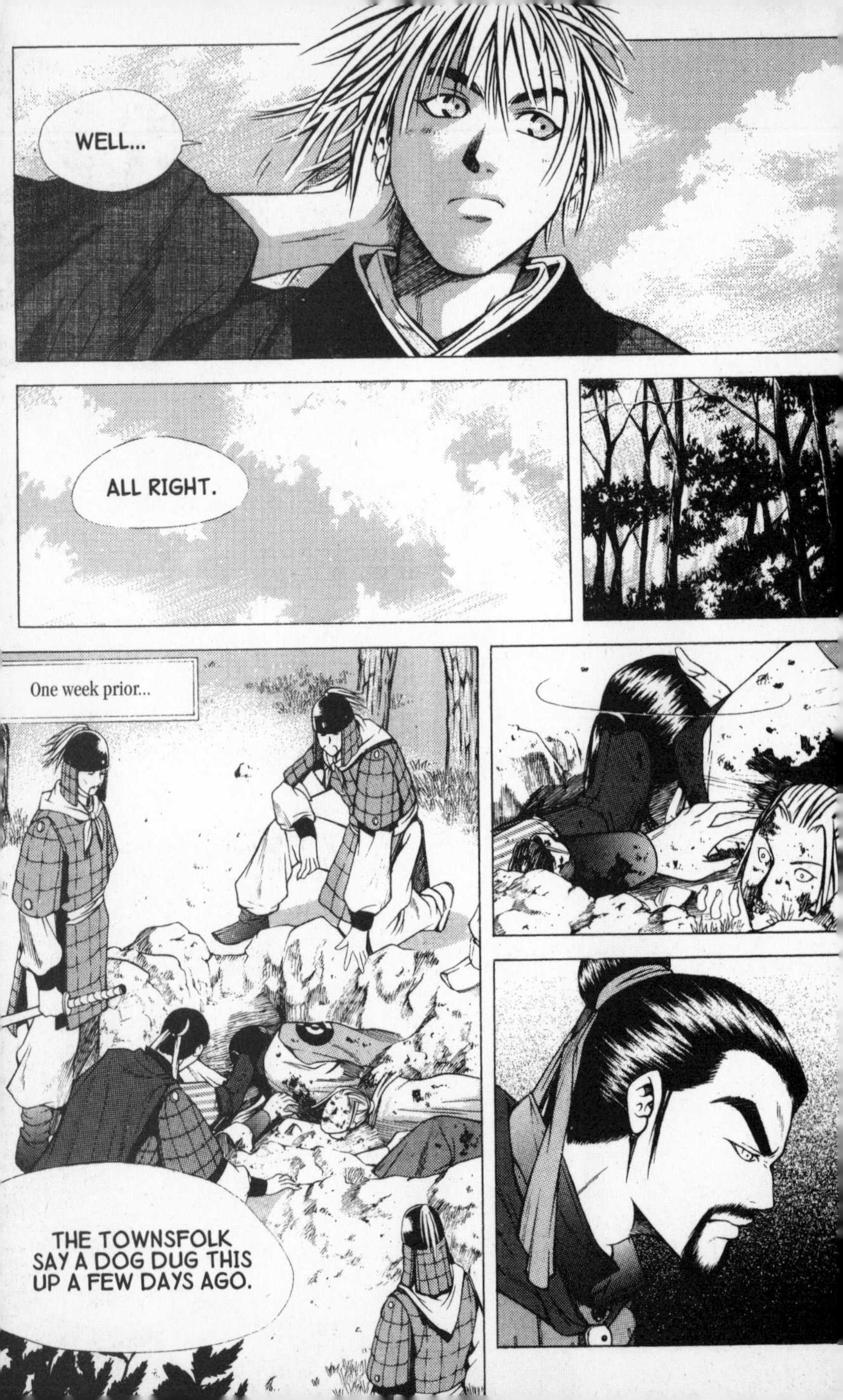
WELL...
ALL RIGHT.
One week prior...
THE TOWNSFOLK SAY A DOG DUG THIS UP A FEW DAYS AGO.

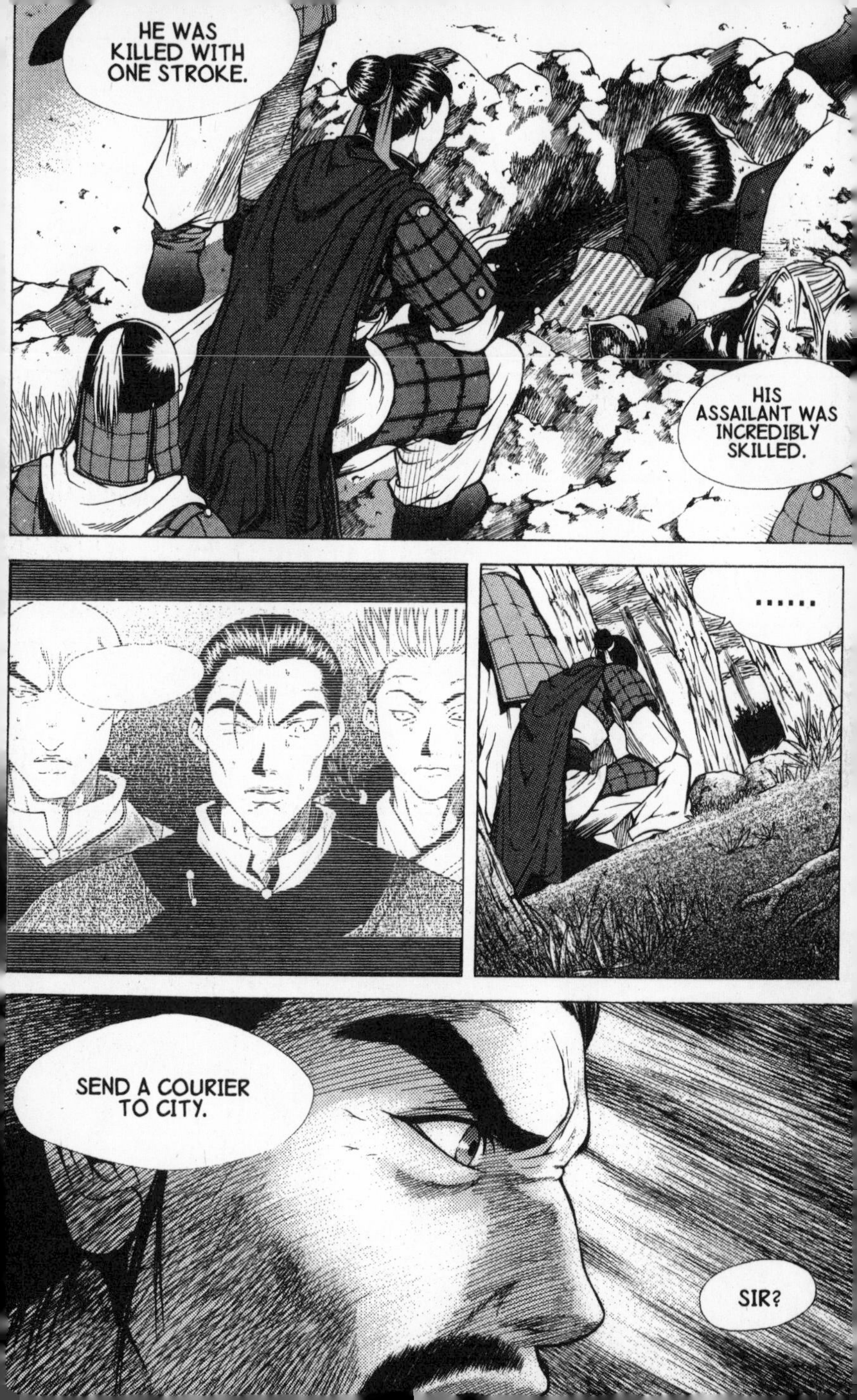
HE WAS KILLED WITH ONE STROKE.
HIS ASSAILANT WAS INCREDIBLY SKILLED.
......
SEND A COURIER TO CITY.
SIR?

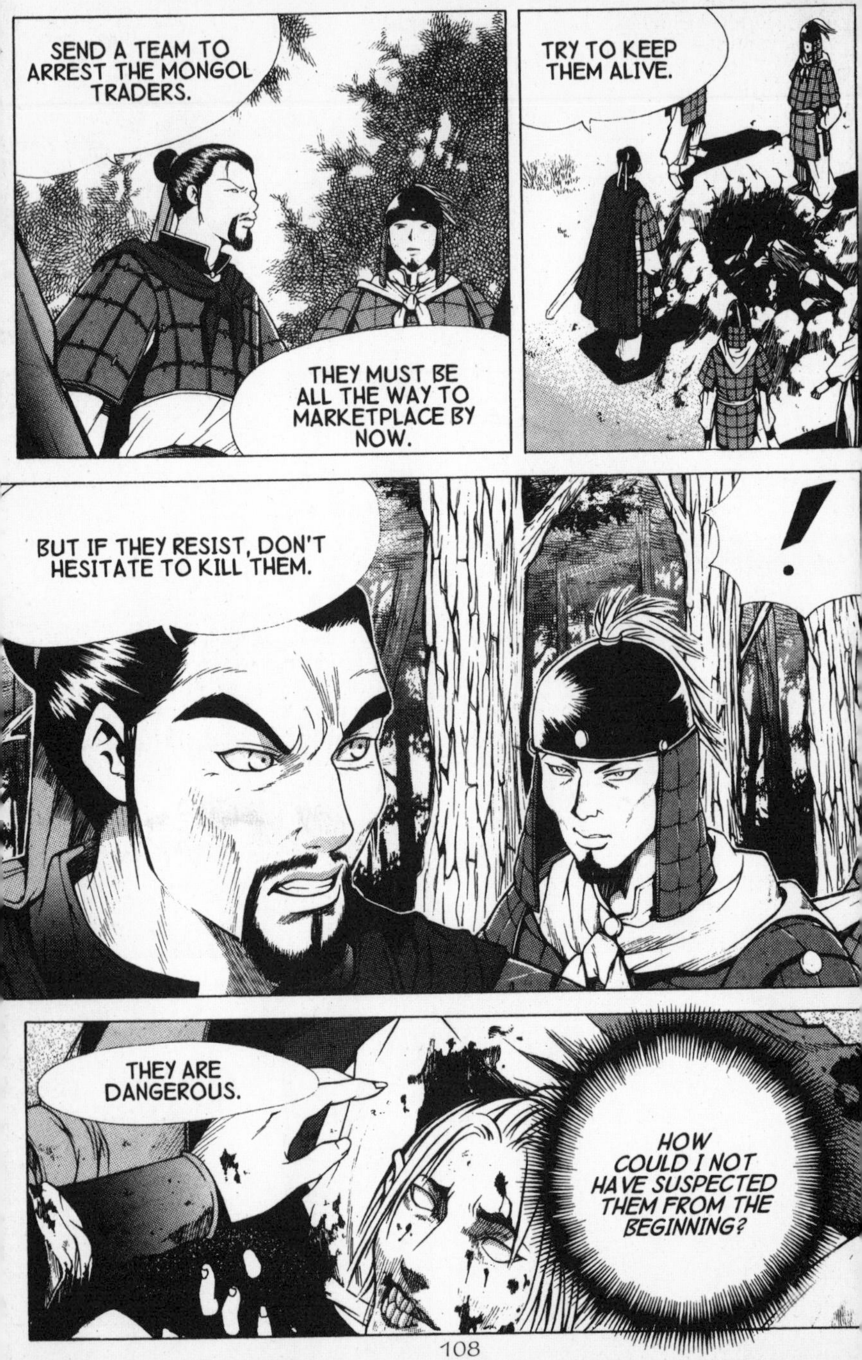
SEND A TEAM TO ARREST THE MONGOL TRADERS.
THEY MUST BE ALL THE WAY TO MARKETPLACE BY NOW.
TRY TO KEEP THEM ALIVE.
BUT IF THEY RESIST, DON'T HESITATE TO KILL THEM.
!
THEY ARE DANGEROUS.
HOW COULD I NOT HAVE SUSPECTED THEM FROM THE BEGINNING?

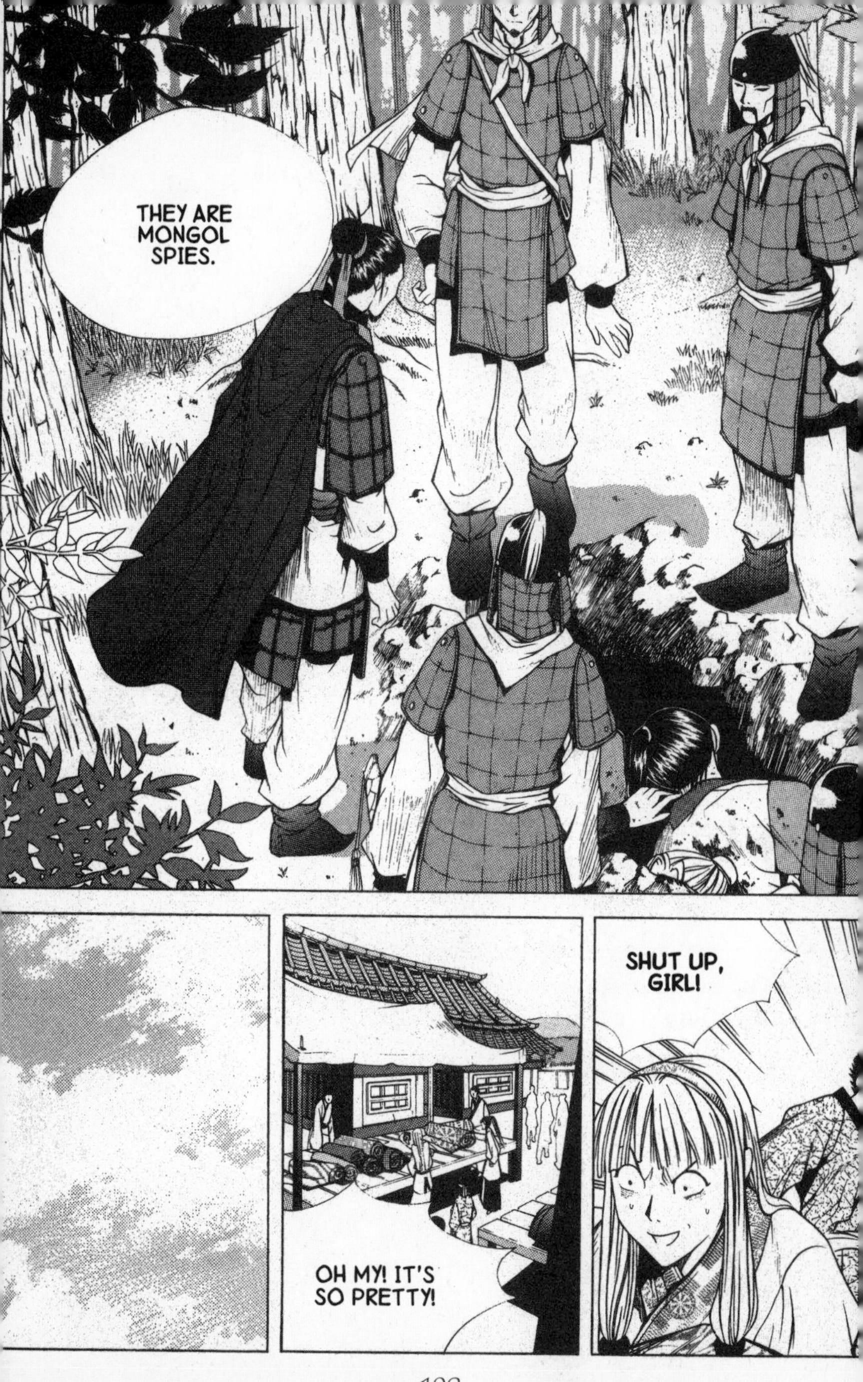
THEY ARE MONGOL SPIES.
OH MY! IT'S SO PRETTY!
SHUT UP, GIRL!

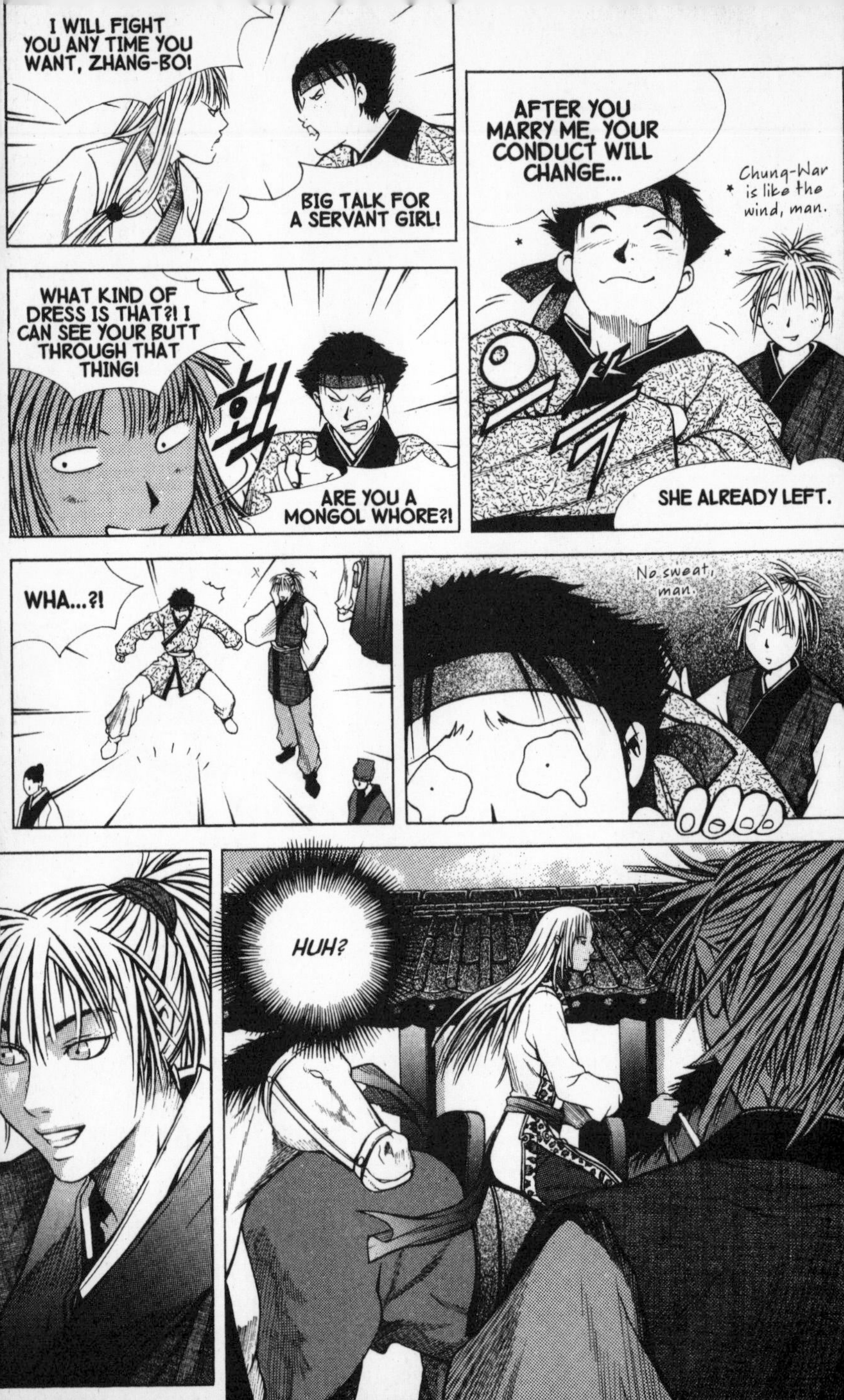
I WILL FIGHT YOU ANY TIME YOU WANT, ZHANG-BO!
BIG TALK FOR A SERVANT GIRL!
WHAT KIND OF DRESS IS THAT?! I CAN SEE YOUR BUTT THROUGH THAT THING!
홱
ARE YOU A MONGOL WHORE?!
AFTER YOU MARRY ME, YOUR CONDUCT WILL CHANGE...
Chung-War is like the wind, man.
SHE ALREADY LEFT.
WHA...?!
No sweat, man.
HUH?

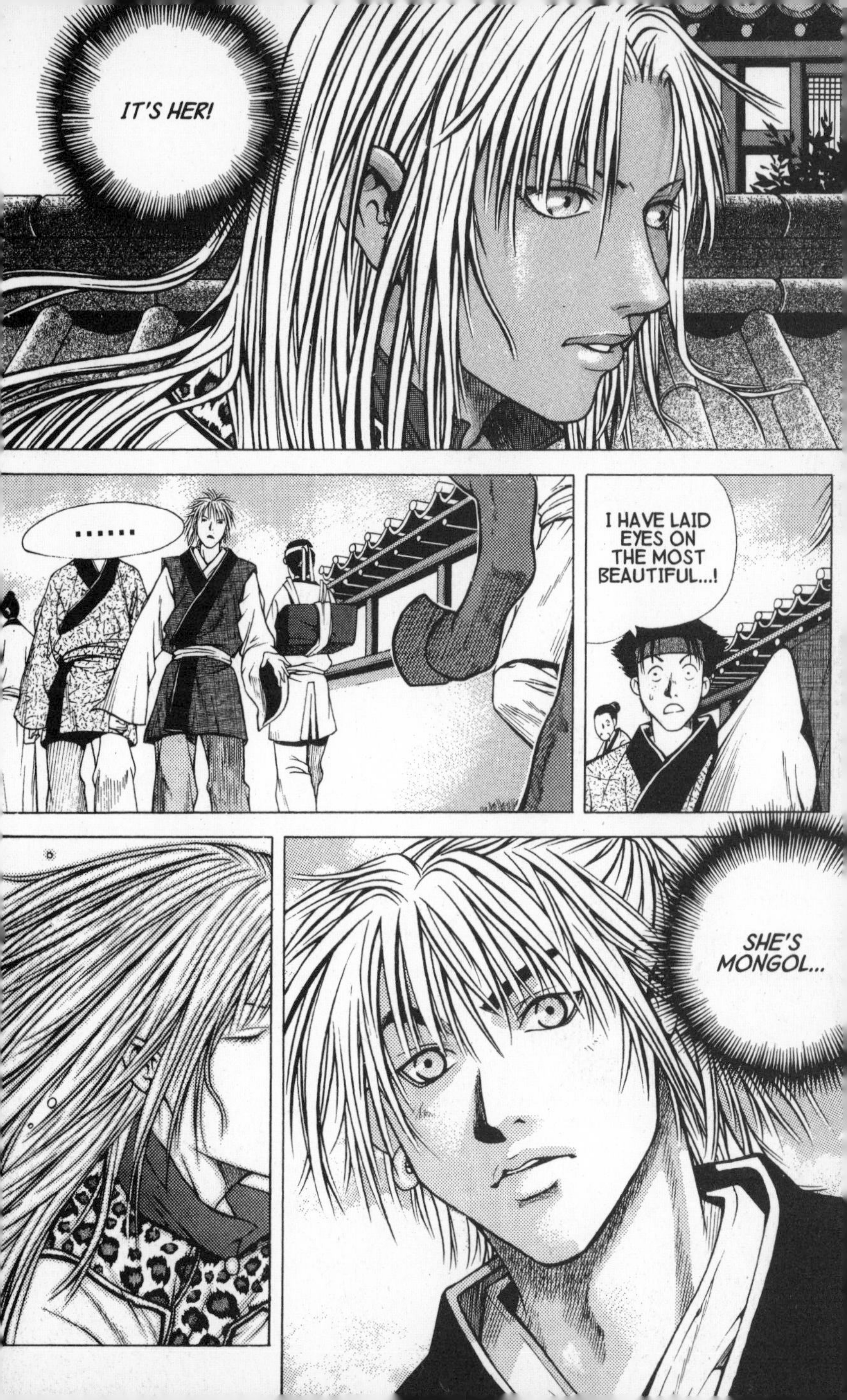
IT'S HER!
......
I HAVE LAID EYES ON THE MOST BEAUTIFUL...!
SHE'S MONGOL...

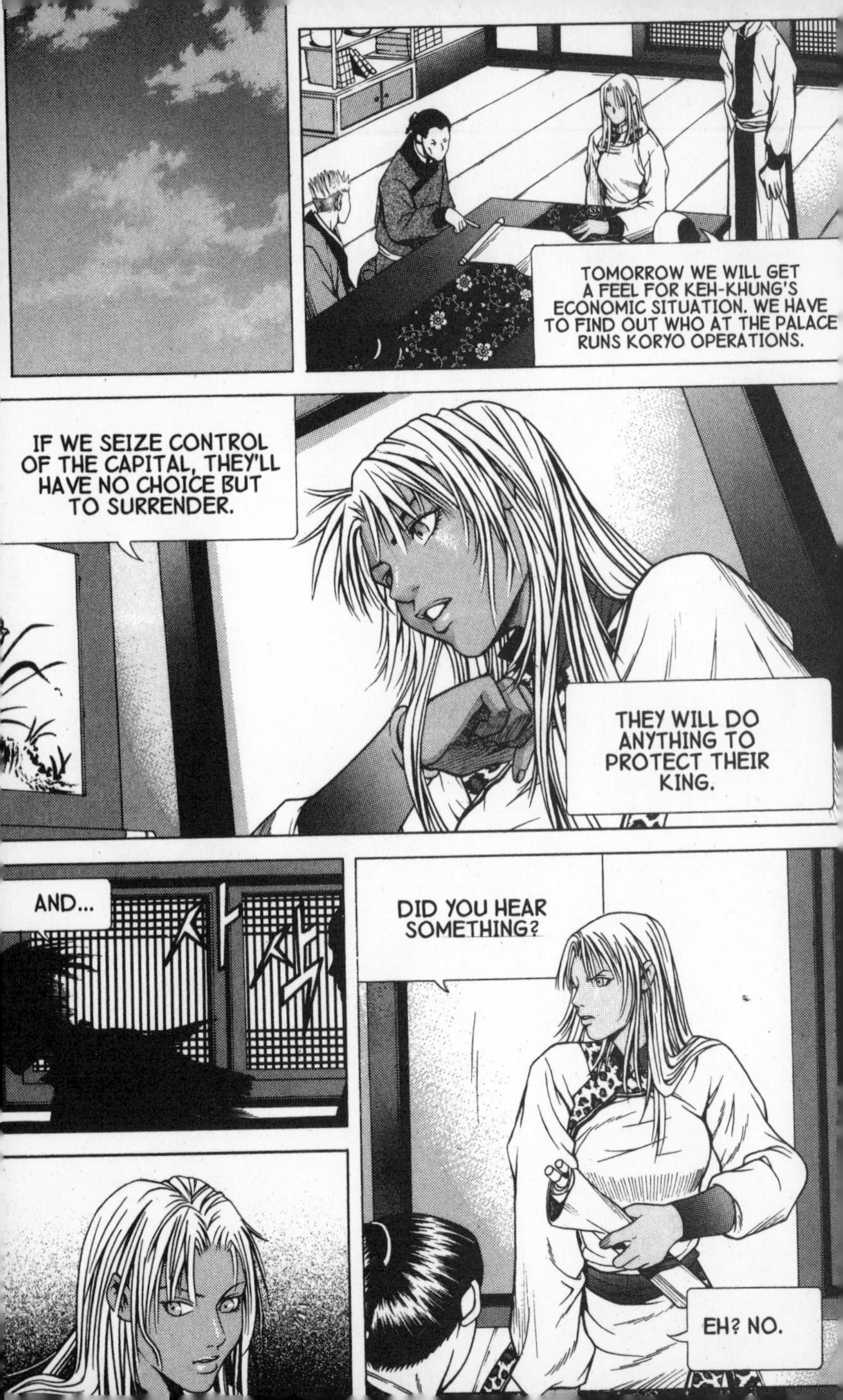
TOMORROW WE WILL GET A FEEL FOR KEH-KHUNG'S ECONOMIC SITUATION. WE HAVE TO FIND OUT WHO AT THE PALACE RUNS KORYO OPERATIONS.
IF WE SEIZE CONTROL OF THE CAPITAL, THEY'LL HAVE NO CHOICE BUT TO SURRENDER.
THEY WILL DO ANYTHING TO PROTECT THEIR KING.
AND...
DID YOU HEAR SOMETHING?
EH? NO.

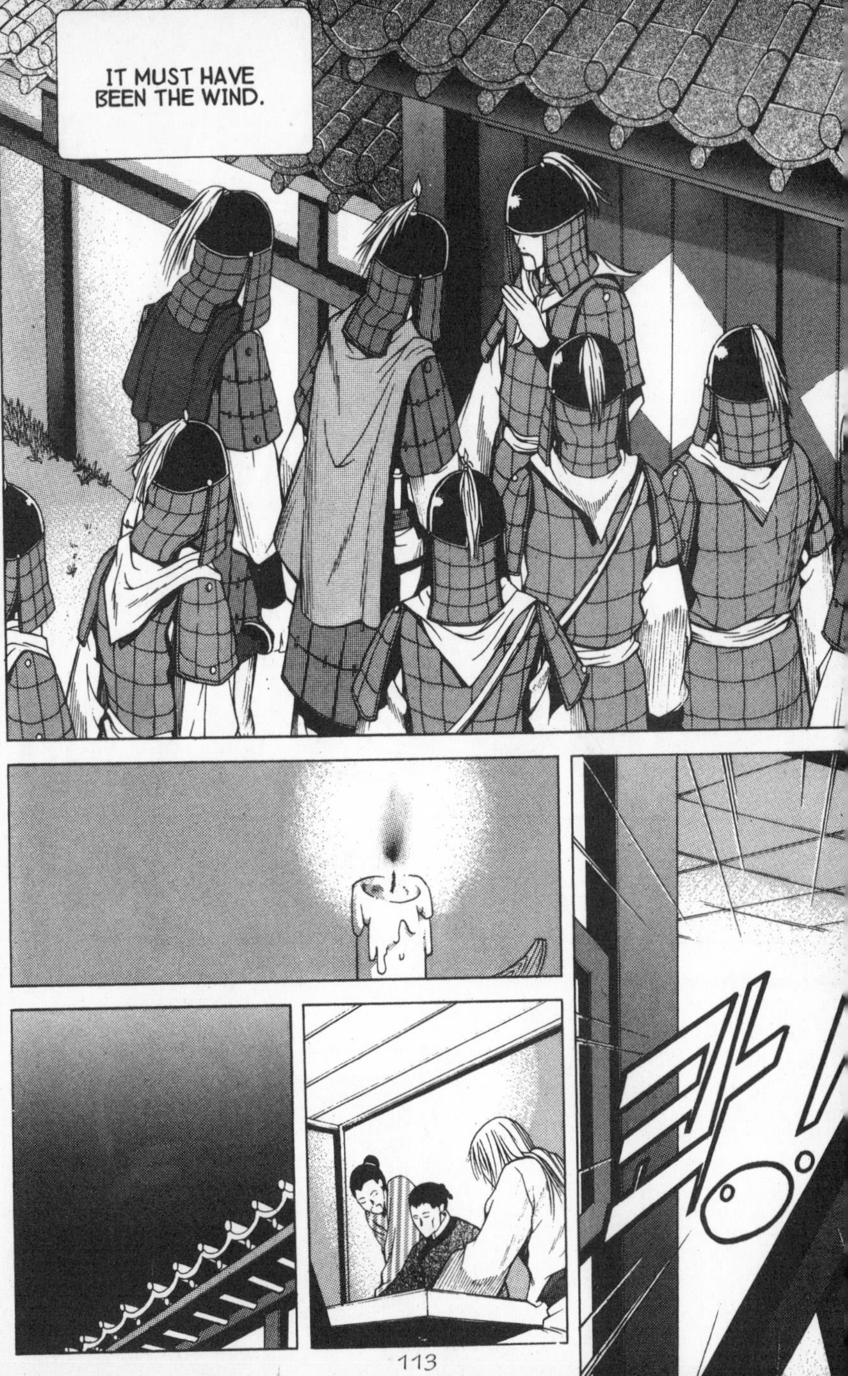
IT MUST HAVE BEEN THE WIND.

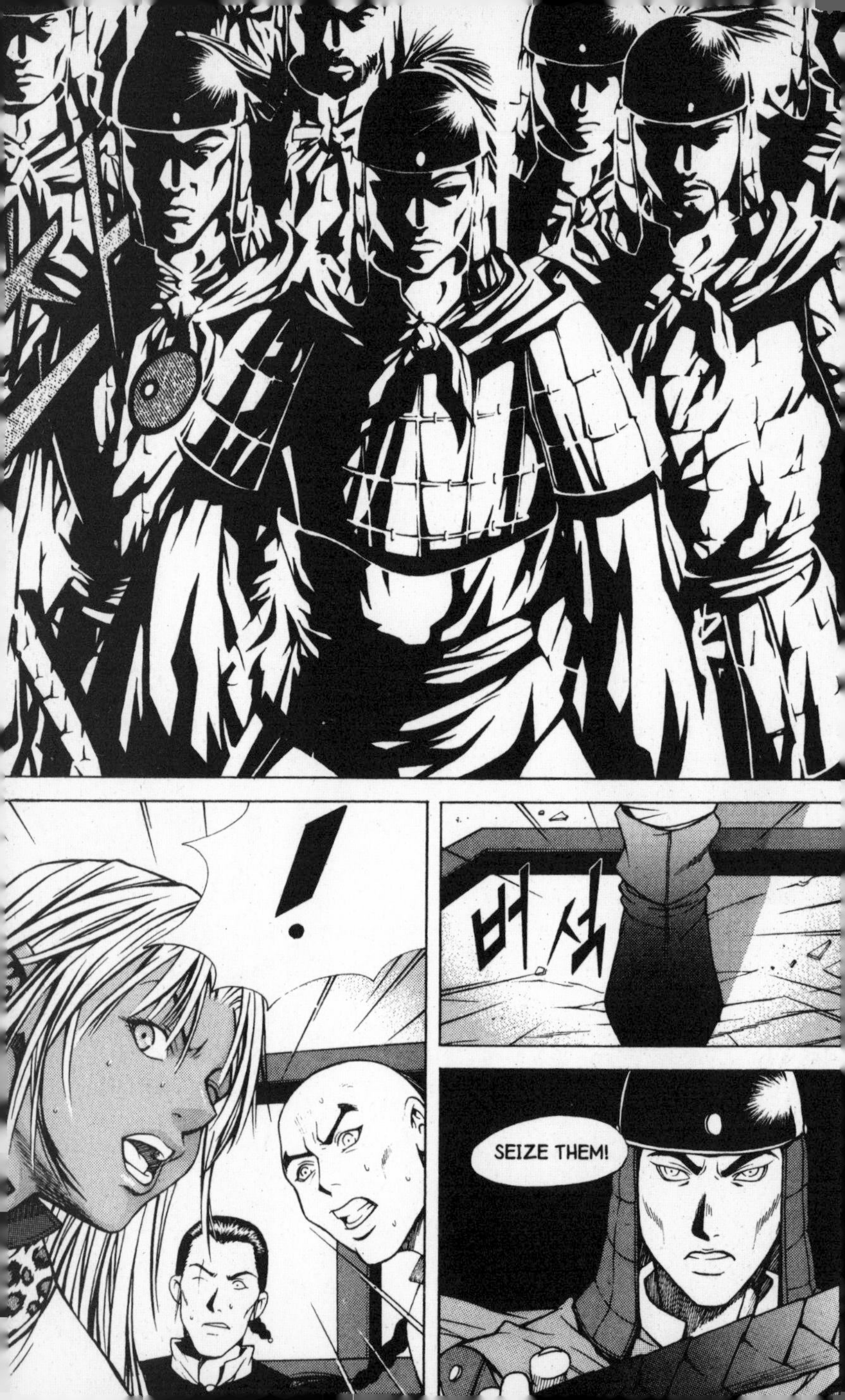
버석
SEIZE THEM!

우우어

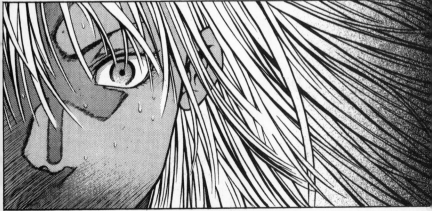

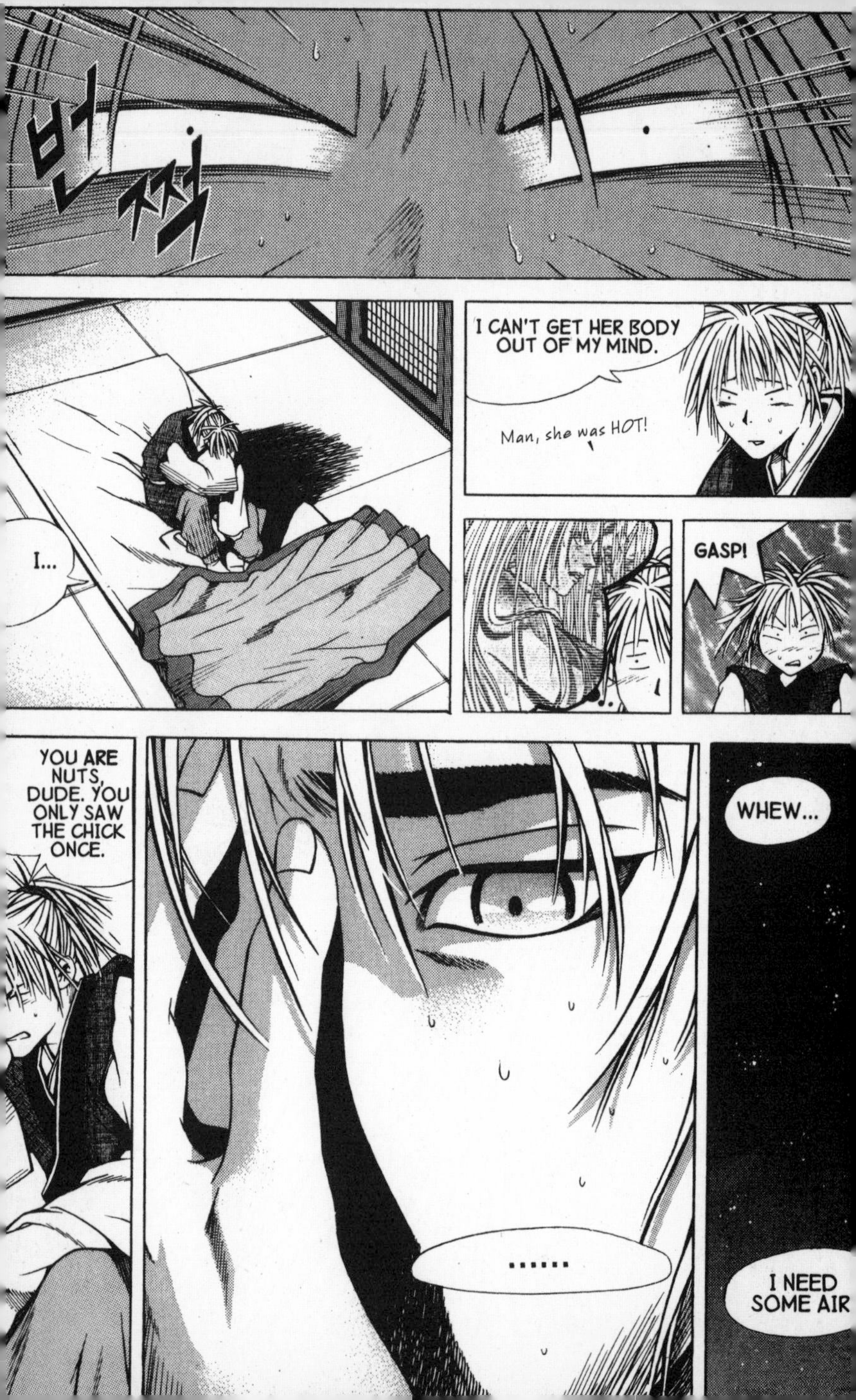
번쩍
I...
I CAN'T GET HER BODY OUT OF MY MIND.
Man, she was HOT!
GASP!
YOU ARE NUTS, DUDE. YOU ONLY SAW THE CHICK ONCE.
......
WHEW...
I NEED SOME AIR

SORU KAHN!!

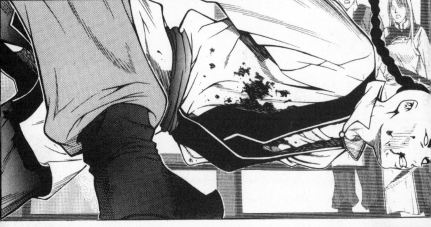

RUN, PRINCESS!!

I ENTRUST THE PRINCESS TO YOU! PROTECT HER WITH YOUR LIFE!

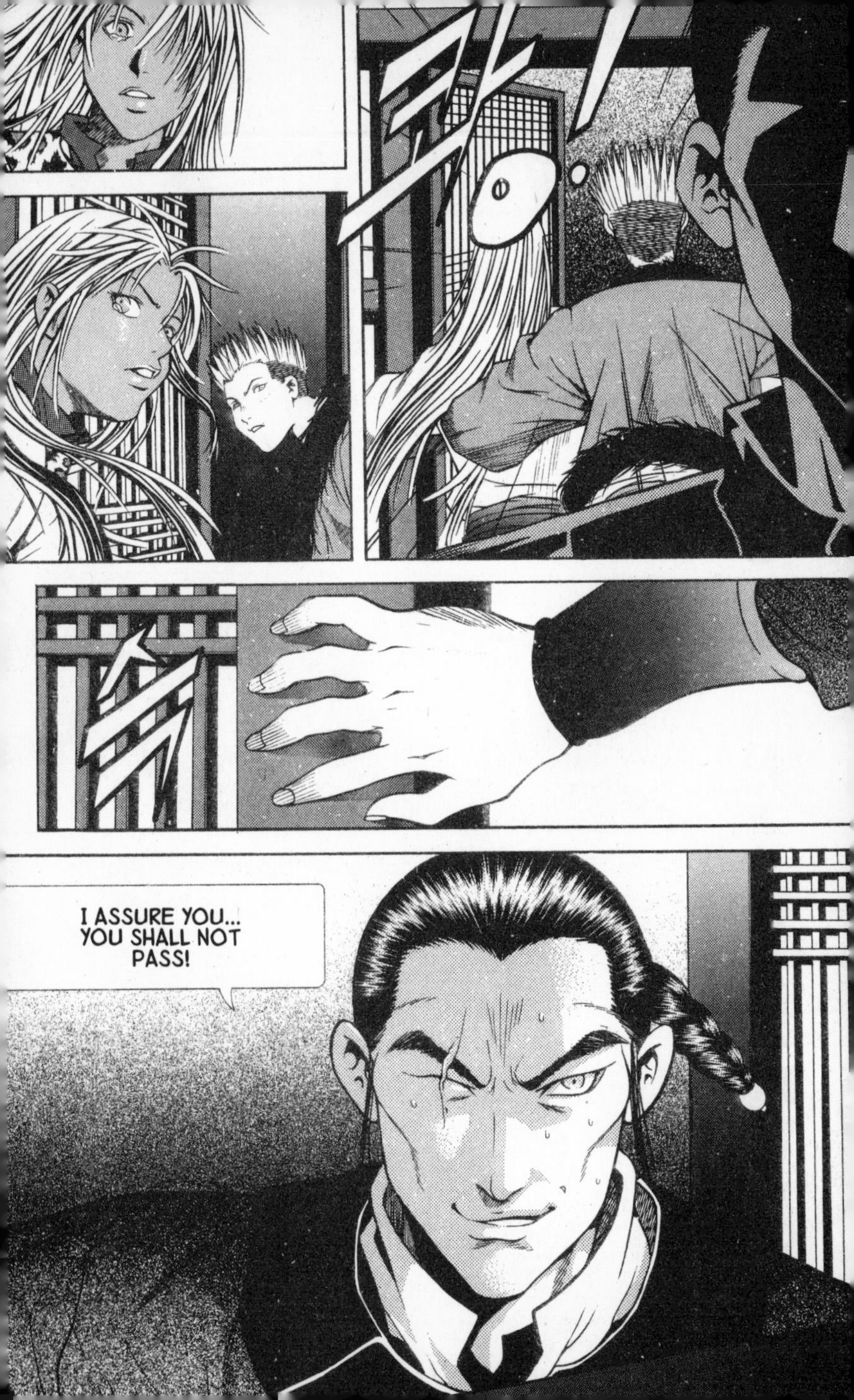
I ASSURE YOU... YOU SHALL NOT PASS!

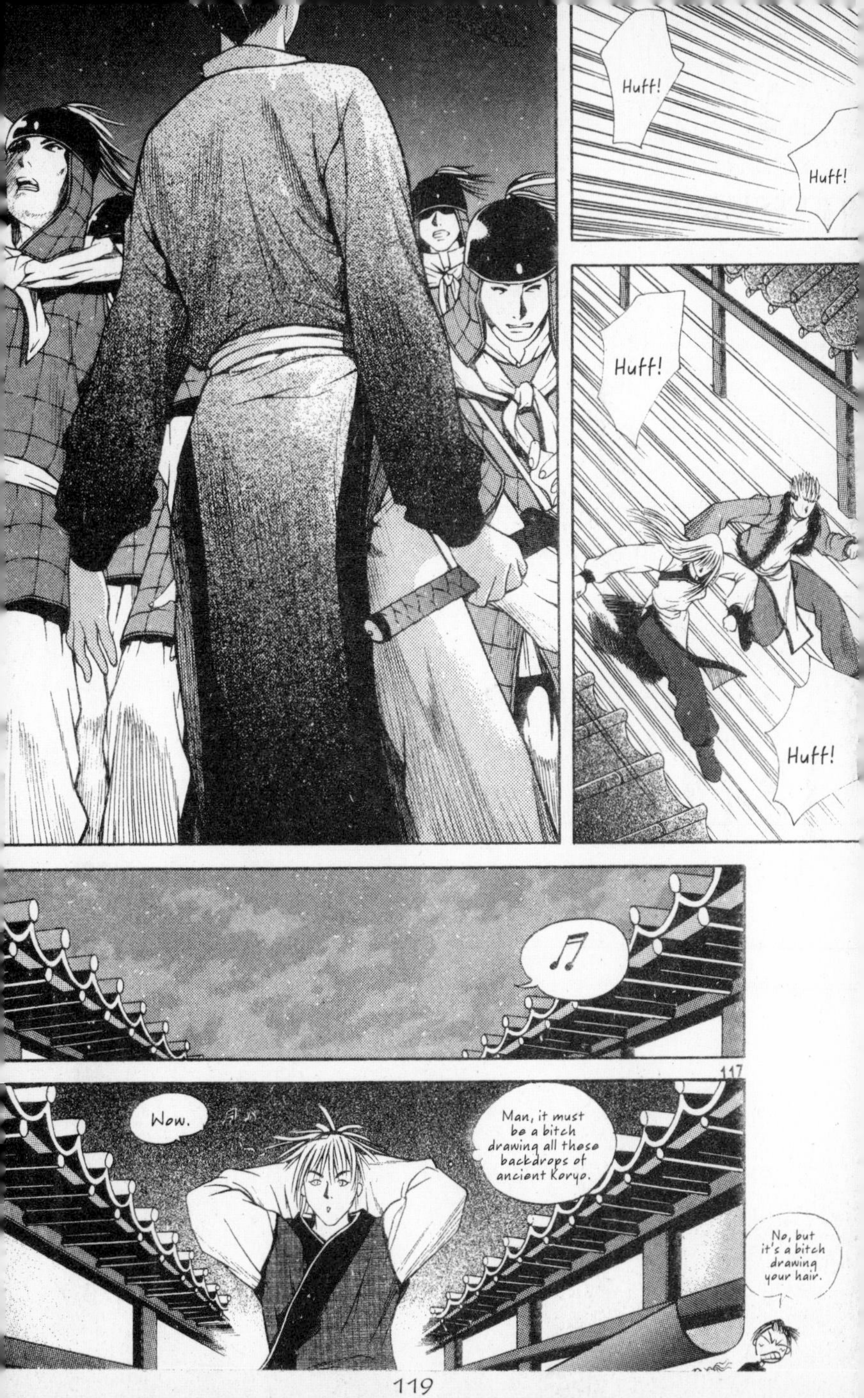
Huff!
Huff!
Huff!
Huff!
♪
117
Wow.
Man, it must be a bitch drawing all these backdrops of ancient Koryo.
No, but it's a bitch drawing your hair.

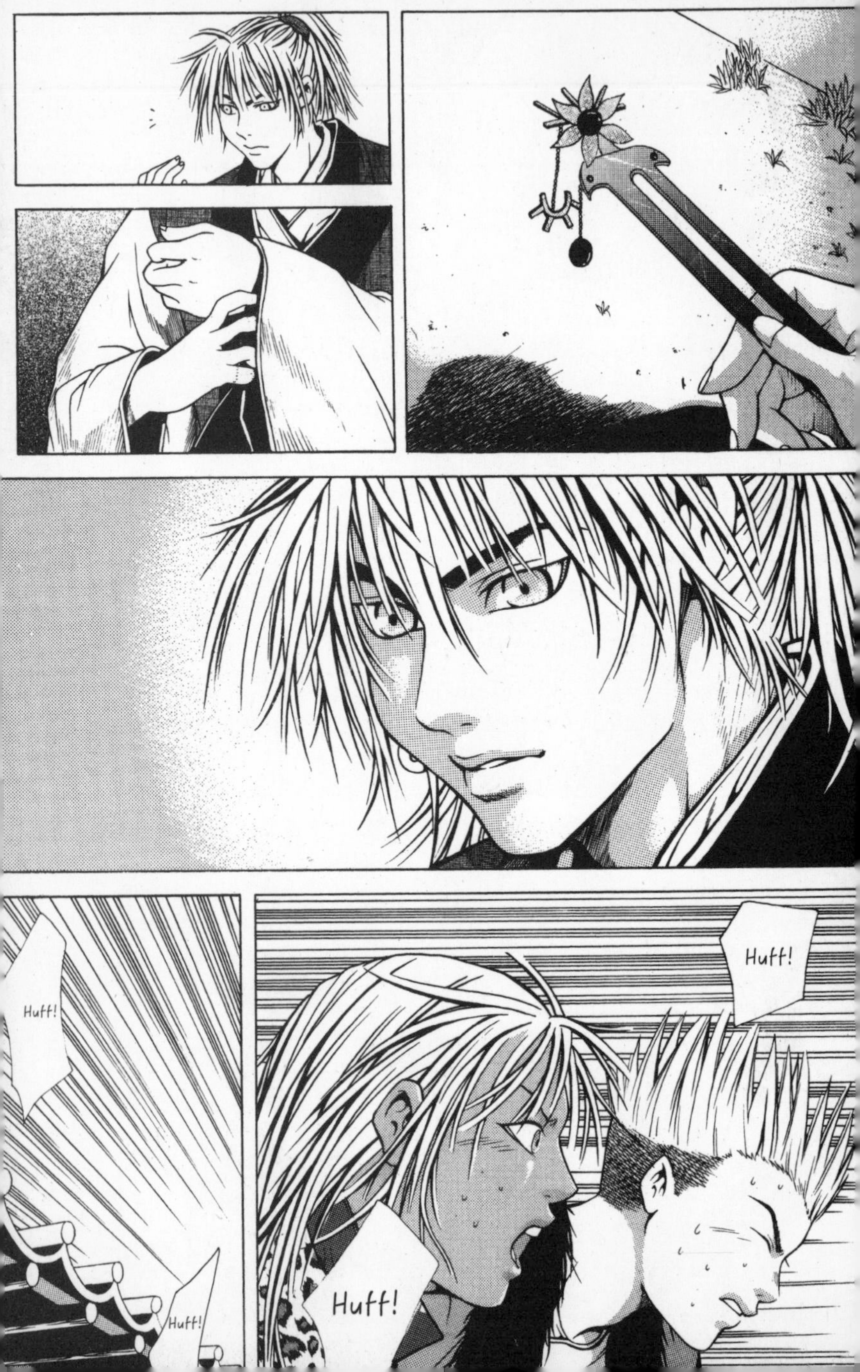
Huff!
Huff!
Huff!
Huff!

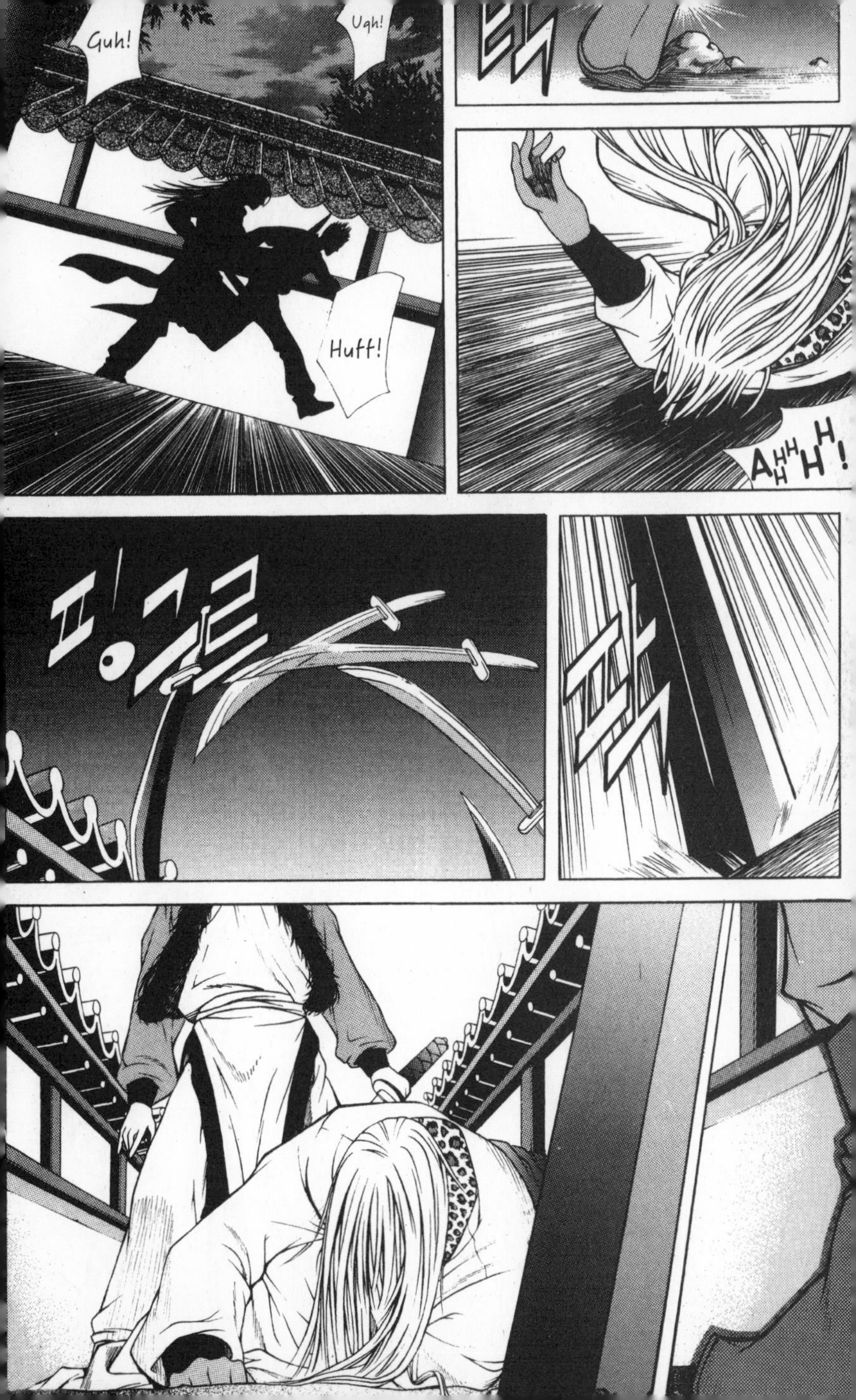
Guh!
Ugh!
Huff!
AHHHHH!
핑그르

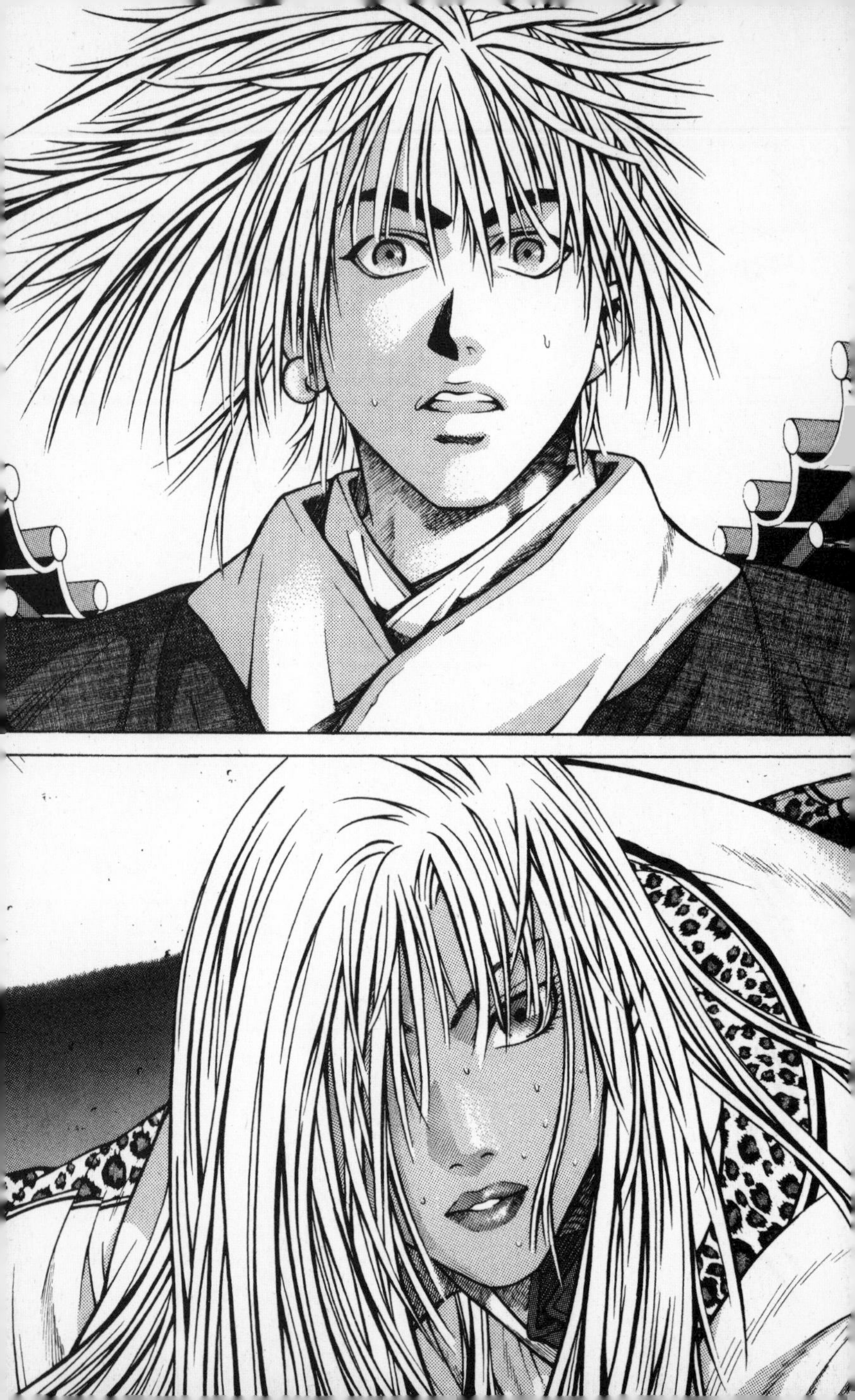

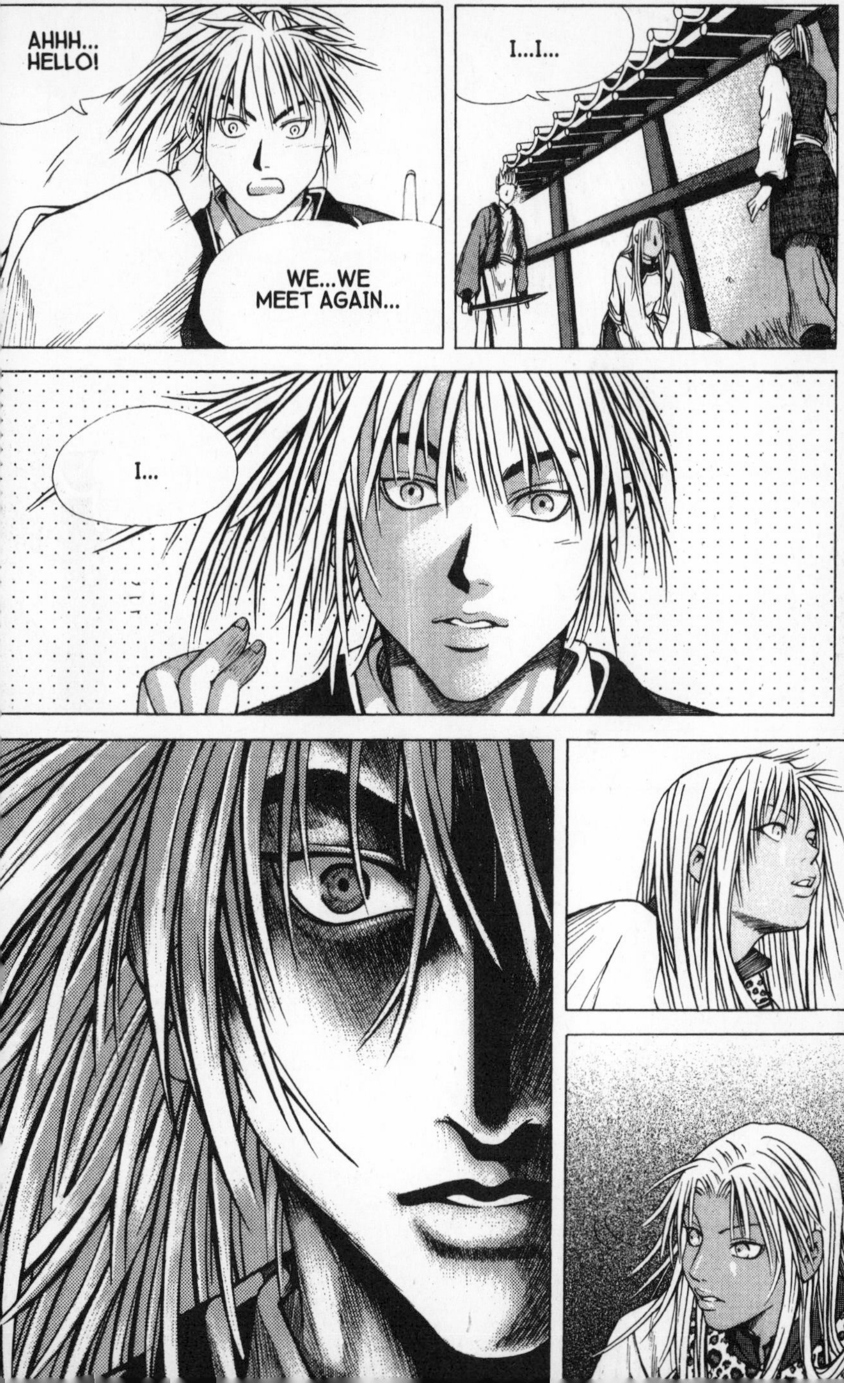
AHHH... HELLO!
WE...WE MEET AGAIN...
I...I...
I...

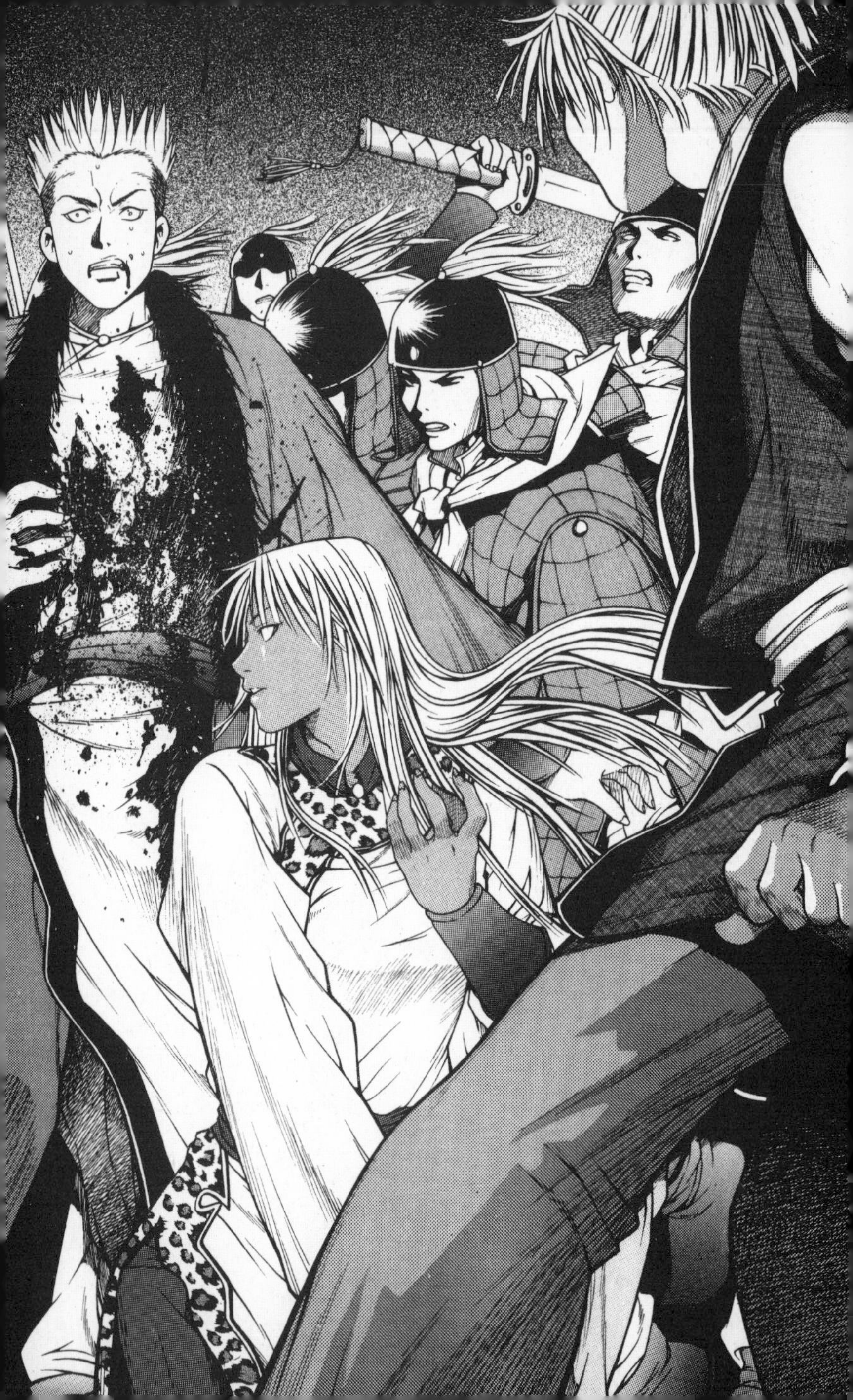

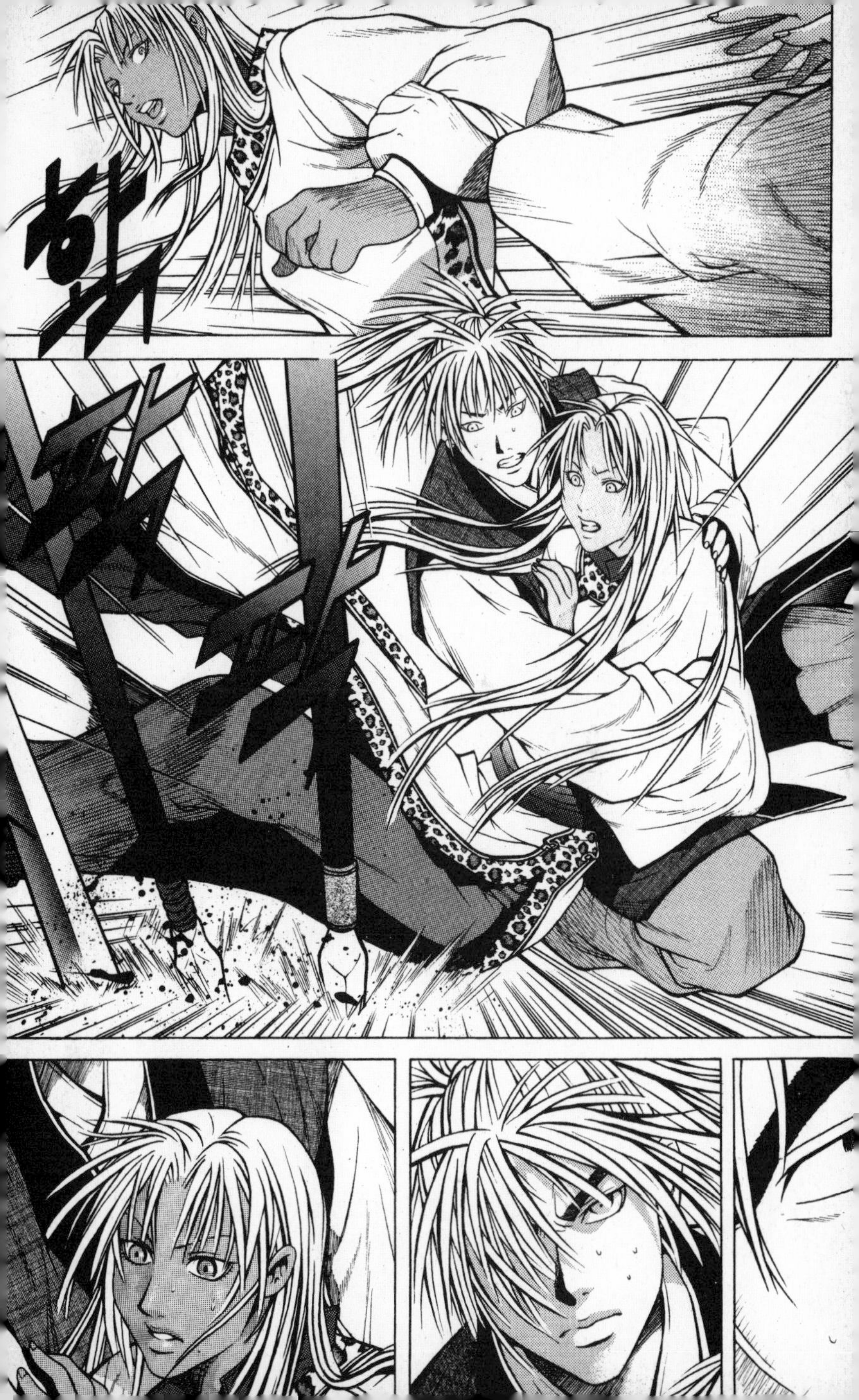

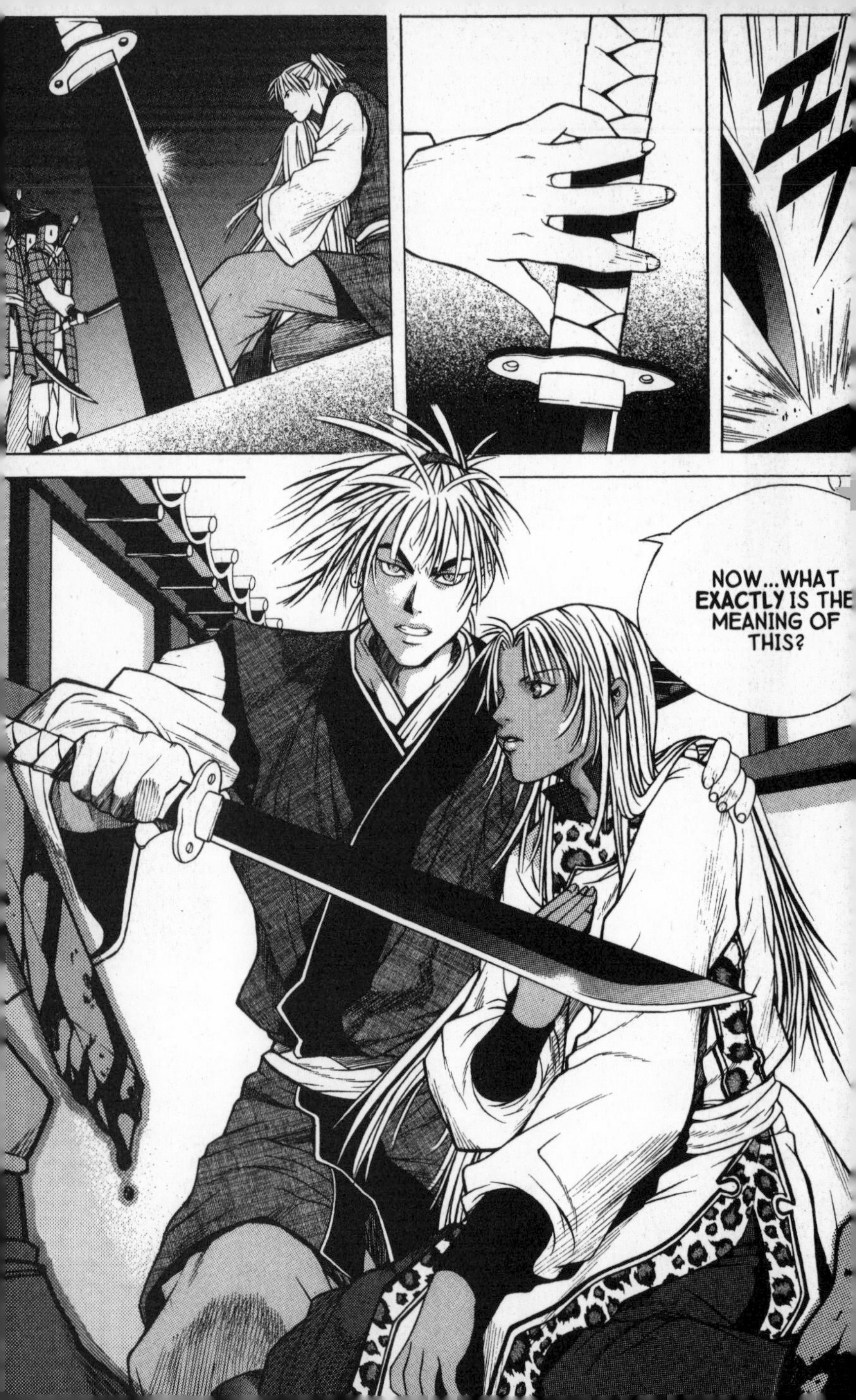
NOW...WHAT EXACTLY IS THE MEANING OF THIS?

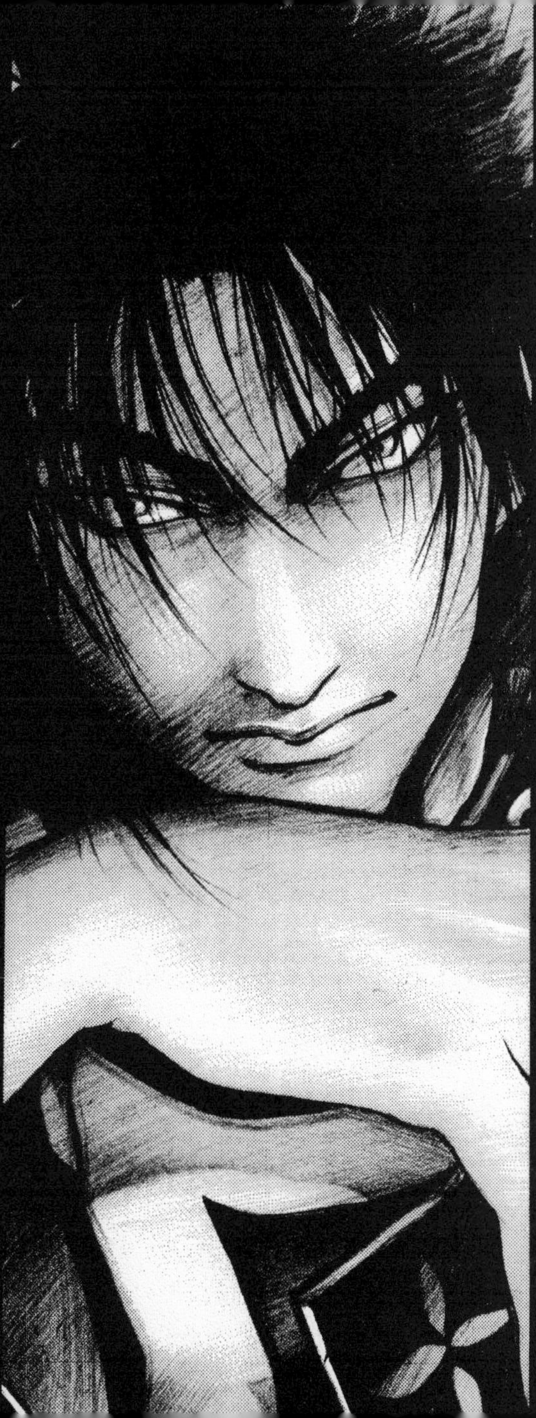

Chapter 9
Fate

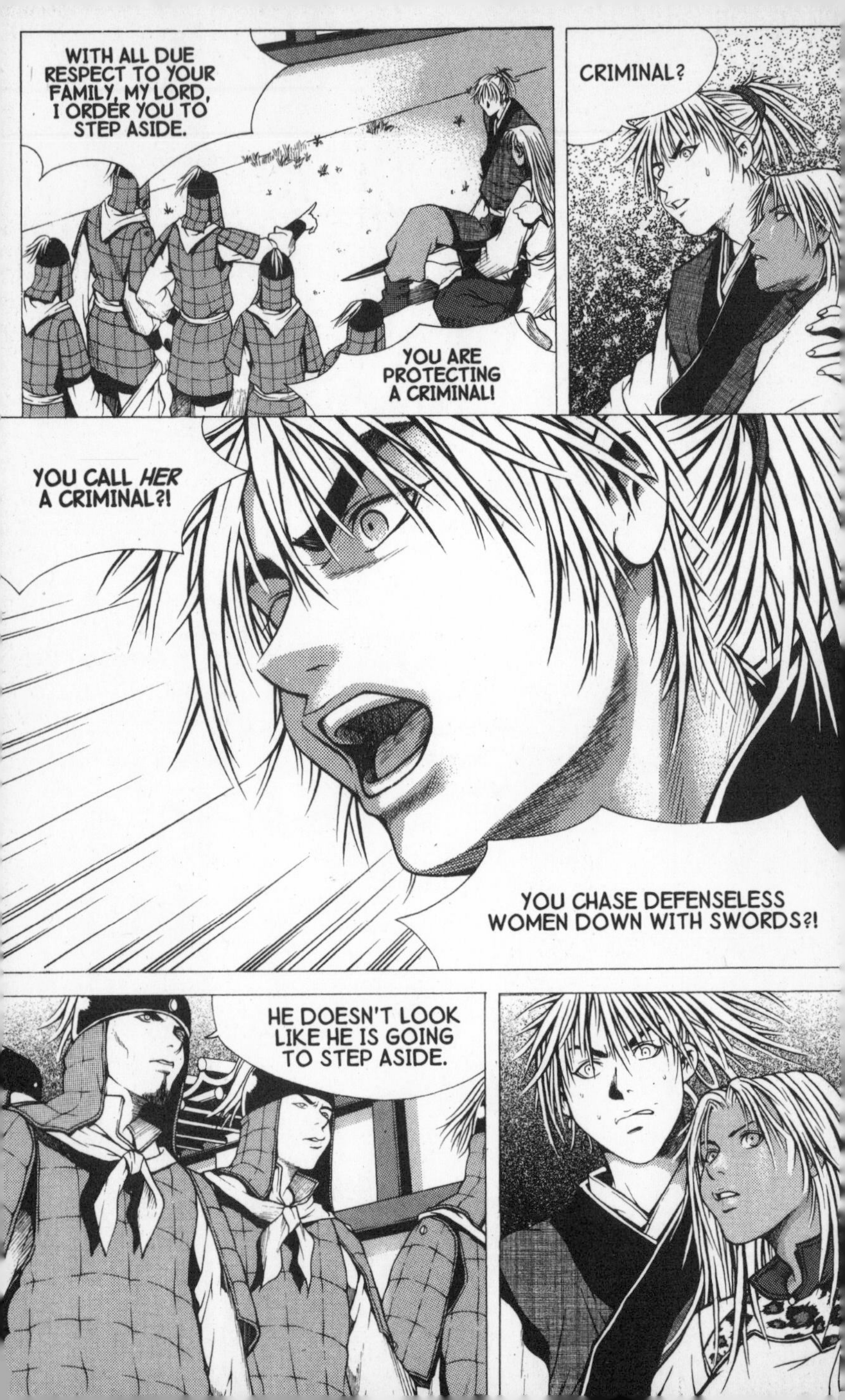
WITH ALL DUE RESPECT TO YOUR FAMILY, MY LORD, I ORDER YOU TO STEP ASIDE.
YOU ARE PROTECTING A CRIMINAL!
CRIMINAL?
YOU CALL *HER* A CRIMINAL?!
YOU CHASE DEFENSELESS WOMEN DOWN WITH SWORDS?!
HE DOESN'T LOOK LIKE HE IS GOING TO STEP ASIDE.

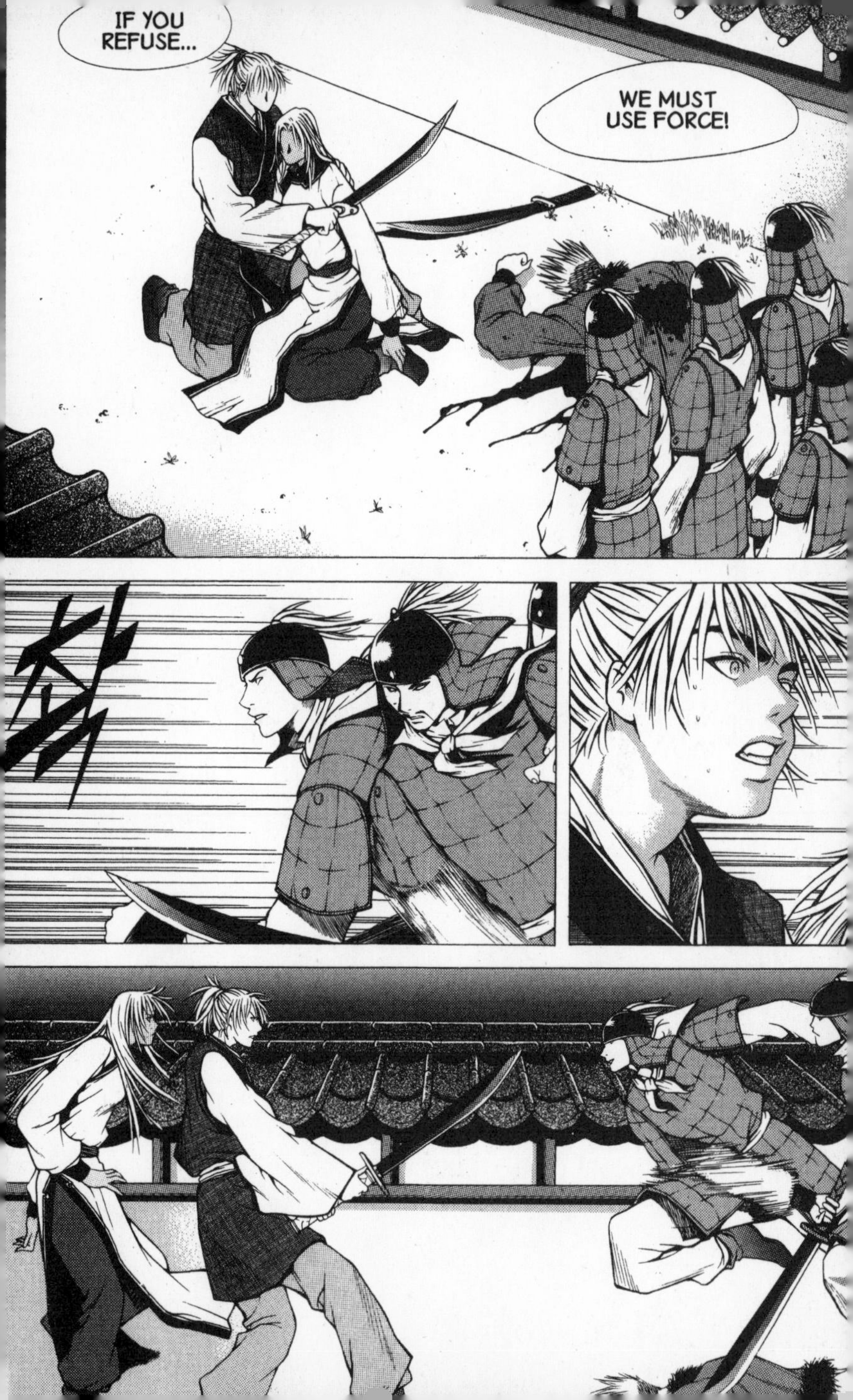
IF YOU REFUSE...
WE MUST USE FORCE!

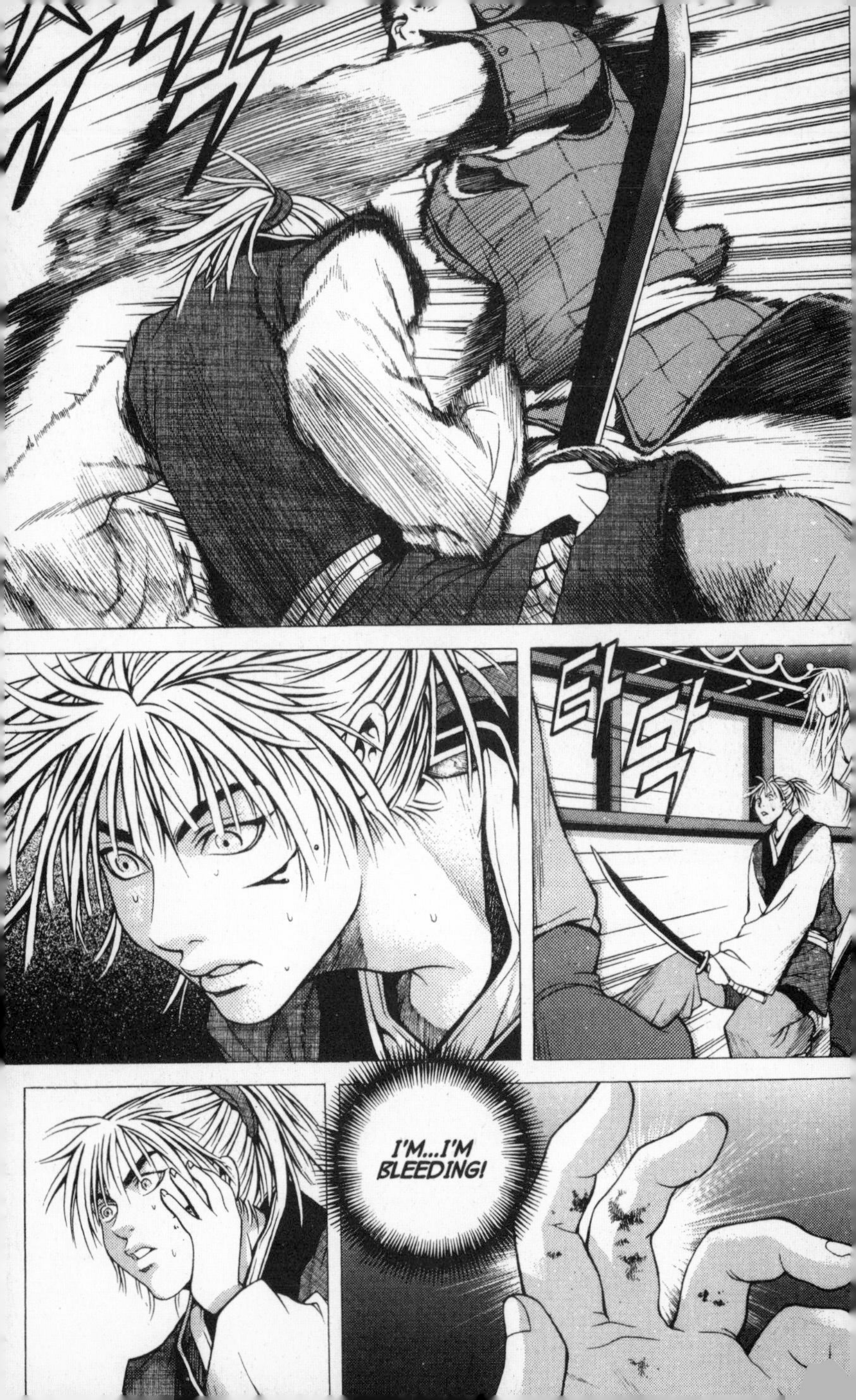
타닥
I'M...I'M BLEEDING!

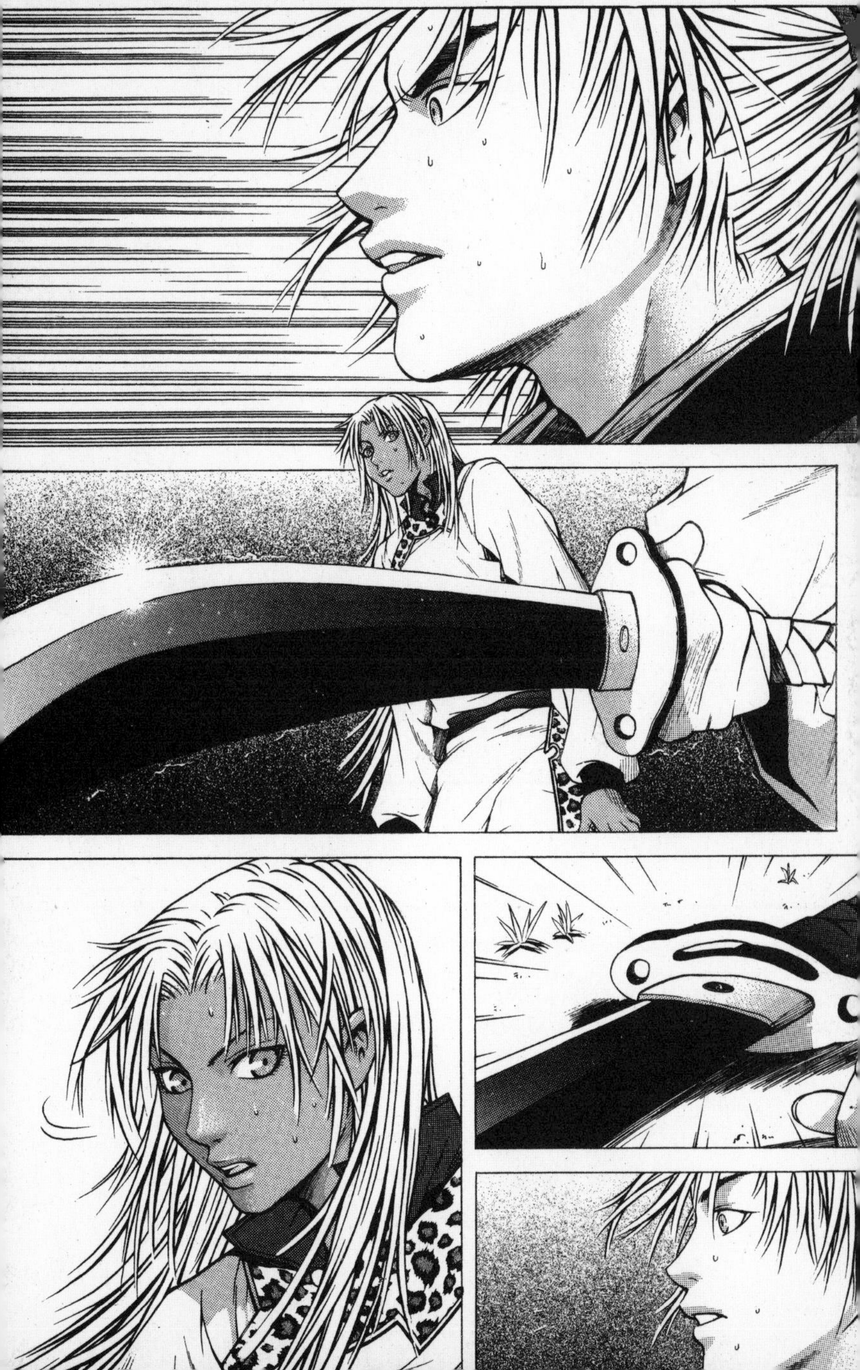

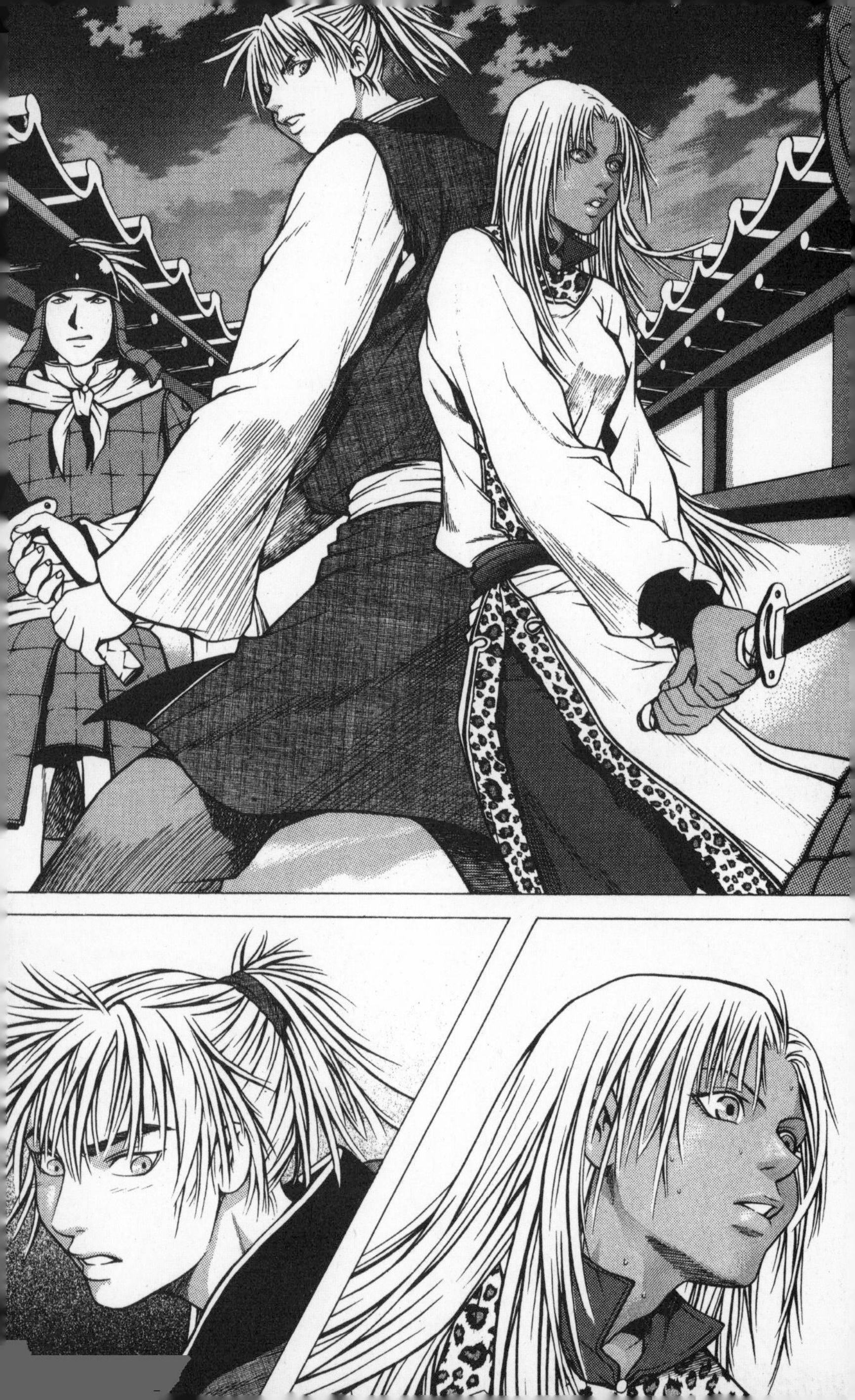

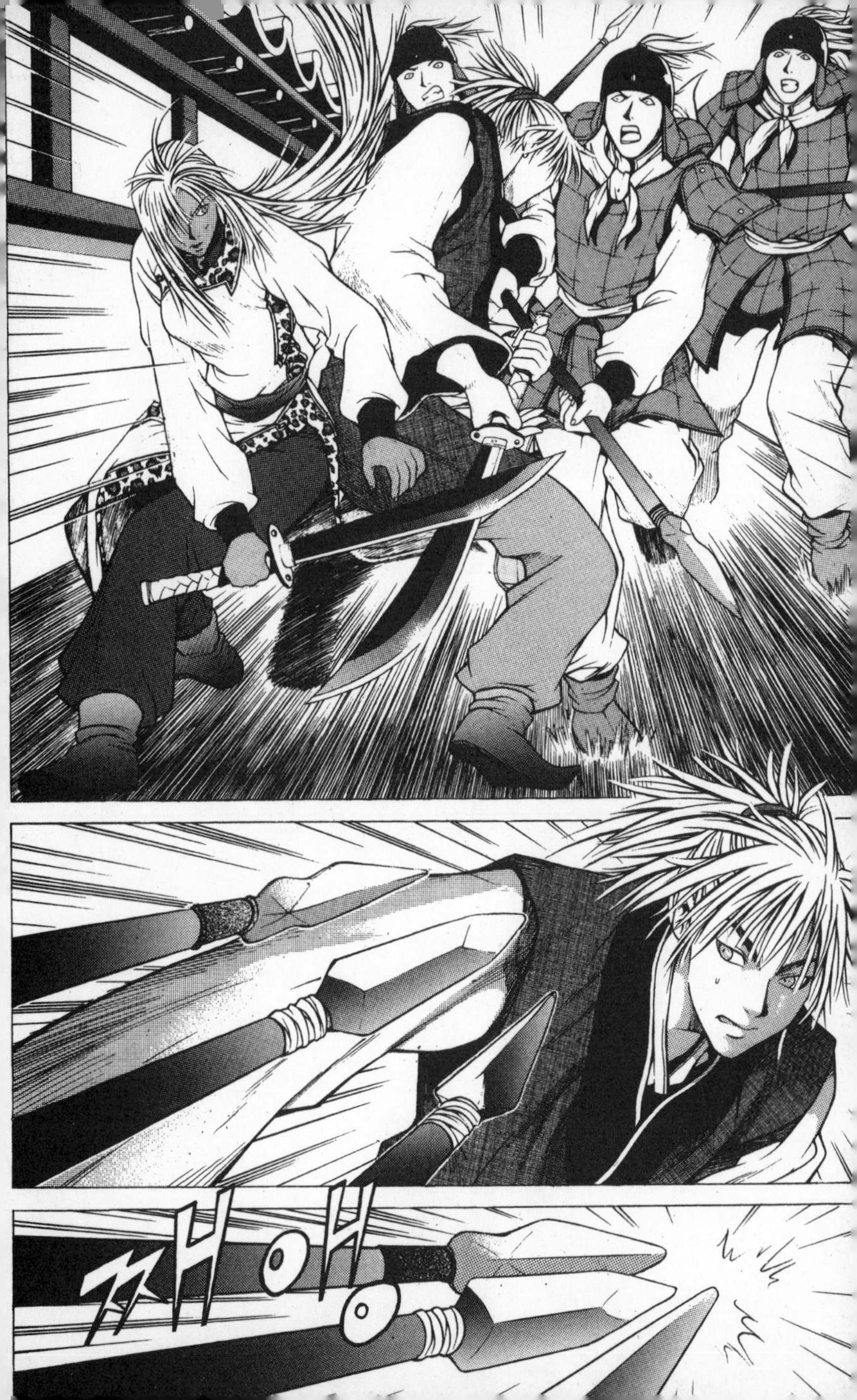

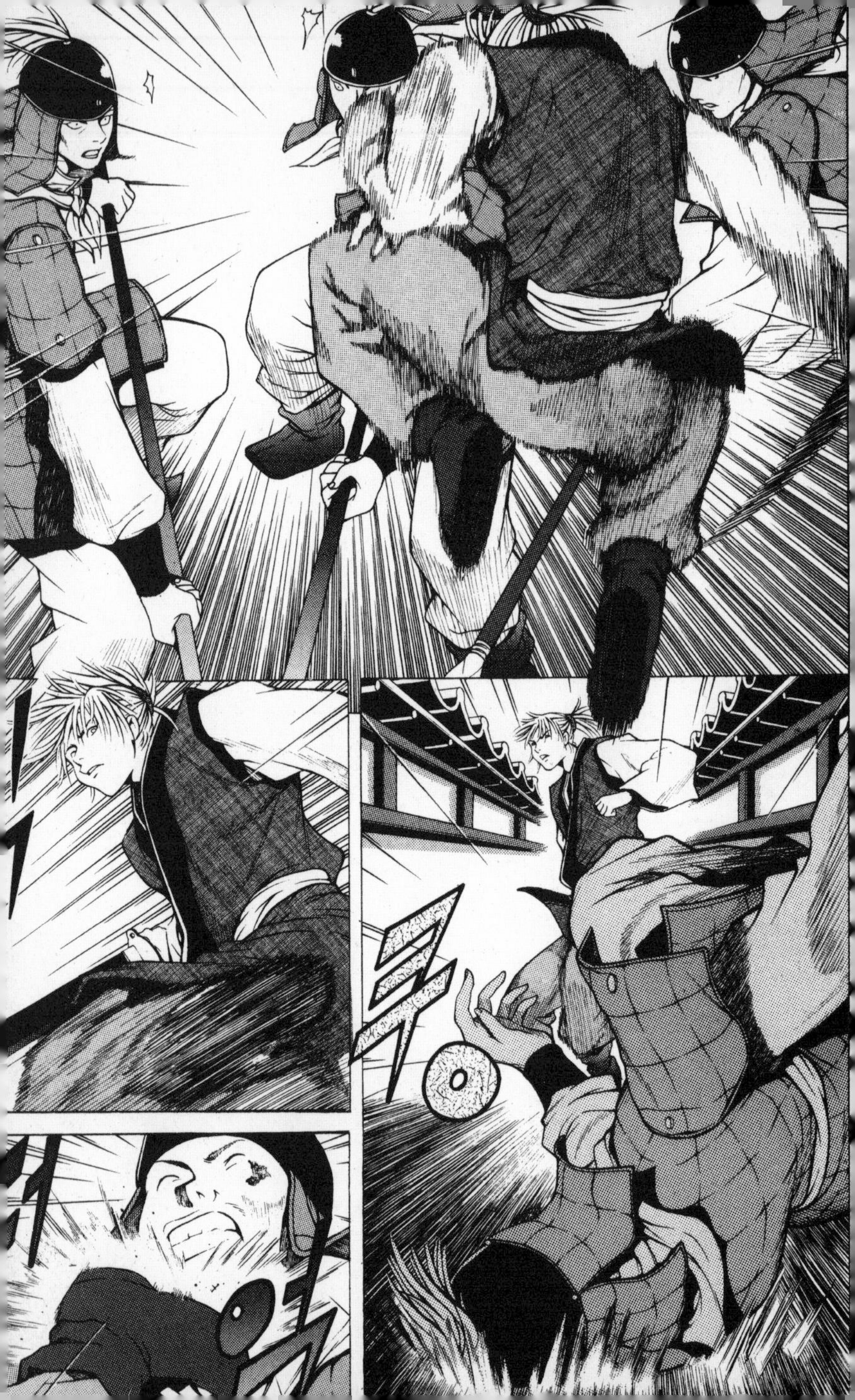

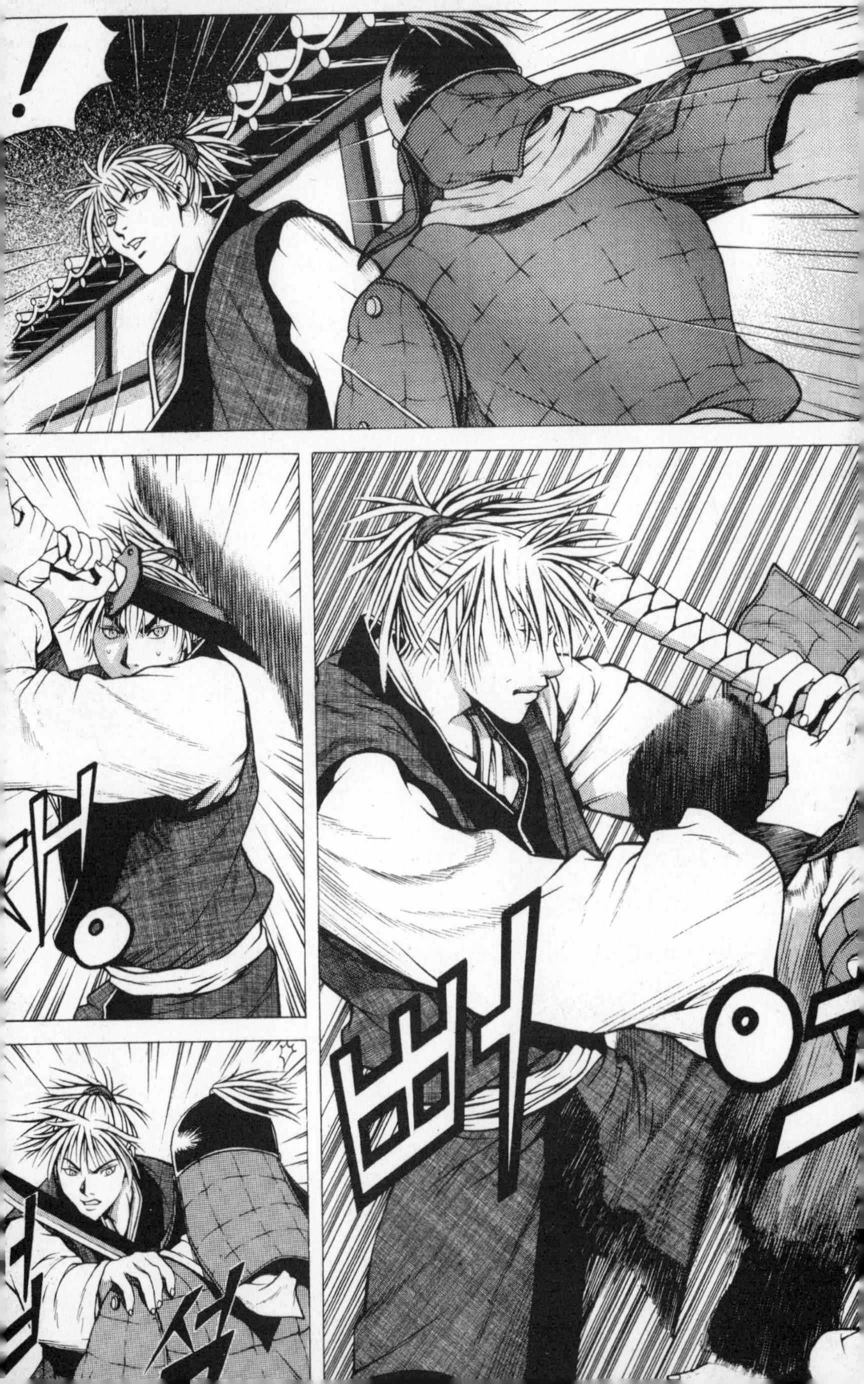
!
벅

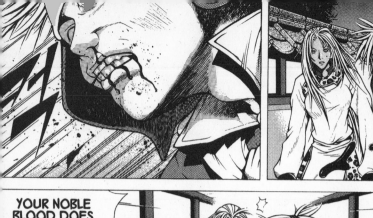

YOUR NOBLE BLOOD DOES NOT ENTITLE YOU TO TREASON!

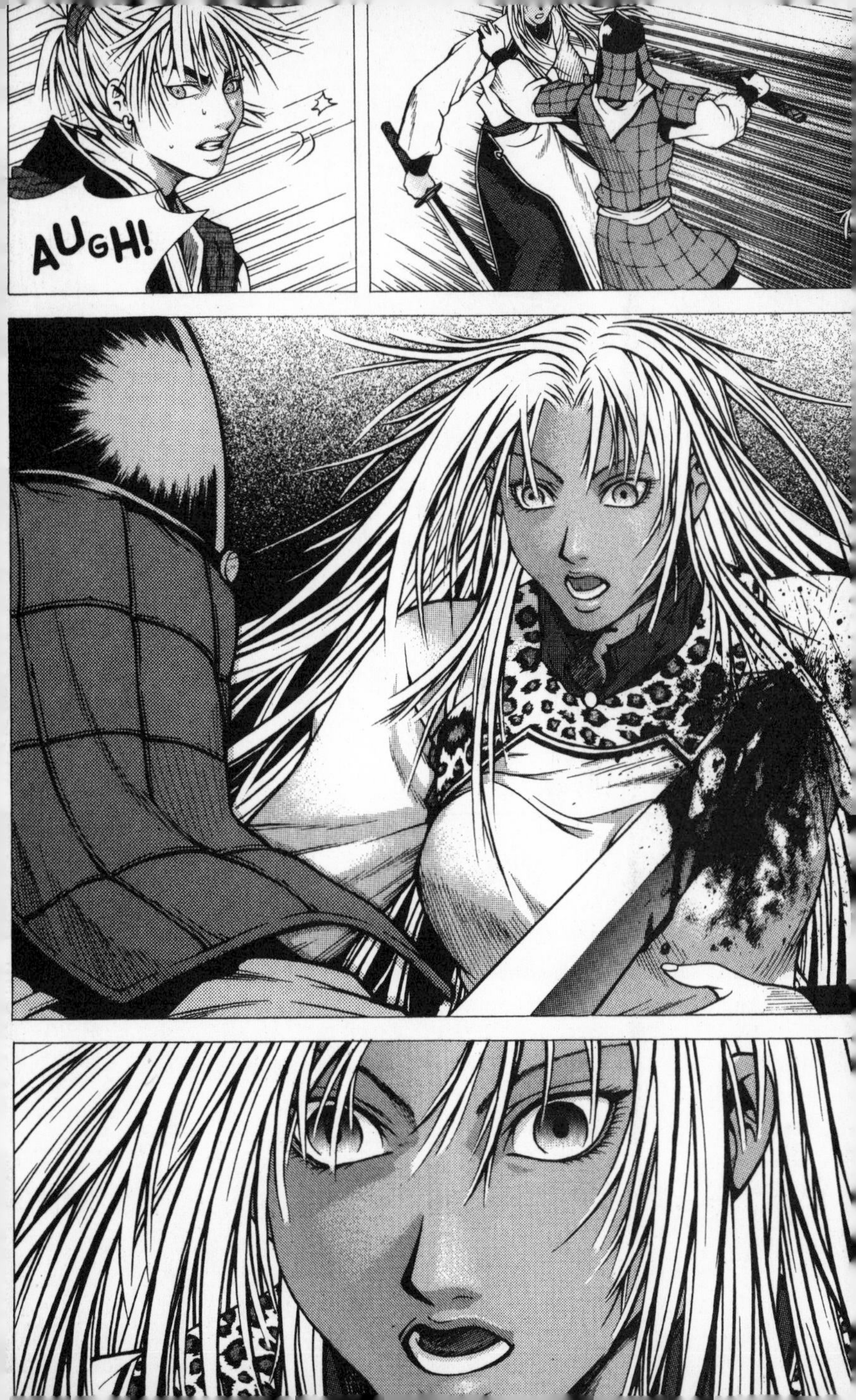
AUGH!

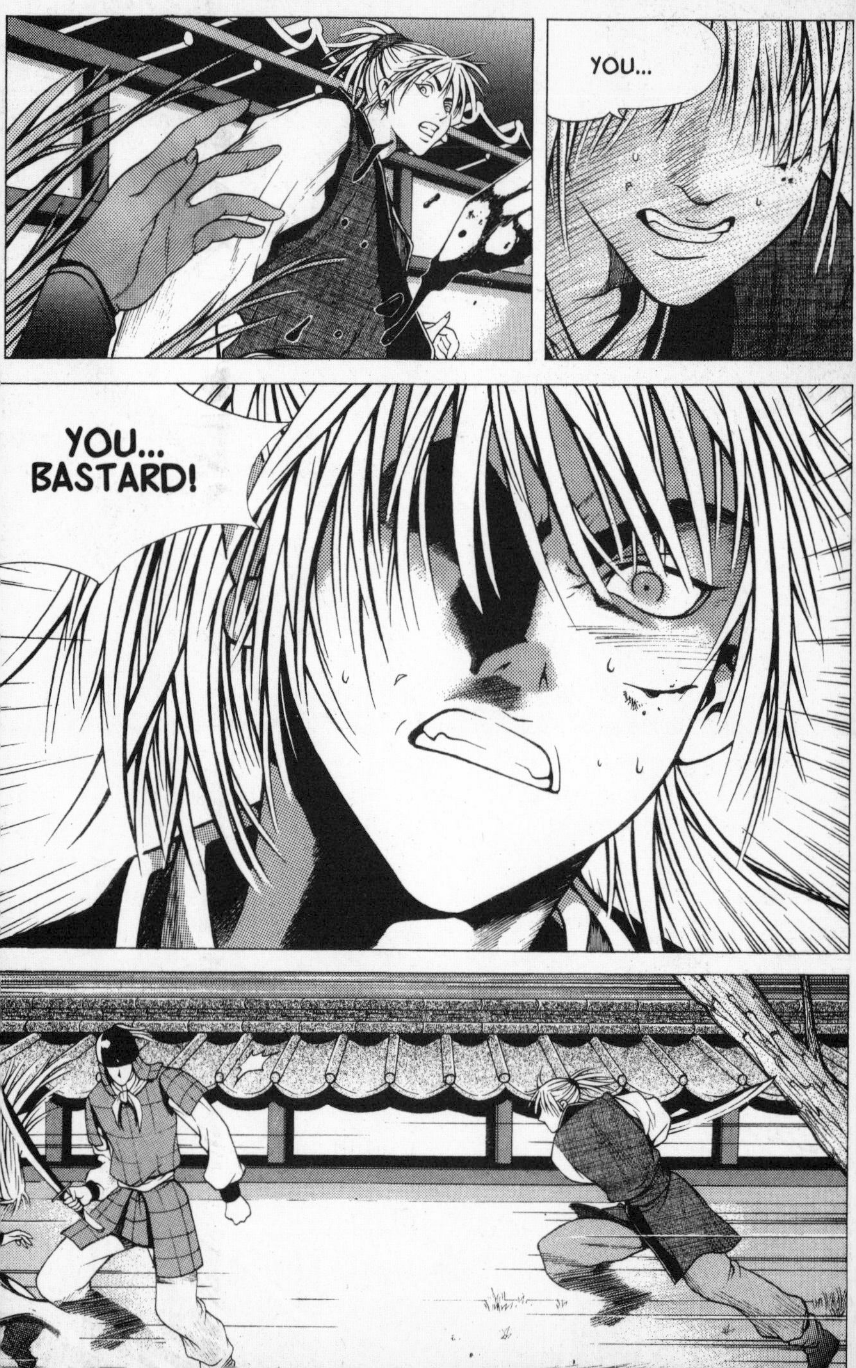
YOU...
YOU... BASTARD!

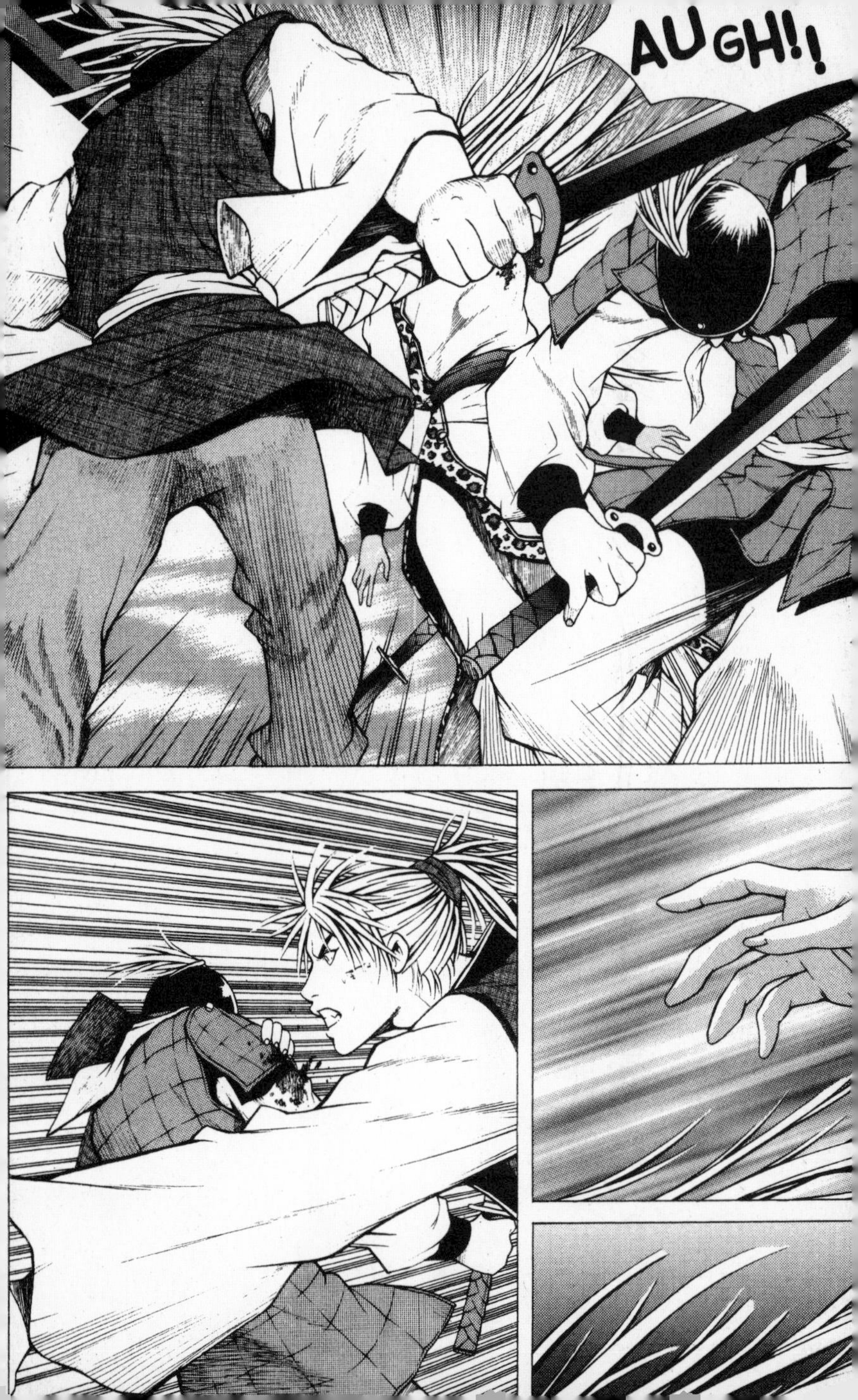
AUGH!!

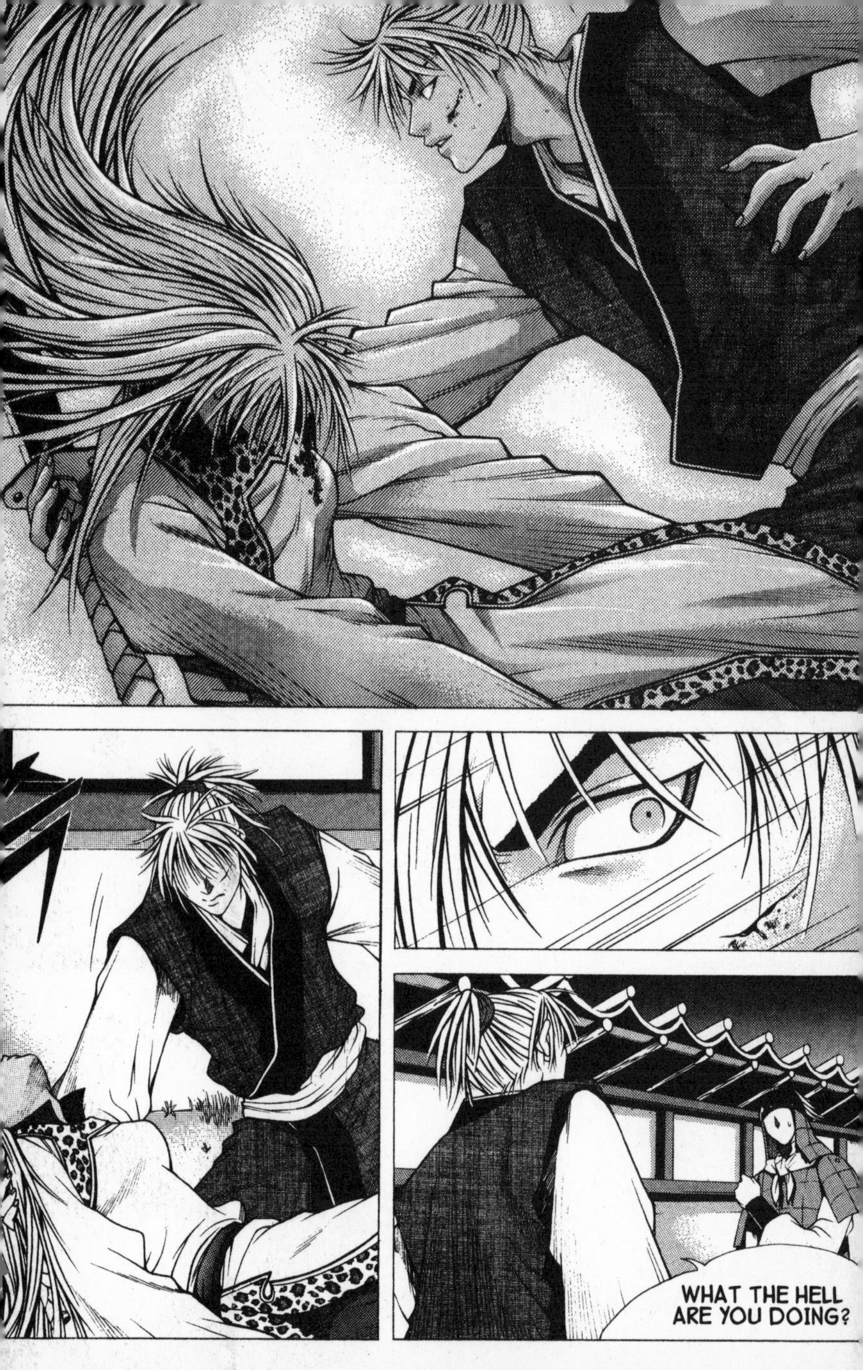
WHAT THE HELL
ARE YOU DOING?

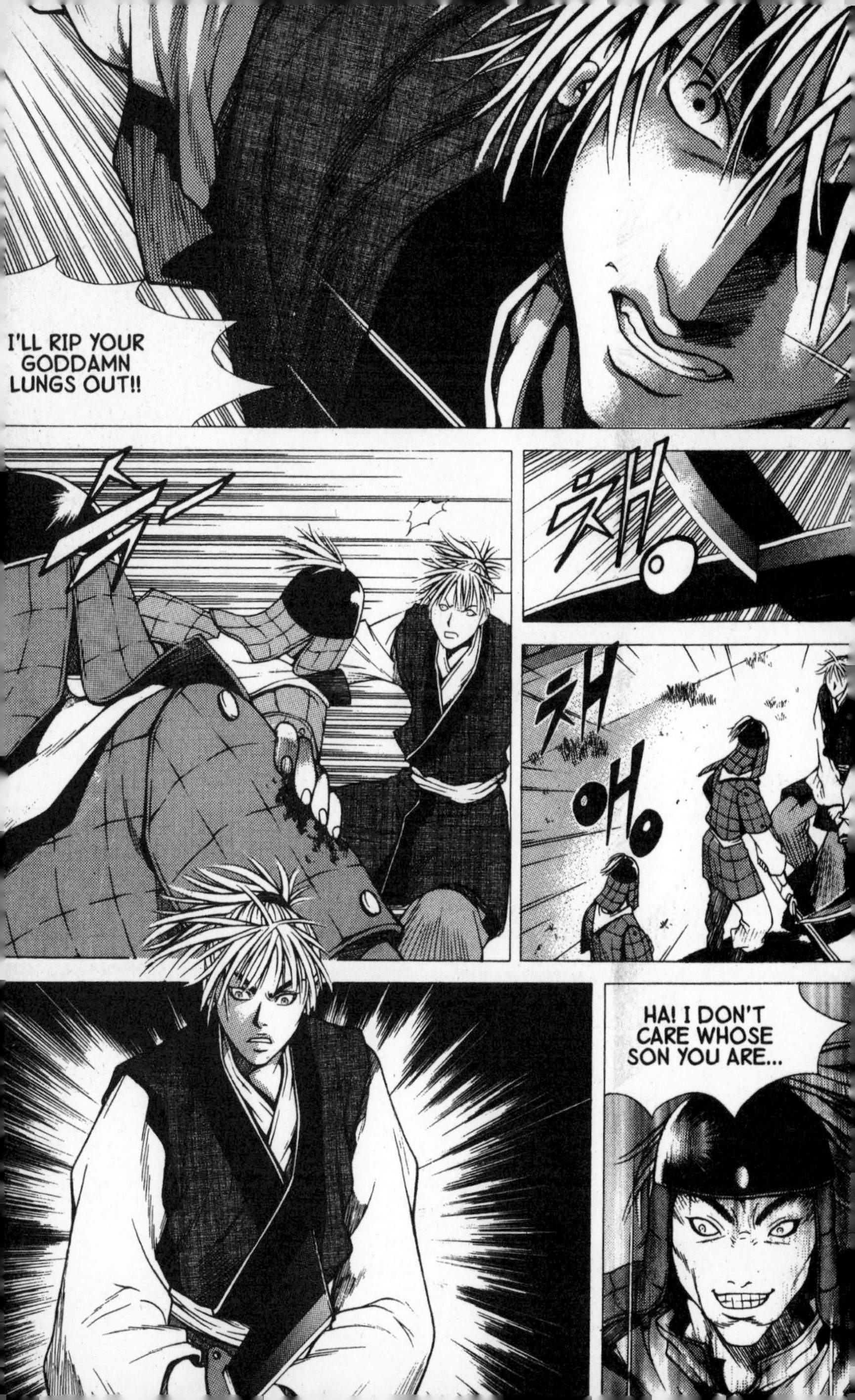
I'LL RIP YOUR GODDAMN LUNGS OUT!!
HA! I DON'T CARE WHOSE SON YOU ARE...

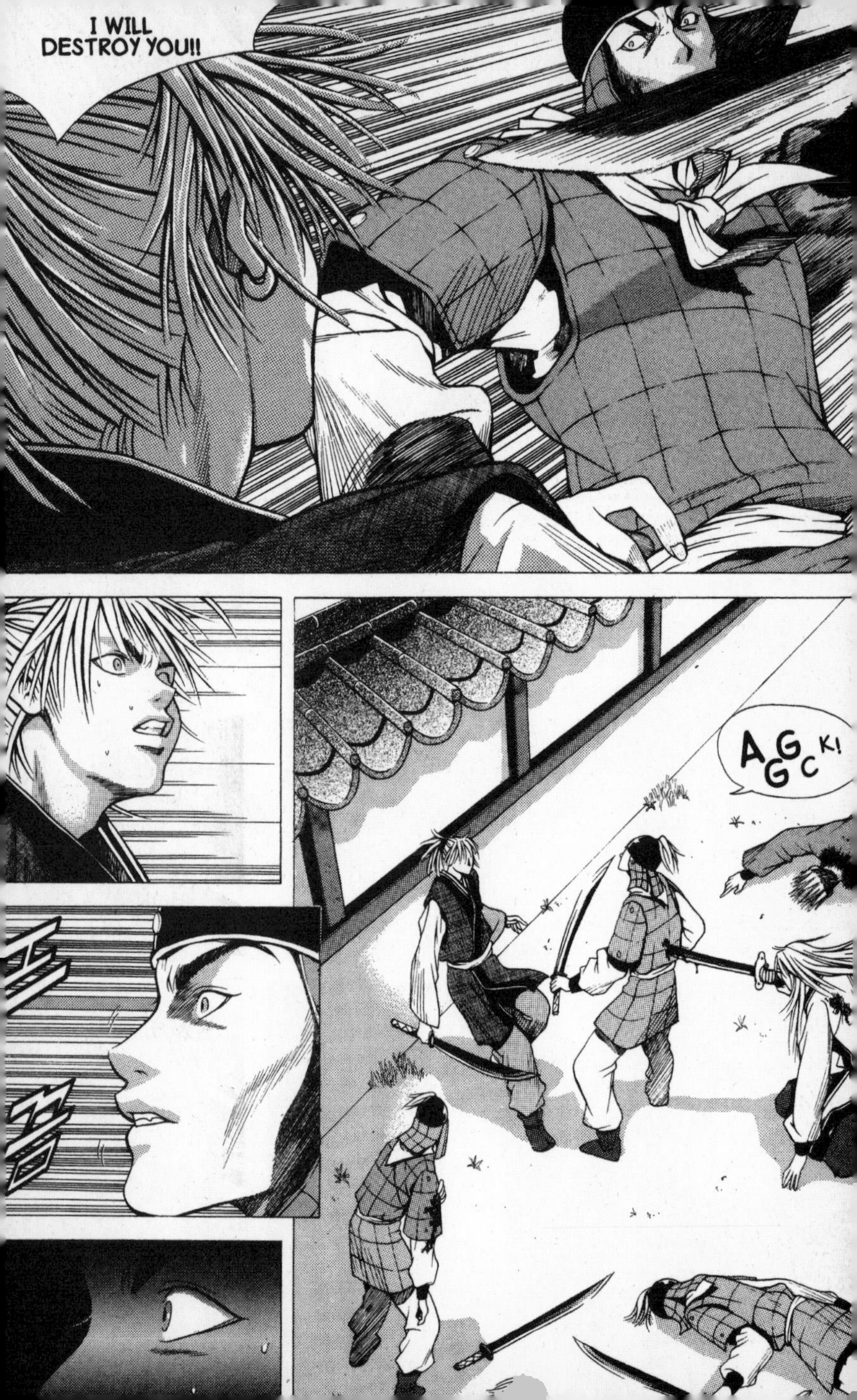
I WILL DESTROY YOU!!
AGGCK!

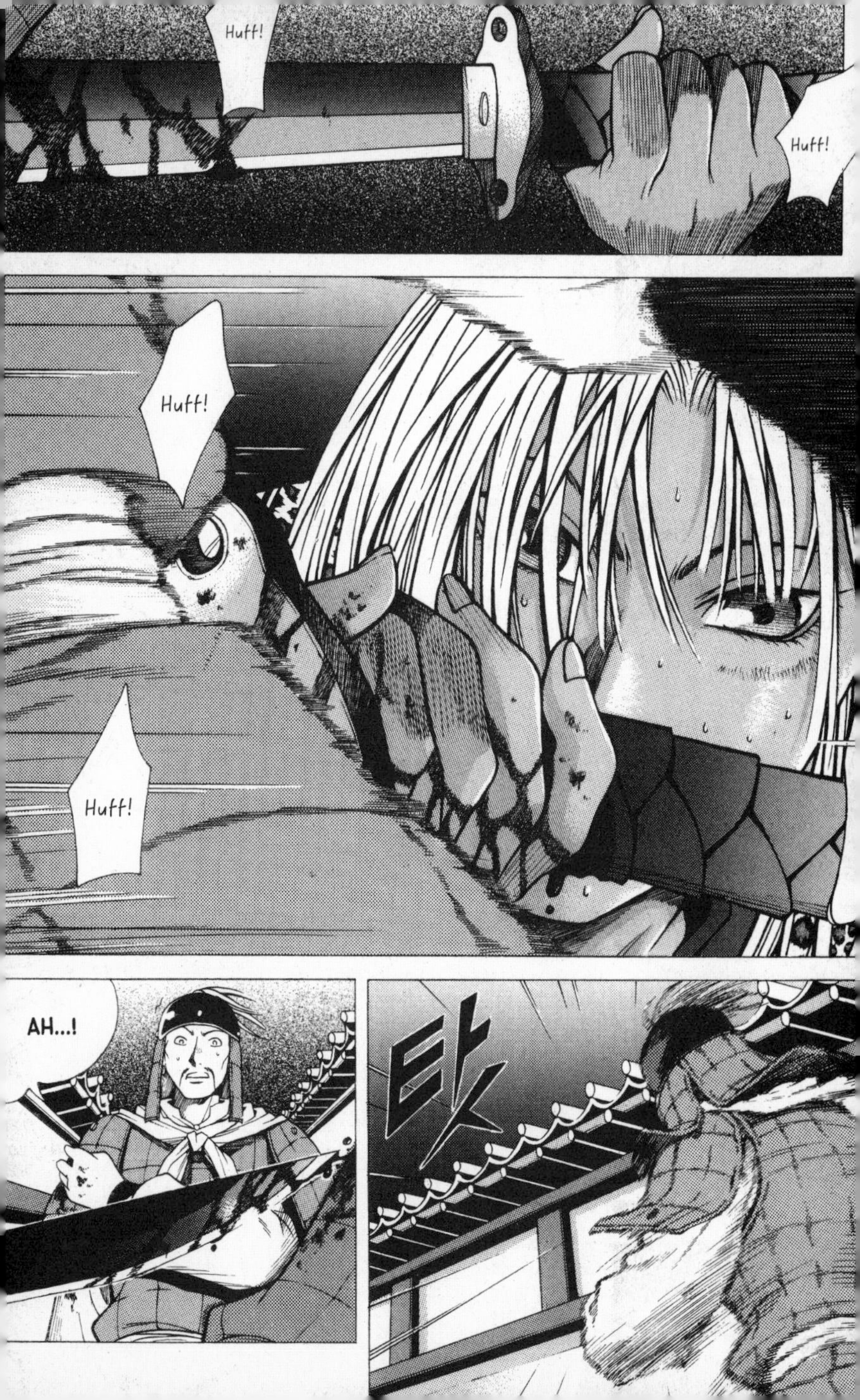
Huff!
Huff!
Huff!
Huff!
AH...!
탁

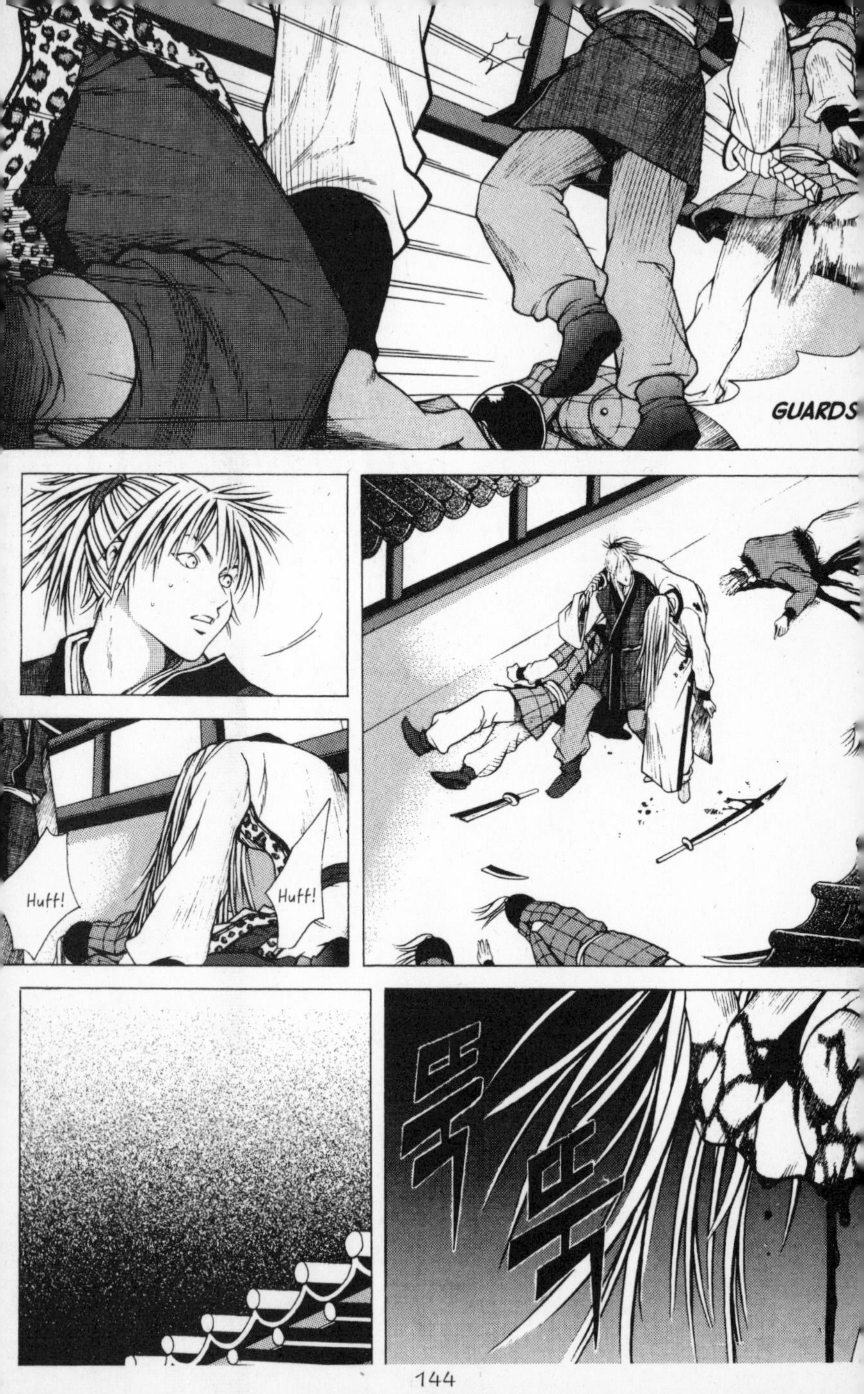
GUARDS
Huff!
Huff!
뚝
뚝

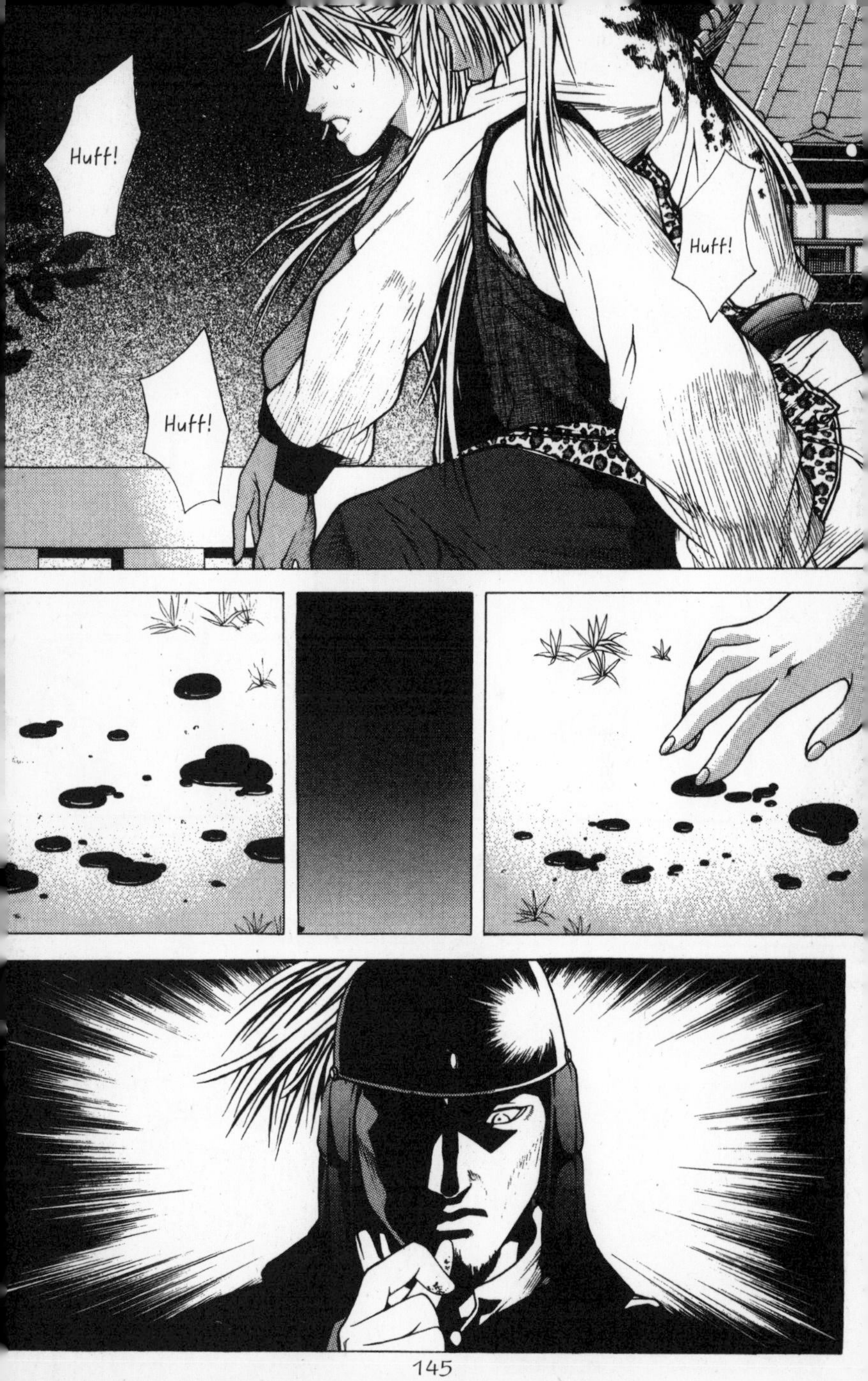
Huff!
Huff!
Huff!

ATTEND TO THE INJURED SOLDIERS AND ORGANIZE A SEARCH OF THE AREA.

Huff!

WITH ONE OF THEM WOUNDED, THEY CAN'T HAVE GOTTEN FAR.

THIS WAY!

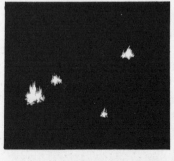

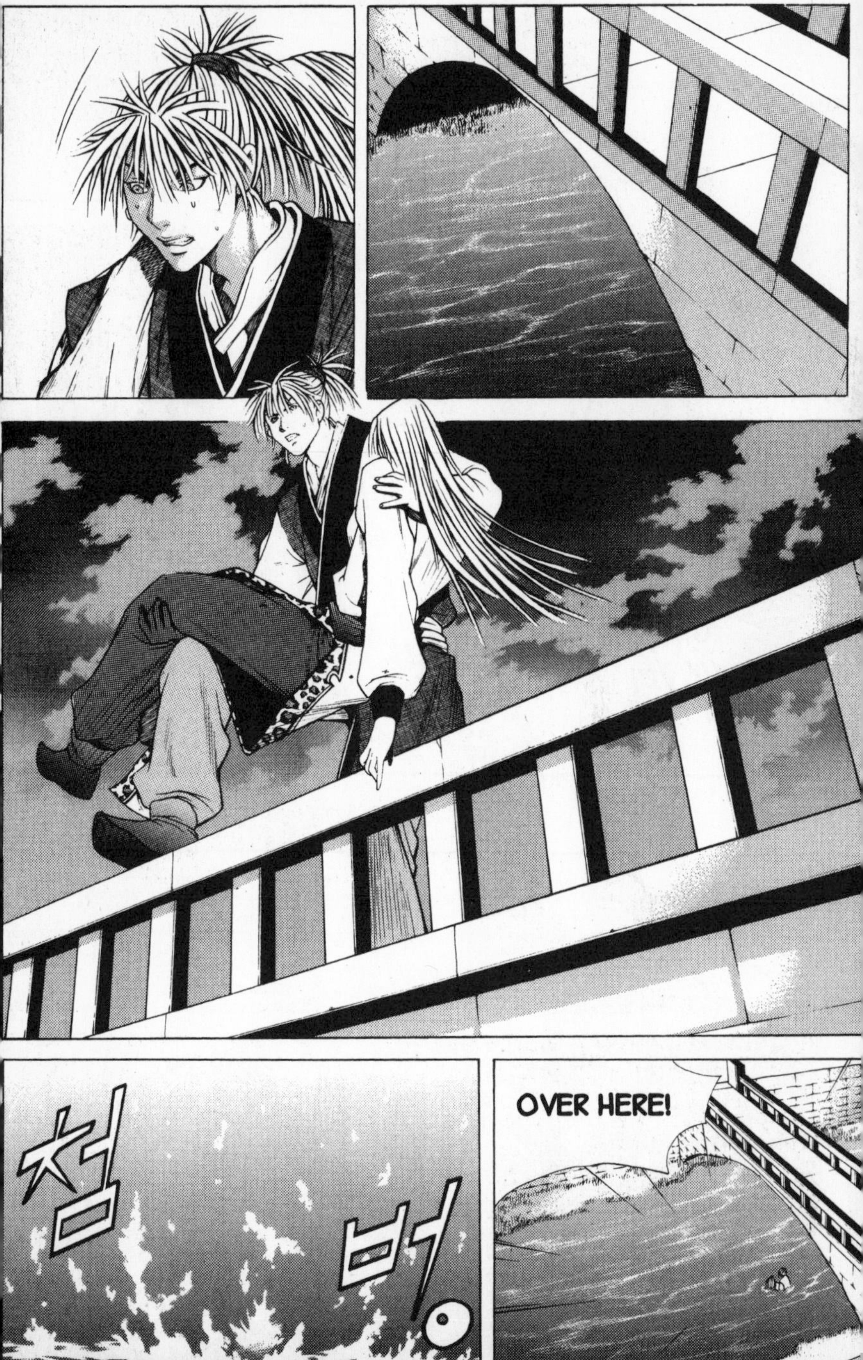
첨벙
OVER HERE!

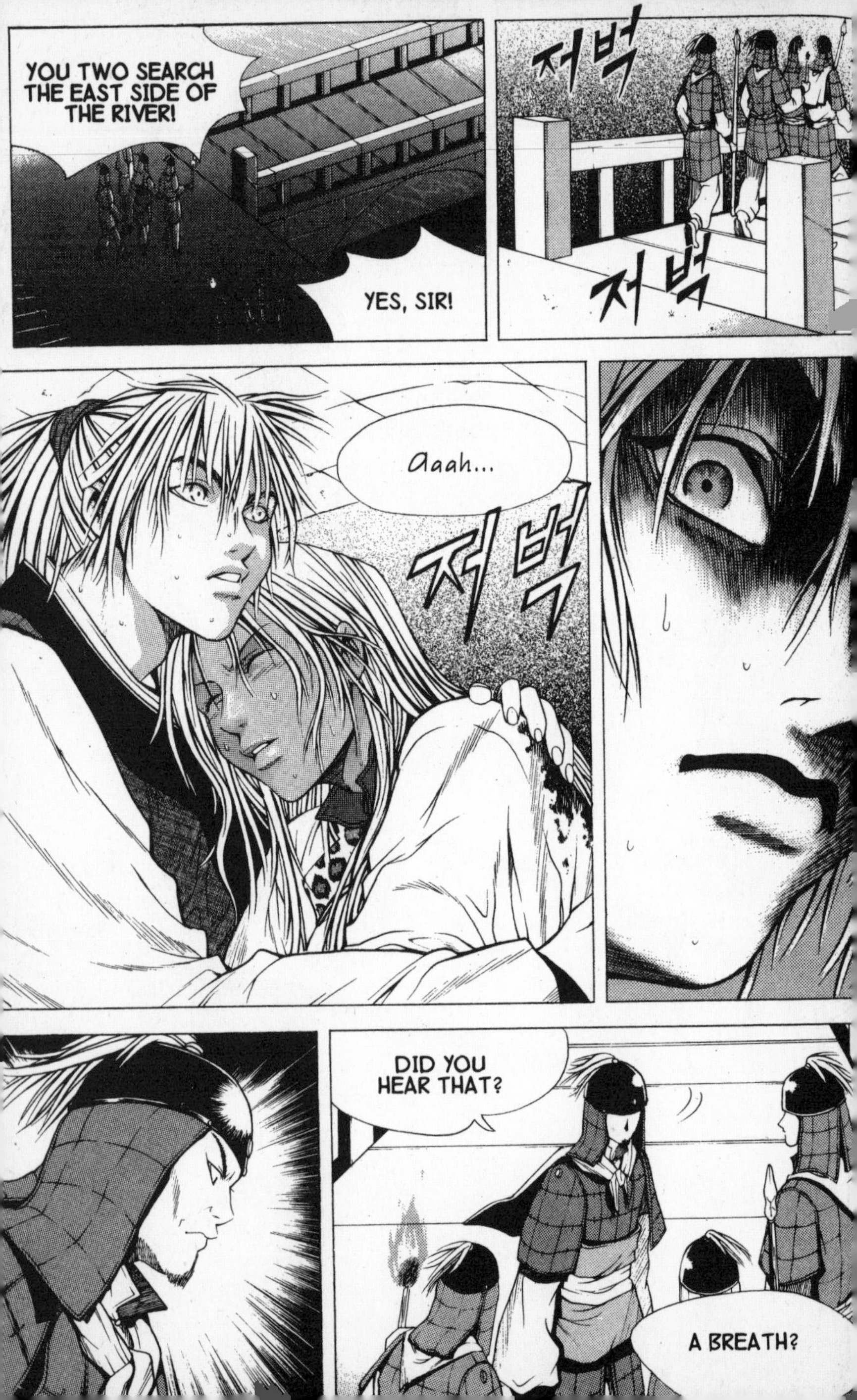
YOU TWO SEARCH THE EAST SIDE OF THE RIVER!
YES, SIR!
저벅
저벅
Aaah...
저벅
DID YOU HEAR THAT?
A BREATH?

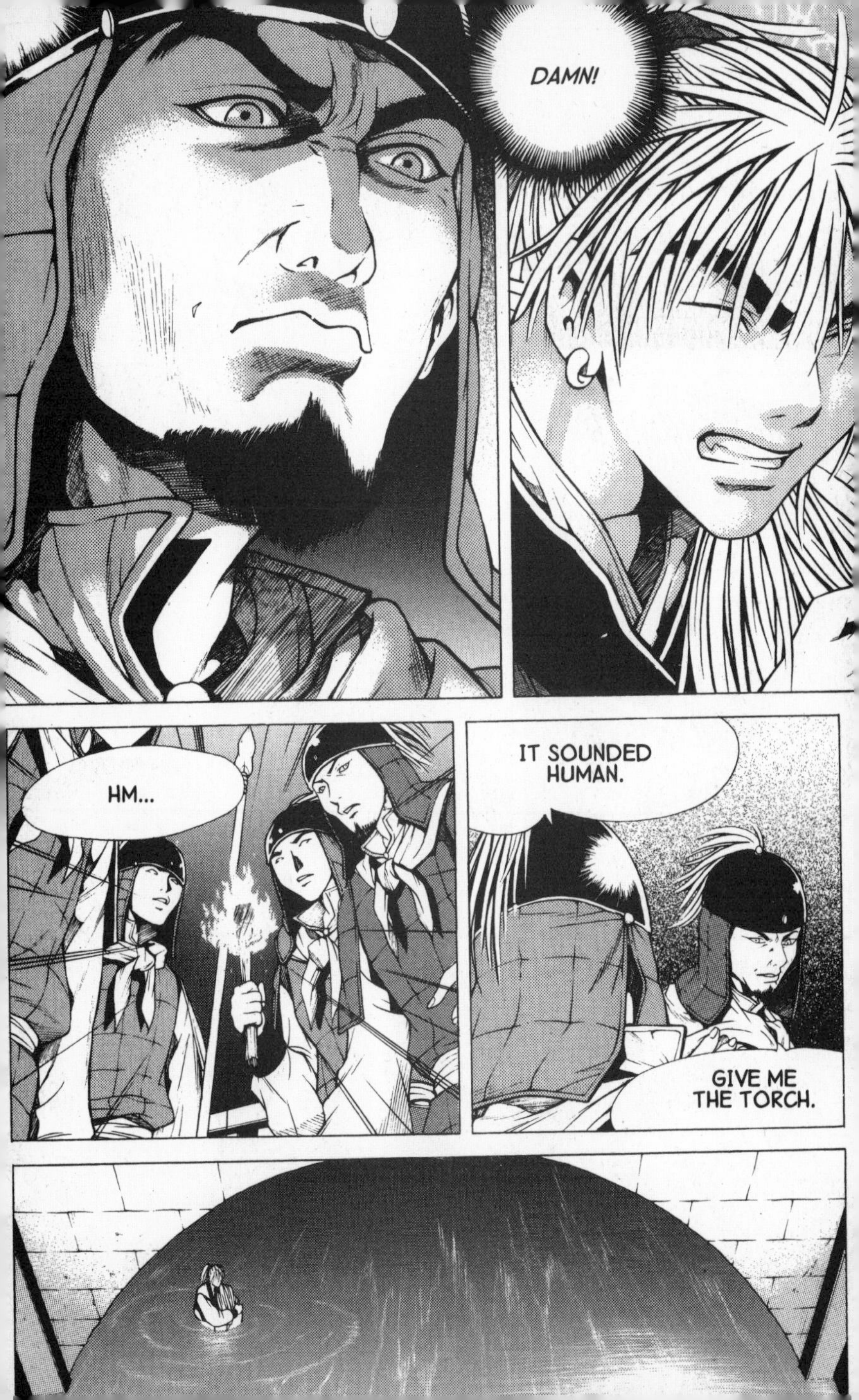
DAMN!
HM...
IT SOUNDED HUMAN.
GIVE ME THE TORCH.

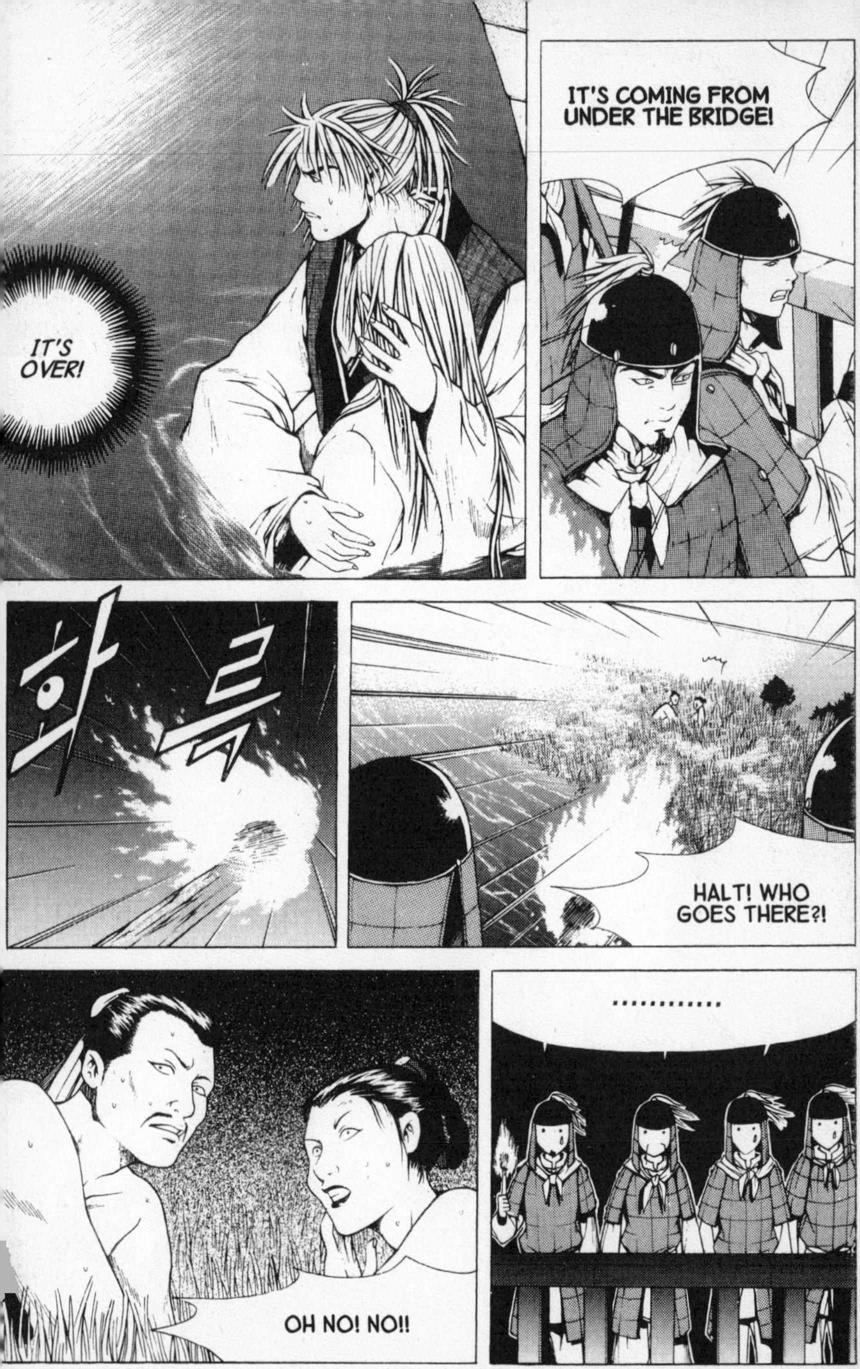
IT'S OVER!
IT'S COMING FROM UNDER THE BRIDGE!
HALT! WHO GOES THERE?!
OH NO! NO!!
....

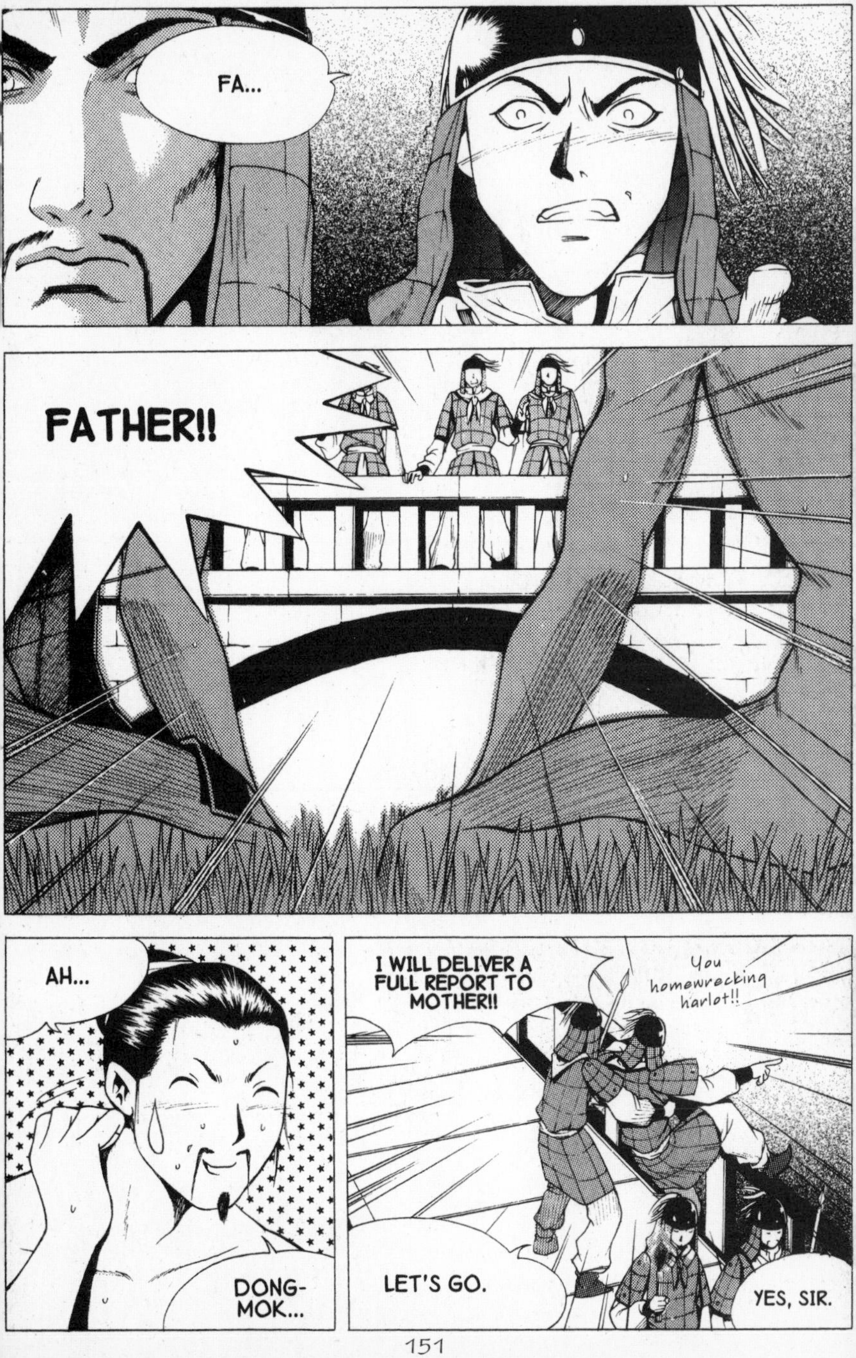
FA...
FATHER!!
AH...
DONG-
MOK...
I WILL DELIVER A FULL REPORT TO MOTHER!!
You homewrecking harlot!!
LET'S GO.
YES, SIR.

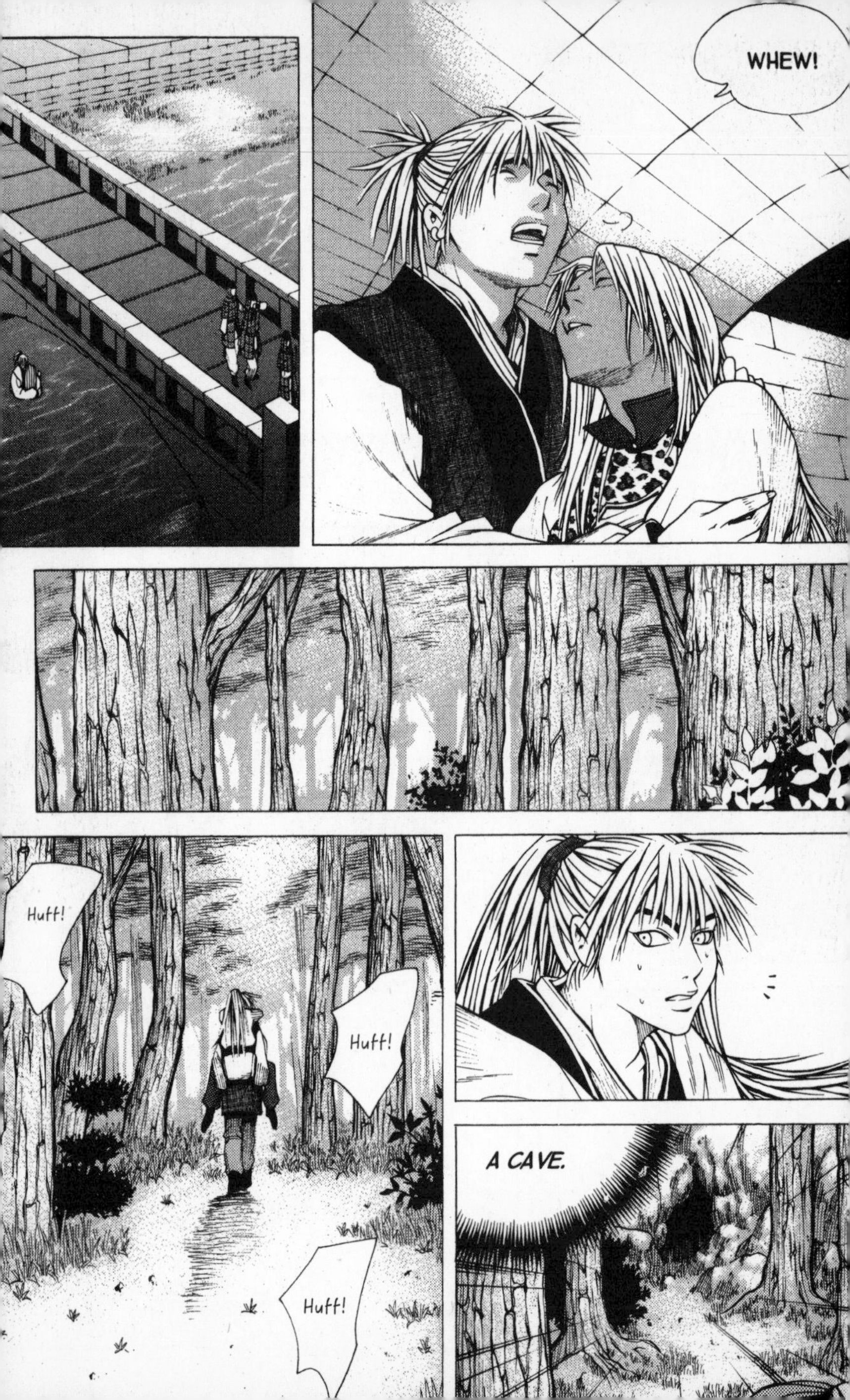
WHEW!
Huff!
Huff!
Huff!
A CAVE.

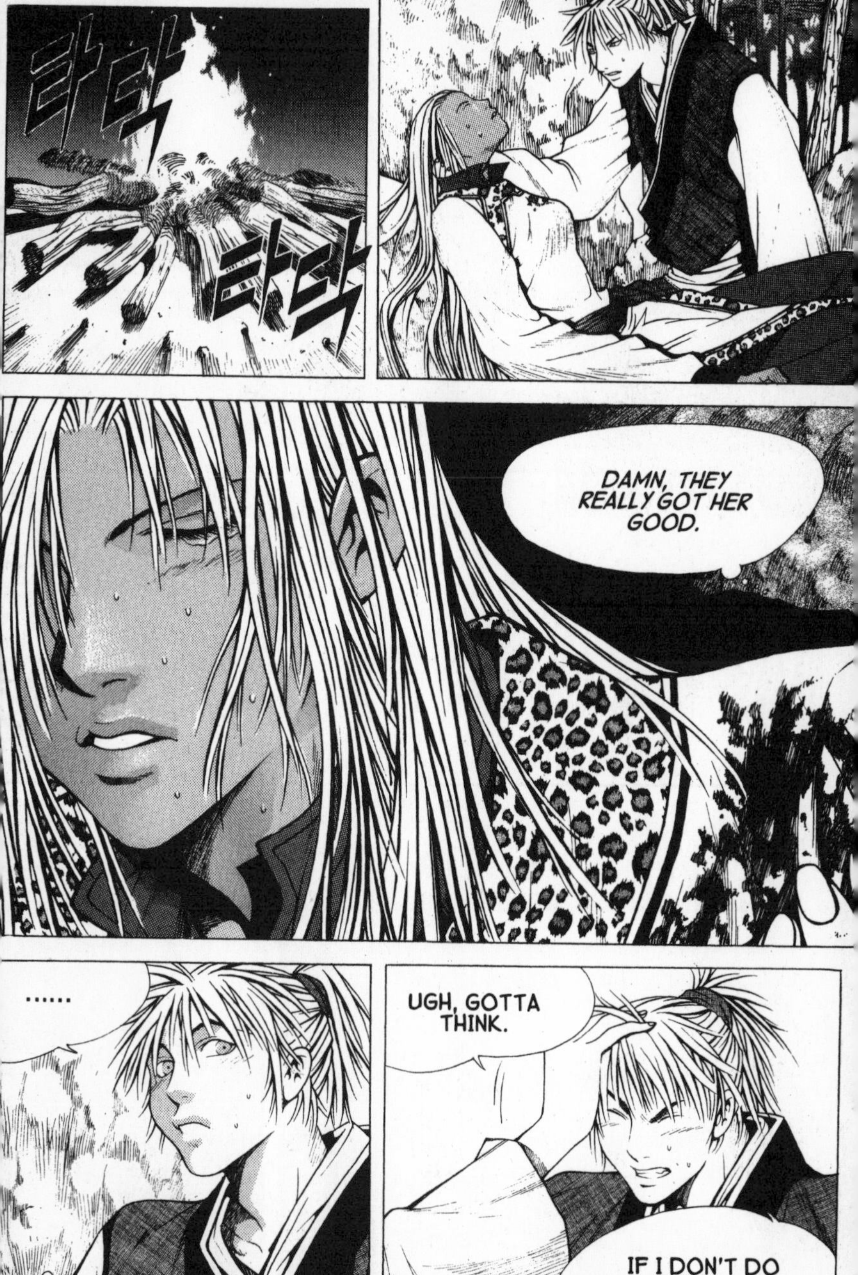
타닥
타닥
DAMN, THEY REALLY GOT HER GOOD.
......
UGH, GOTTA THINK.
IF I DON'T DO SOMETHING SOON, SHE'LL DIE.

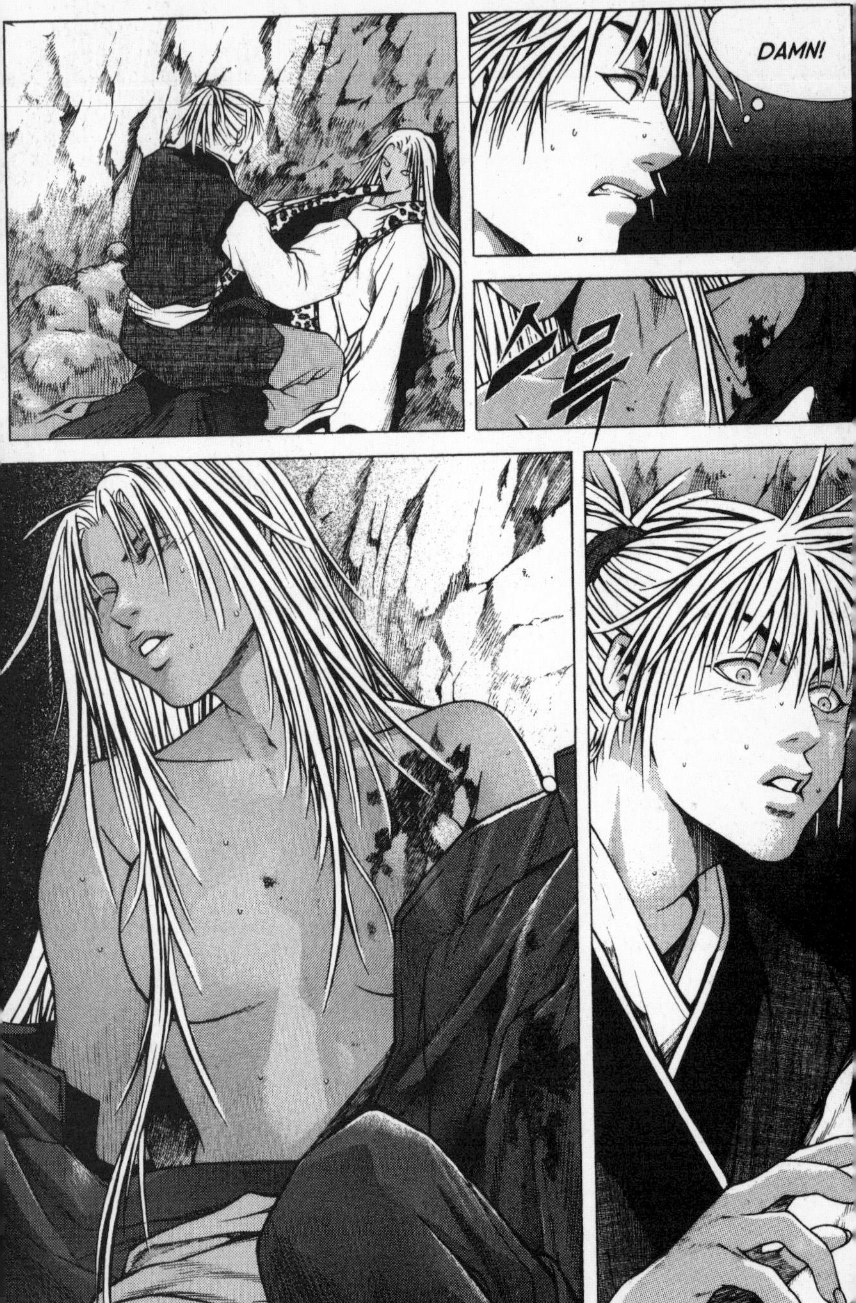
DAMN!
스륵

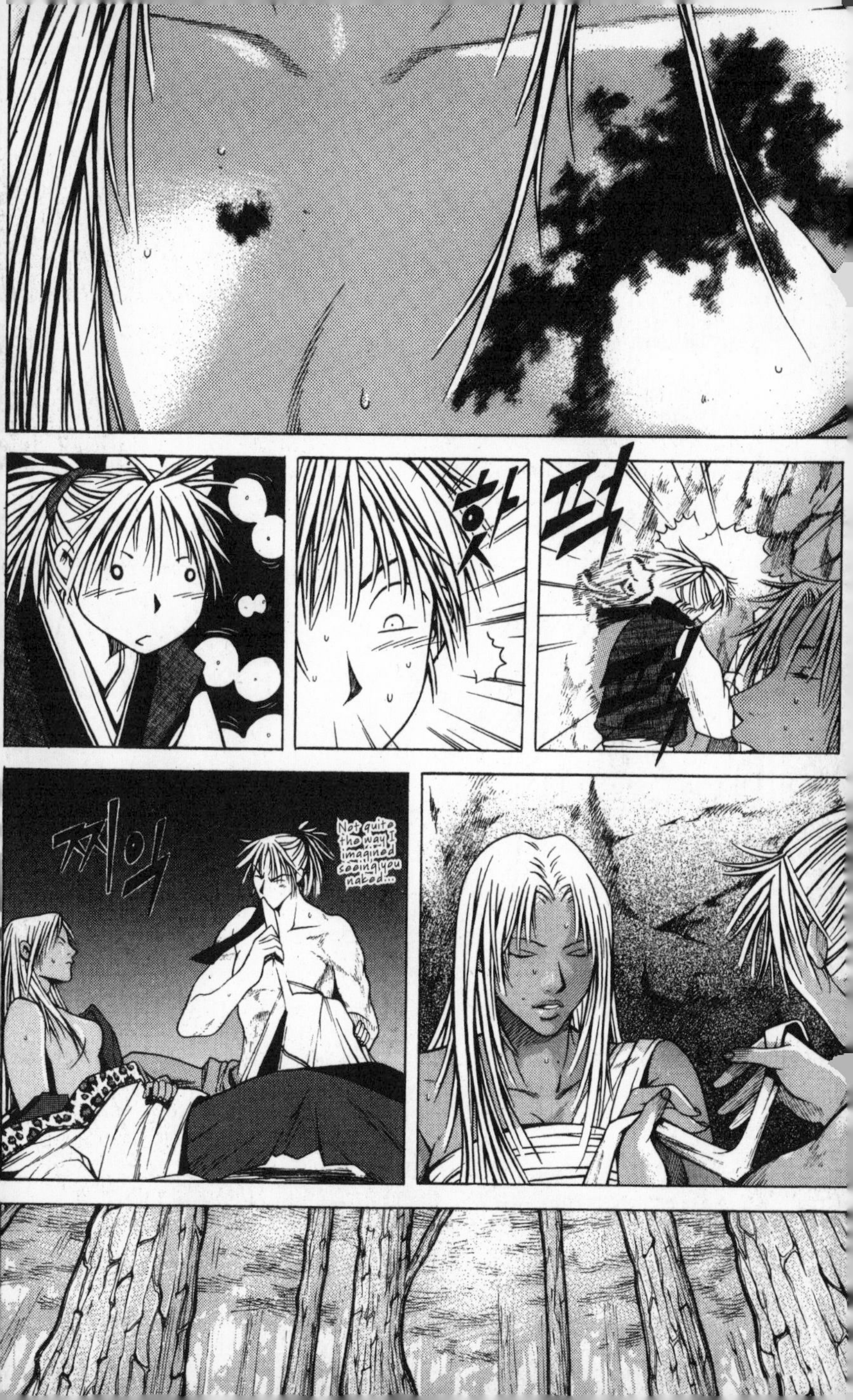

핫
퍽
찌익
Not quite the way I imagined seeing you naked...

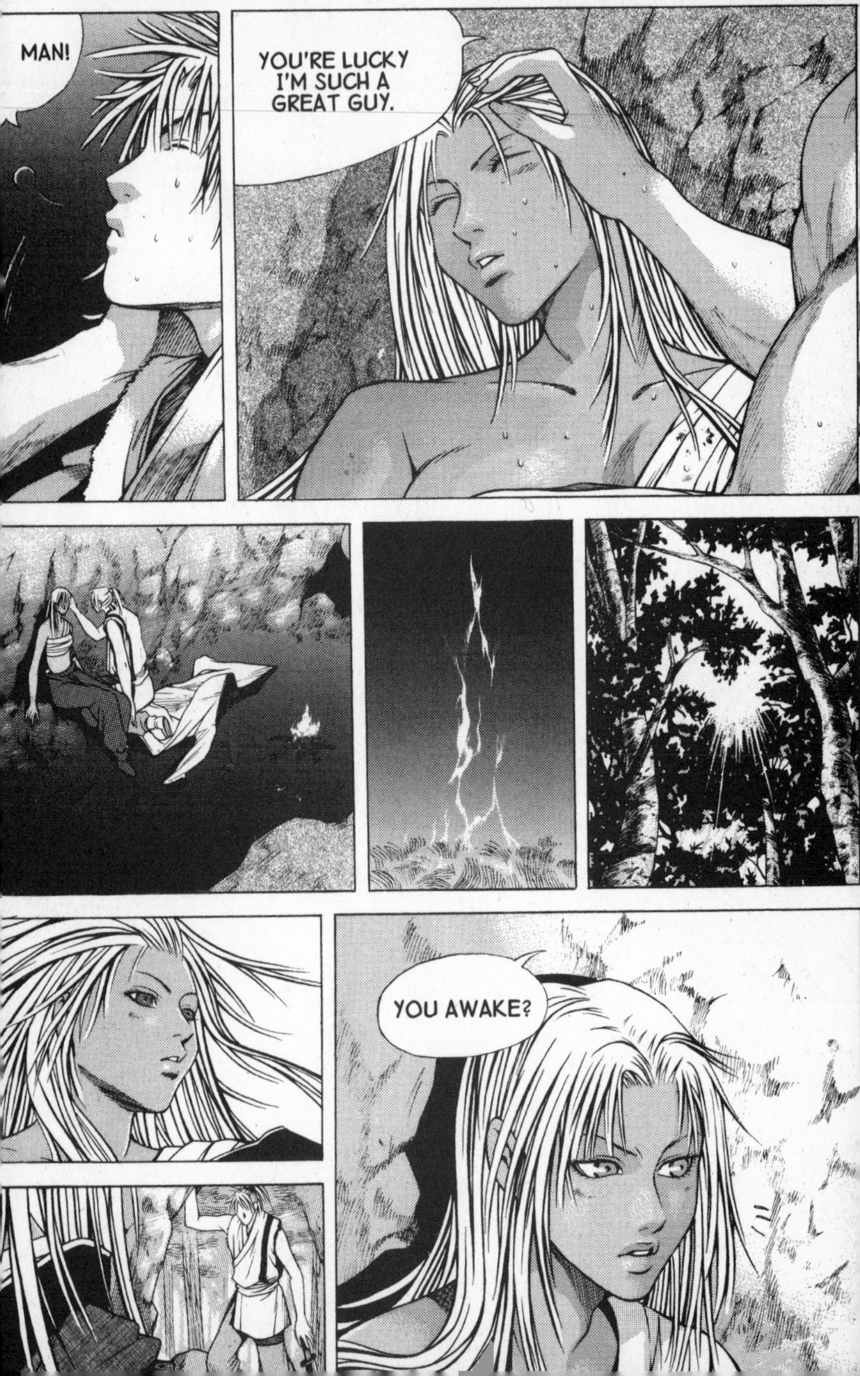
MAN!
YOU'RE LUCKY I'M SUCH A GREAT GUY.
YOU AWAKE?

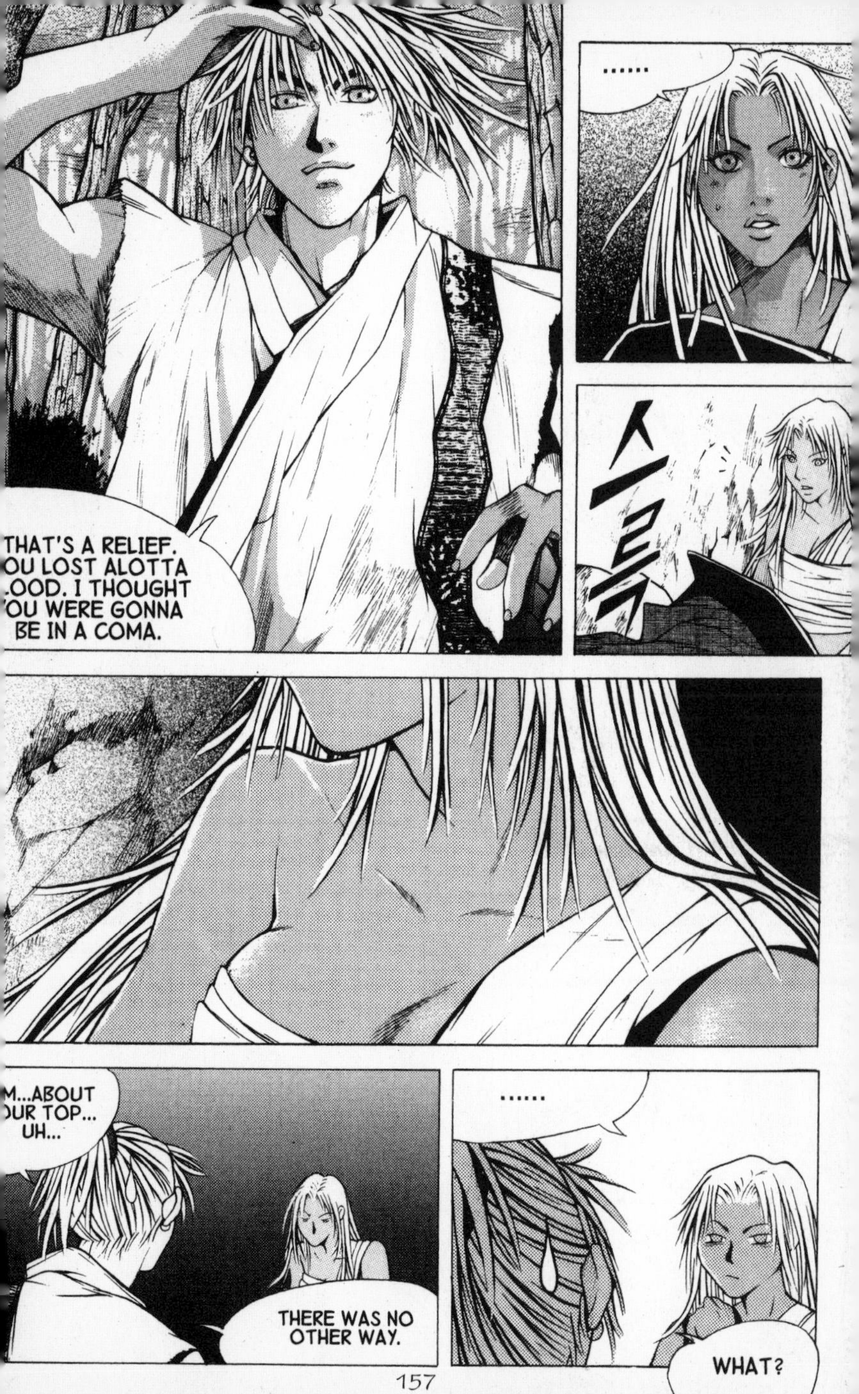

THAT'S A RELIEF. OU LOST ALOTTA LOOD. I THOUGHT OU WERE GONNA BE IN A COMA.
......
M...ABOUT OUR TOP... UH...
THERE WAS NO OTHER WAY.
......
WHAT?

DON'T LOOK AT ME LIKE THAT!

I SAVED YOUR LIFE!

WHAT DO YOU WANT FROM ME? I HAD TO STOP THE BLEEDING!

TH...THANK YOU.

AH!

OH, THIS IS YOURS.

158

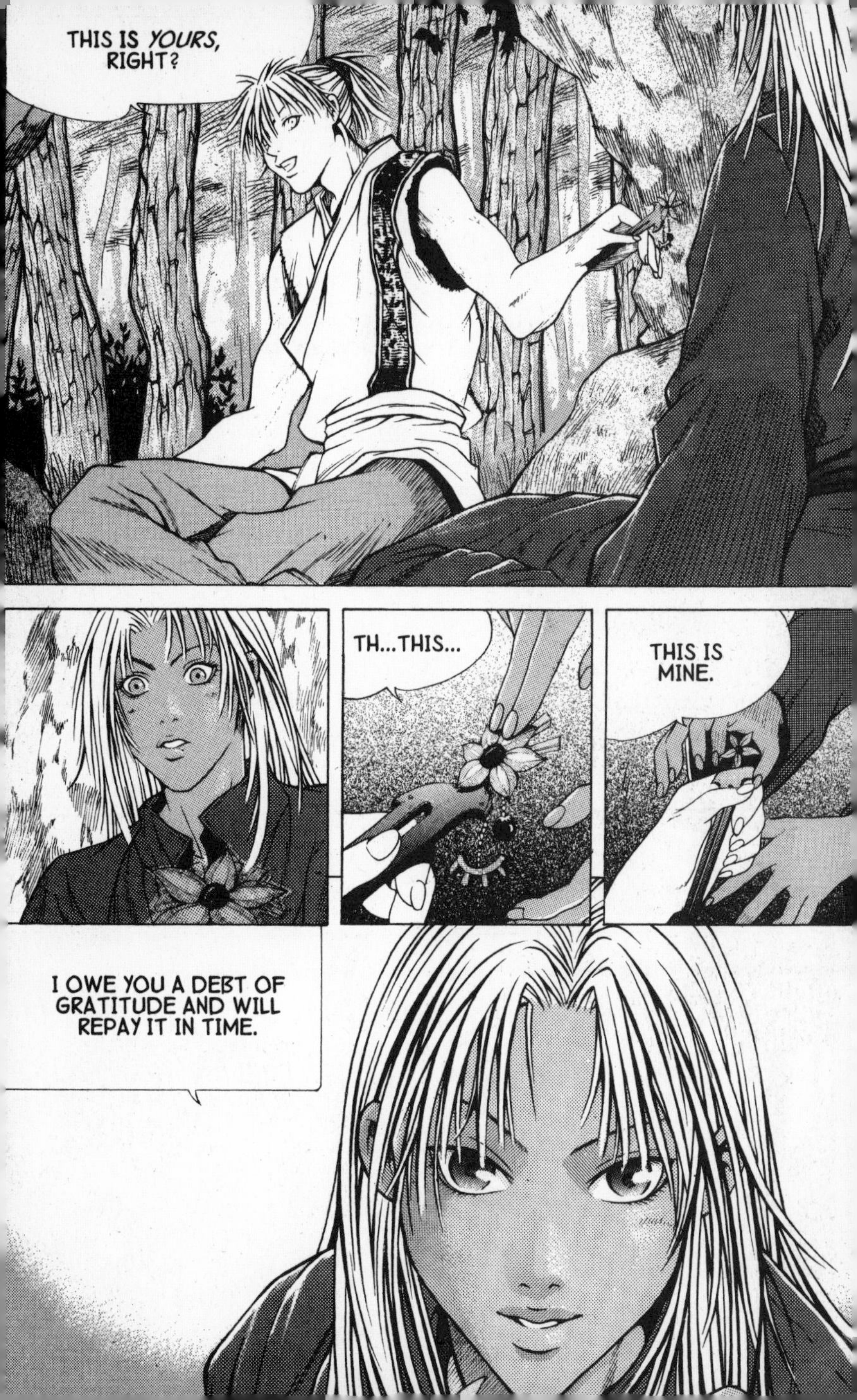
THIS IS *YOURS*, RIGHT?
TH...THIS...
THIS IS MINE.
I OWE YOU A DEBT OF GRATITUDE AND WILL REPAY IT IN TIME.

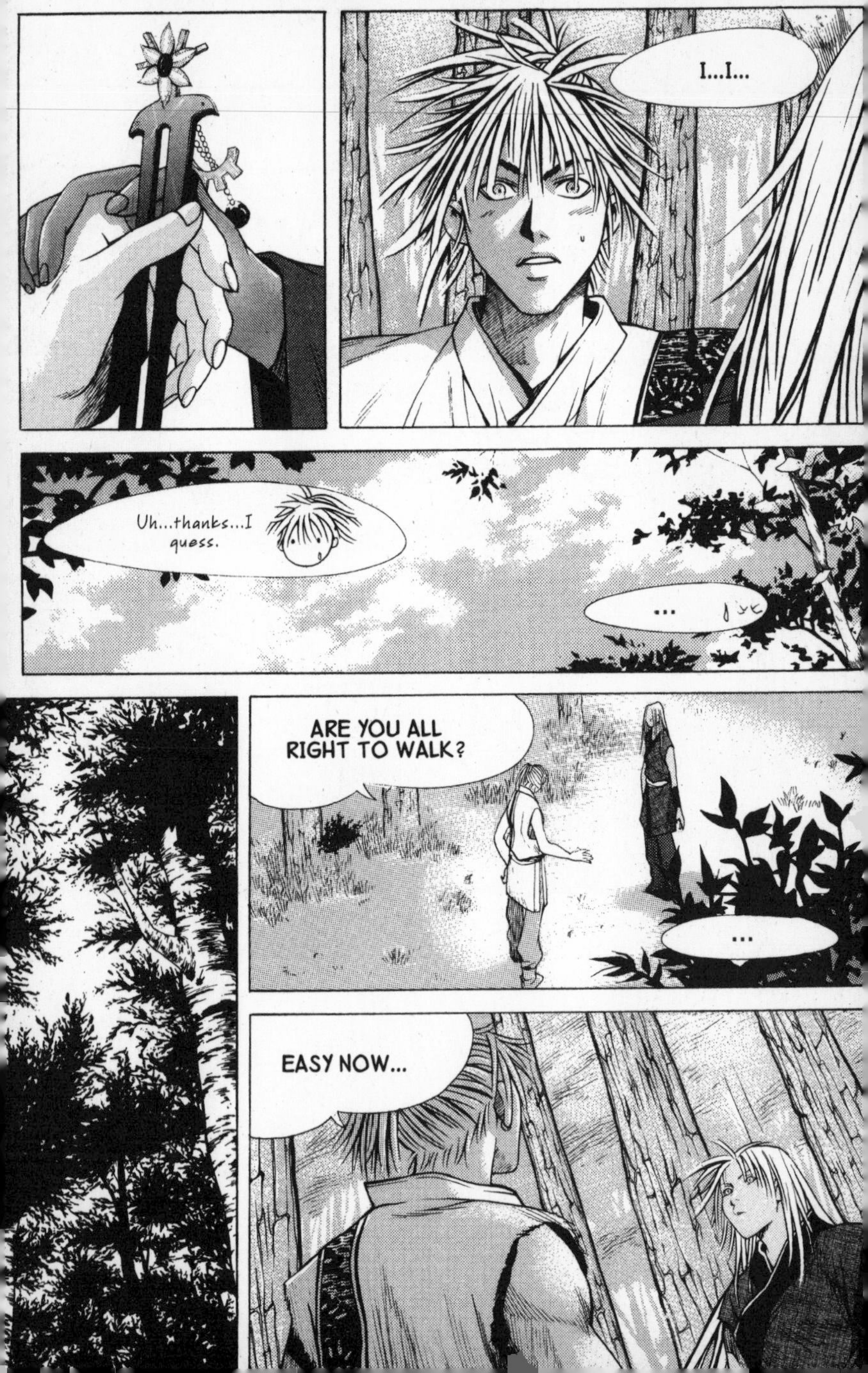
I...I...
Uh...thanks...I guess.
...
ARE YOU ALL RIGHT TO WALK?
...
EASY NOW...

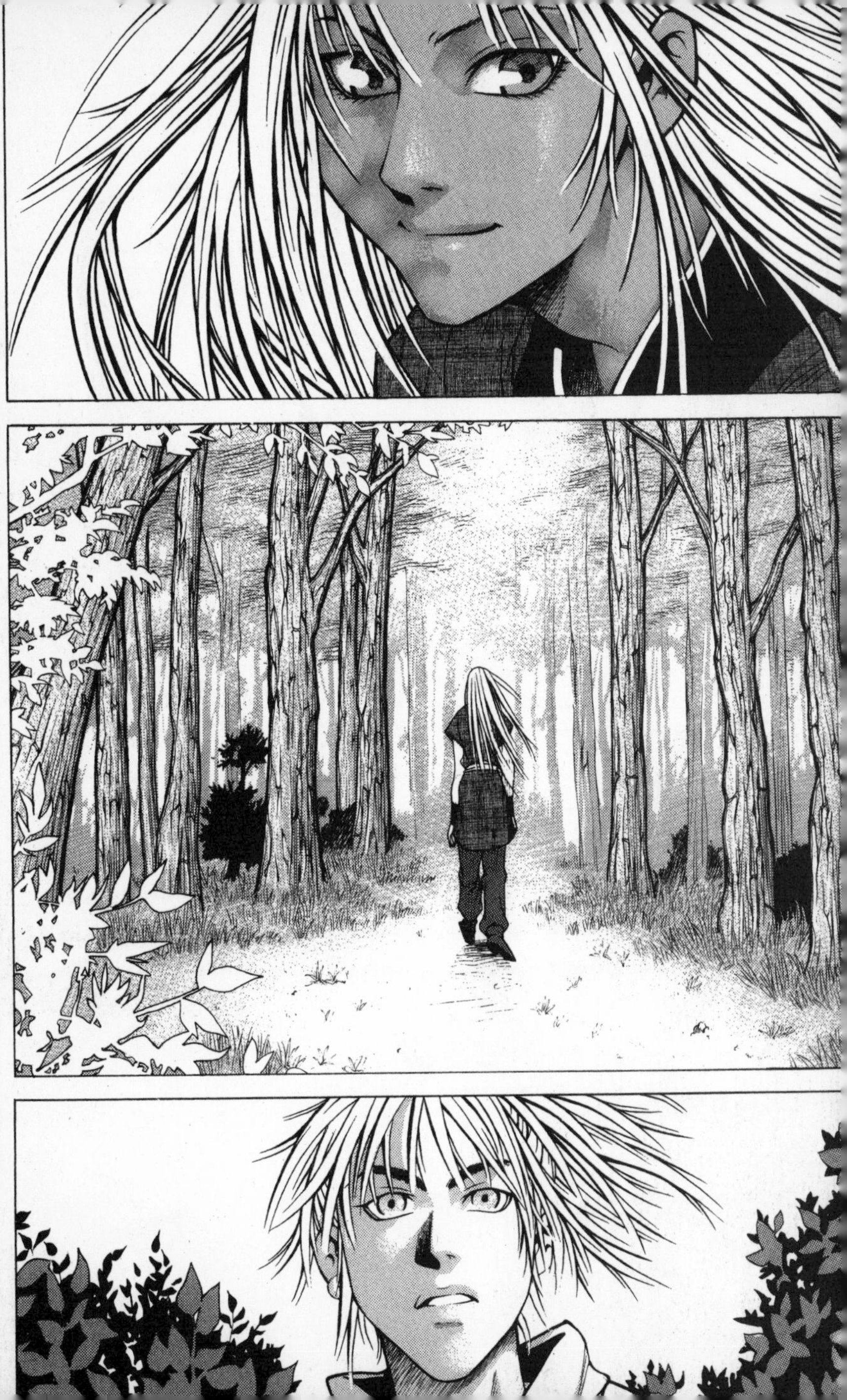

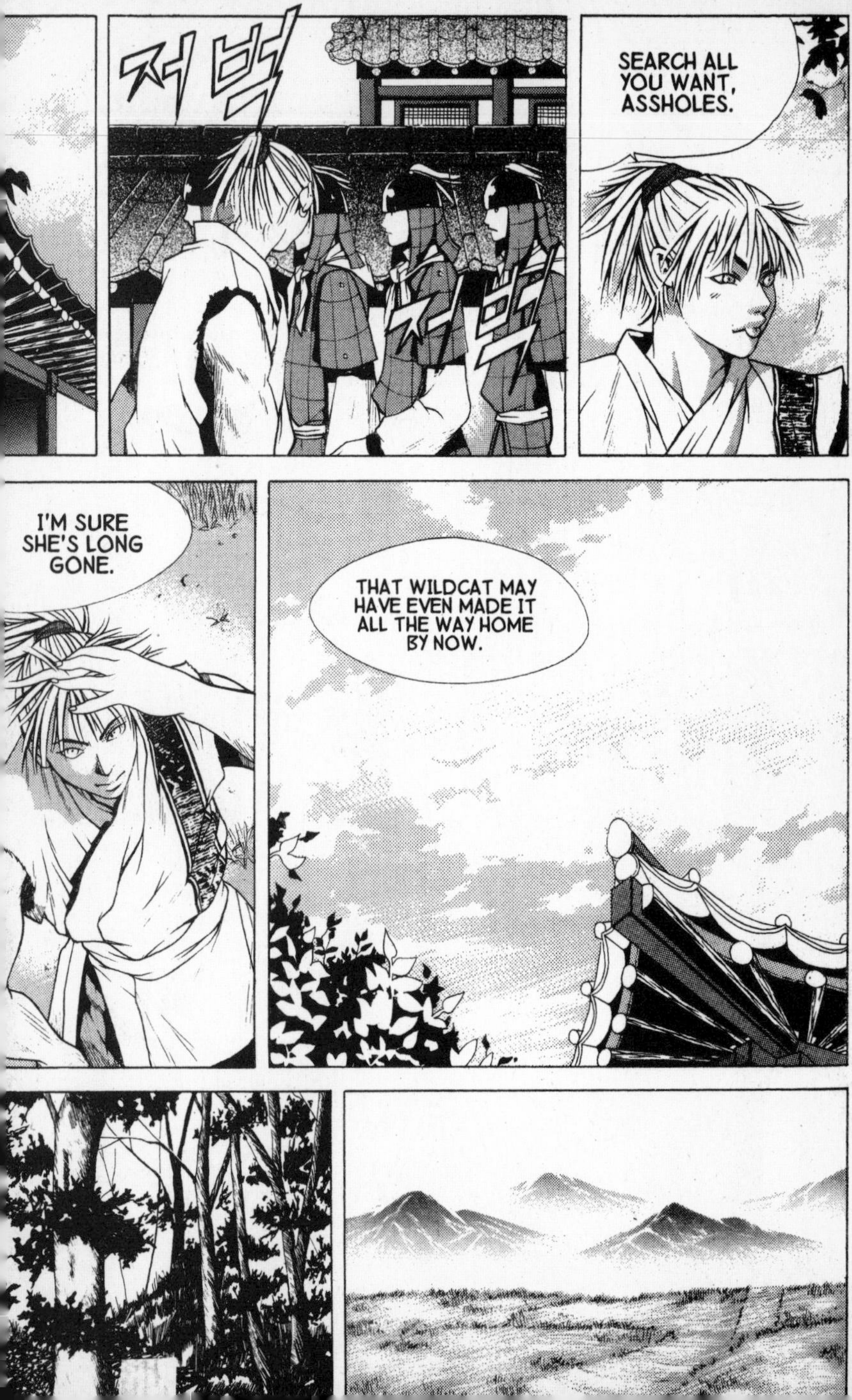
저벅
저벅
SEARCH ALL YOU WANT, ASSHOLES.
I'M SURE SHE'S LONG GONE.
THAT WILDCAT MAY HAVE EVEN MADE IT ALL THE WAY HOME BY NOW.

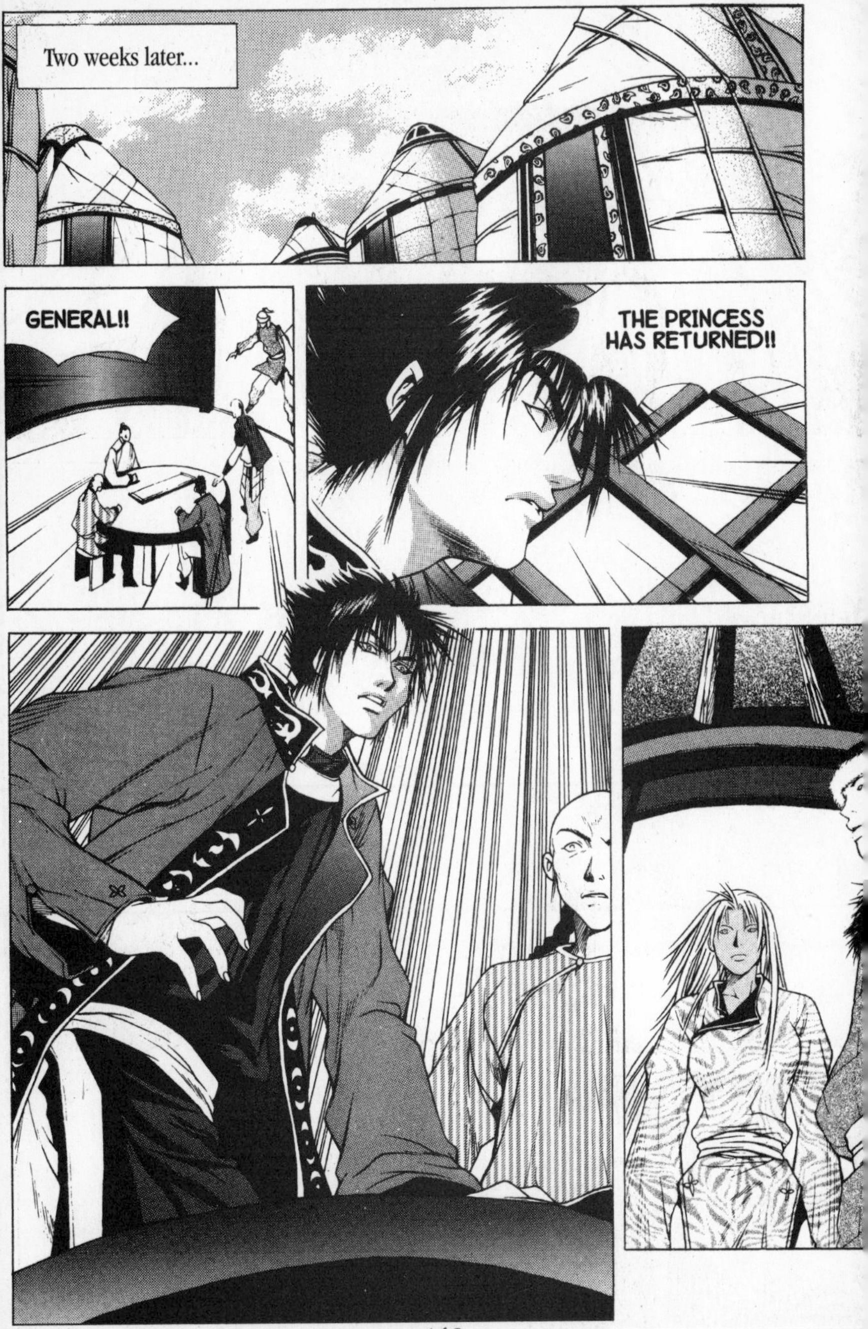
Two weeks later...
GENERAL!!
THE PRINCESS HAS RETURNED!!

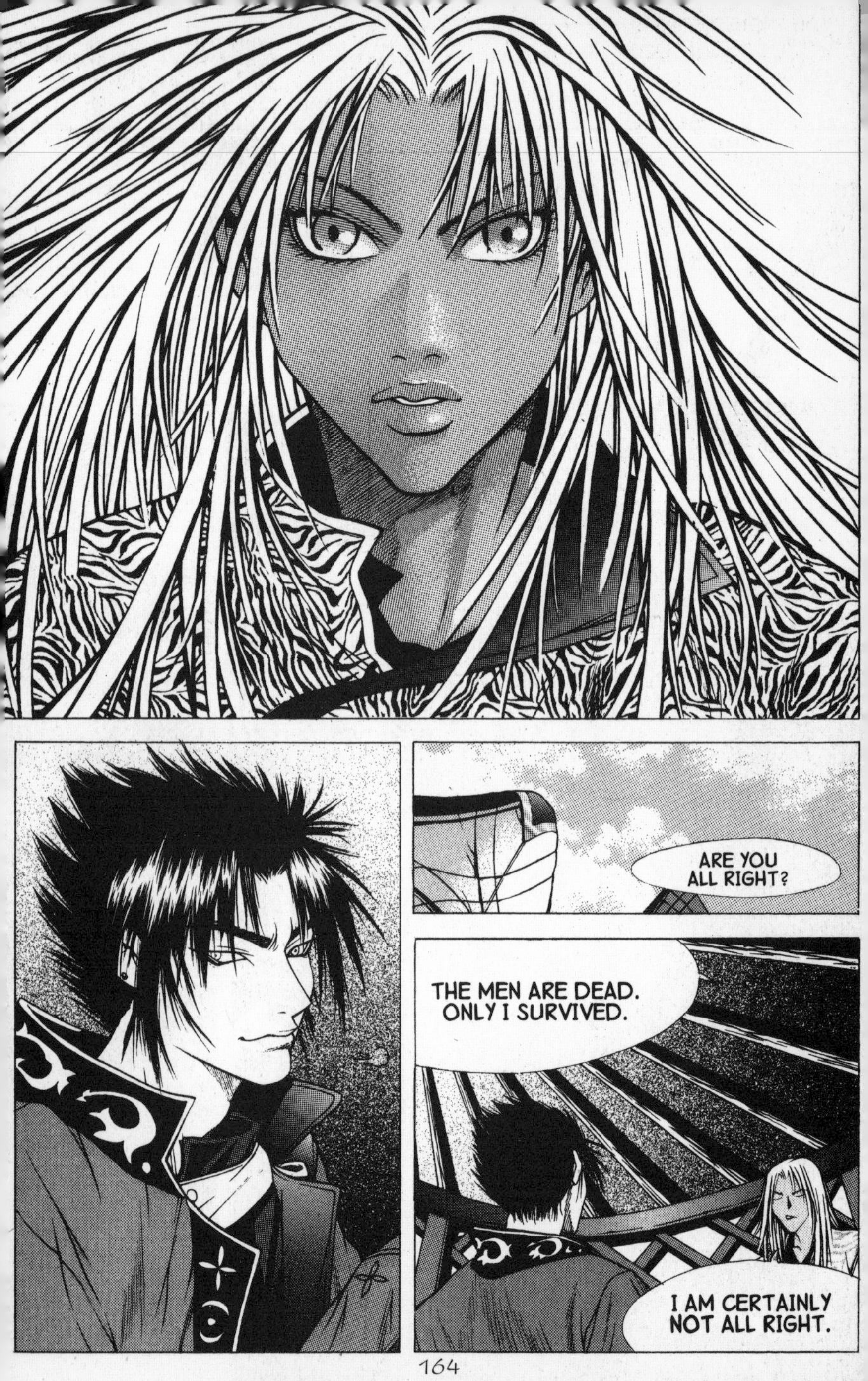
ARE YOU ALL RIGHT?
THE MEN ARE DEAD. ONLY I SURVIVED.
I AM CERTAINLY NOT ALL RIGHT.

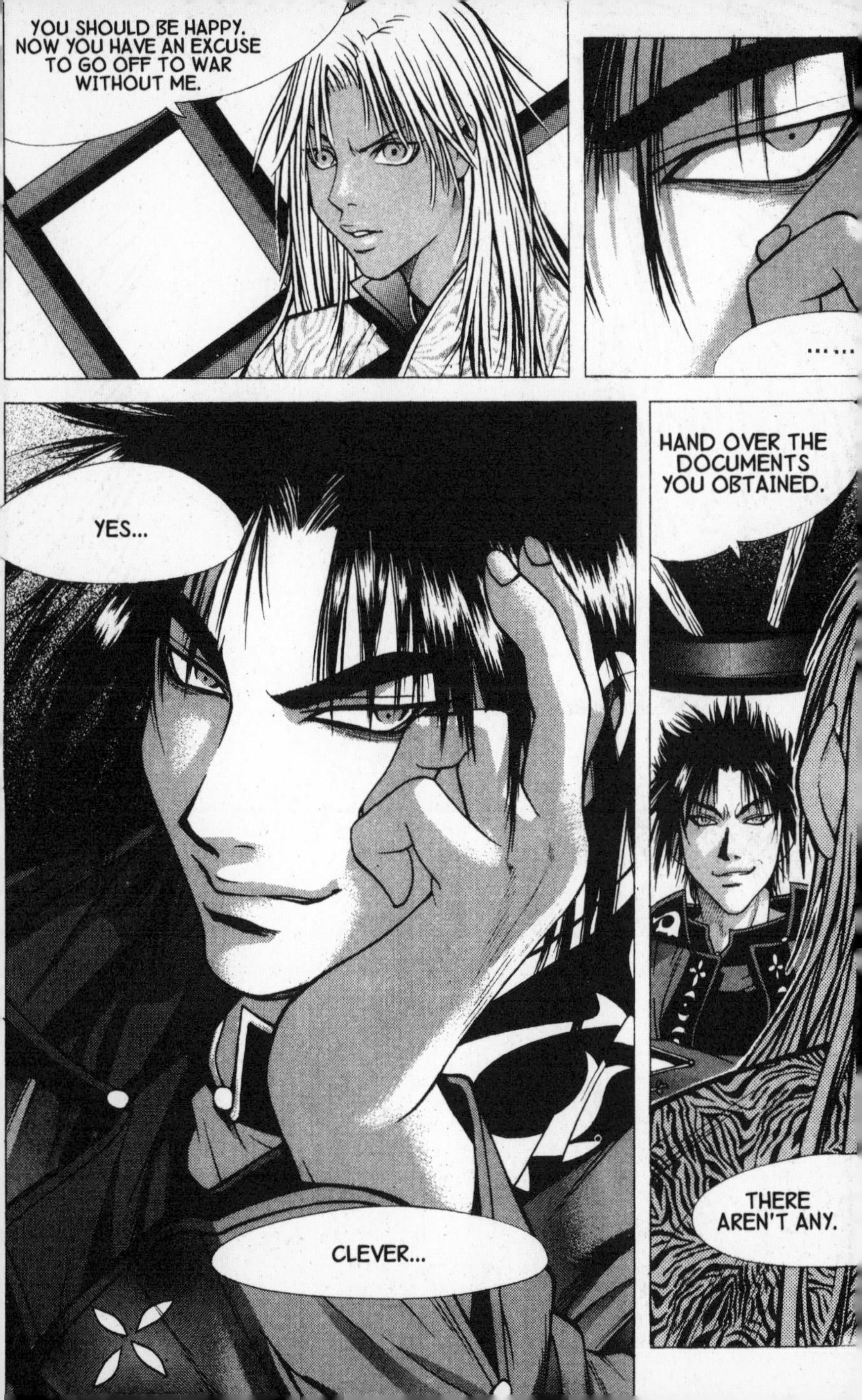
YOU SHOULD BE HAPPY. NOW YOU HAVE AN EXCUSE TO GO OFF TO WAR WITHOUT ME.
......
YES...
CLEVER...
HAND OVER THE DOCUMENTS YOU OBTAINED.
THERE AREN'T ANY.

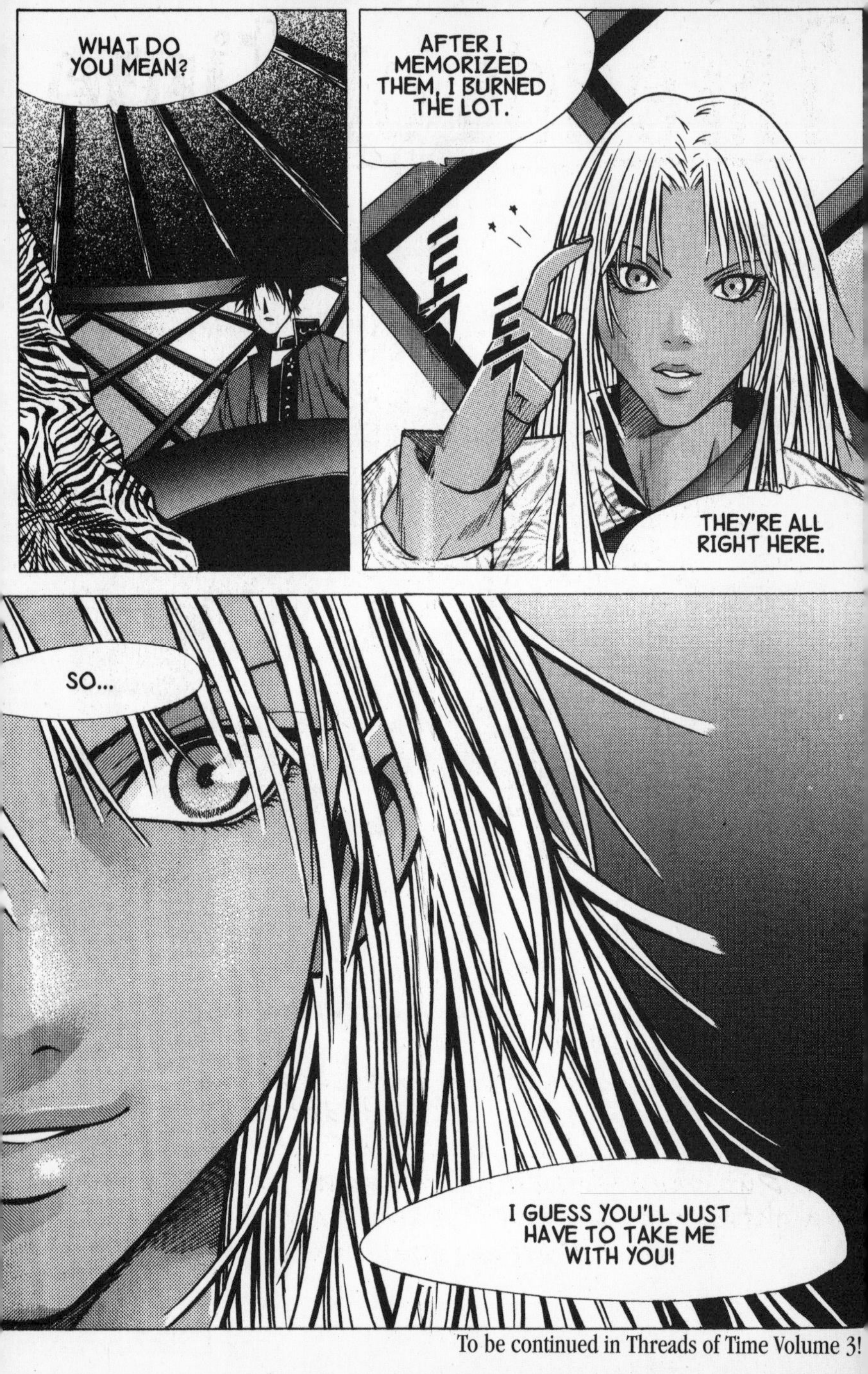
WHAT DO YOU MEAN?
AFTER I MEMORIZED THEM, I BURNED THE LOT.
THEY'RE ALL RIGHT HERE.
SO...
I GUESS YOU'LL JUST HAVE TO TAKE ME WITH YOU!

To be continued in Threads of Time Volume 3!

Threads of Time™

General Sali Tayi offers Koryo an ultimatum—surrender to the Mongol army or go to war with it. Koryo refuses, thereby entering into a blood struggle to retain its freedom against the vast Mongol hordes. And poised on opposite sides of this territorial clash, Atan Hadas and Sa Kyung Kim must decide individually where their hearts lie. But when Sa Kyung Kim begins to have waking nightmares of Moon Bin Kim, he must also deal with his fractured identity.

The Asia of Genghis Khan

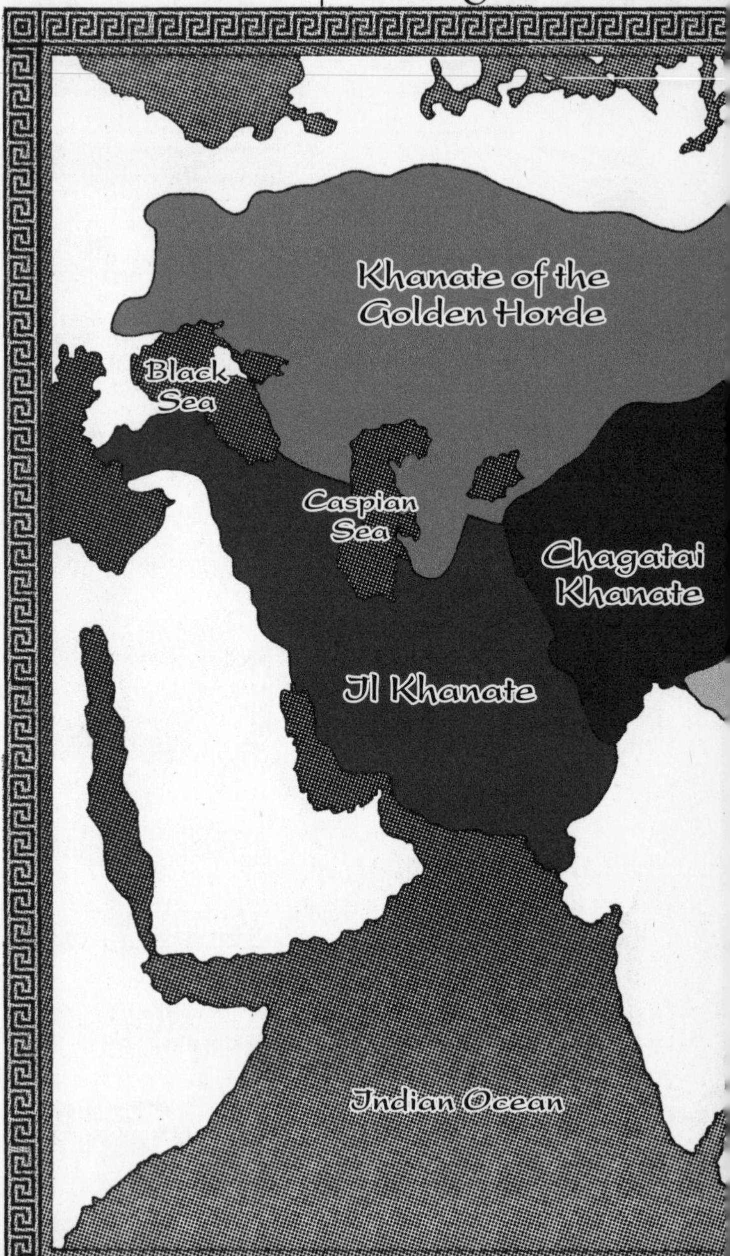

Khanate of the Golden Horde
Black Sea
Caspian Sea
Chagatai Khanate
Il Khanate
Indian Ocean

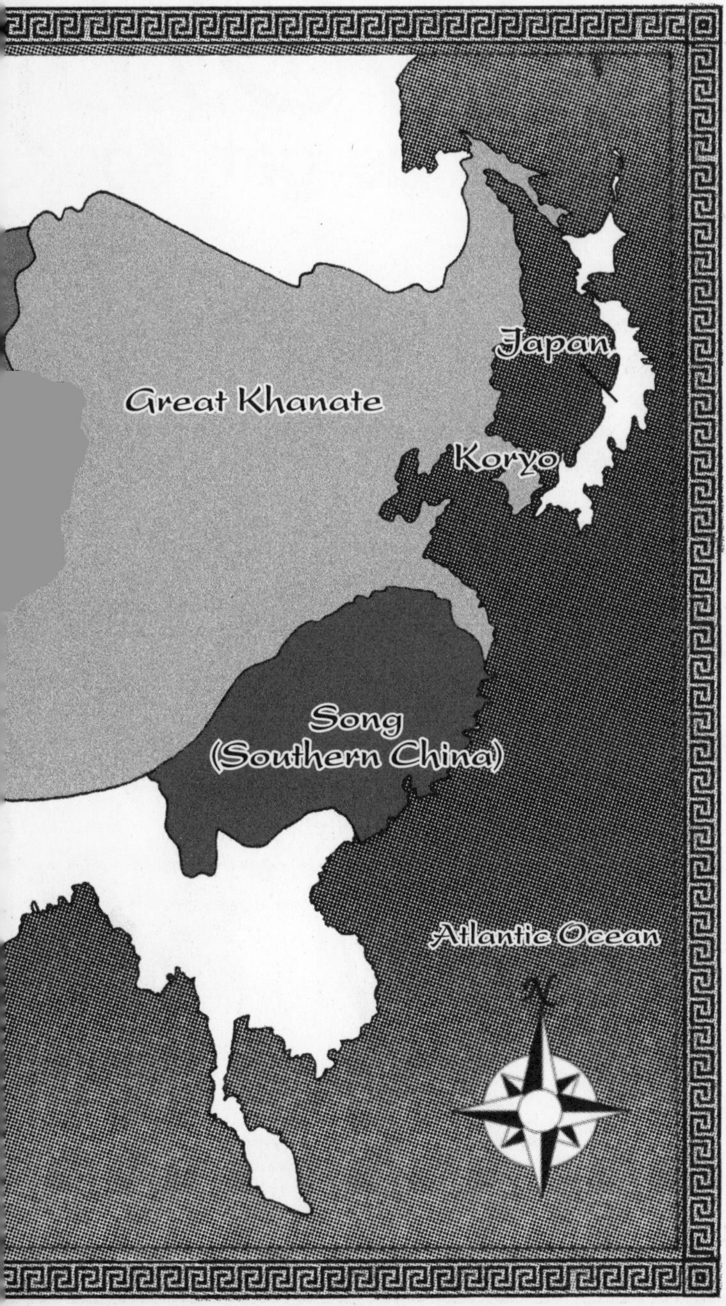
Japan
Great Khanate
Koryo
Song
(Southern China)
Atlantic Ocean
N

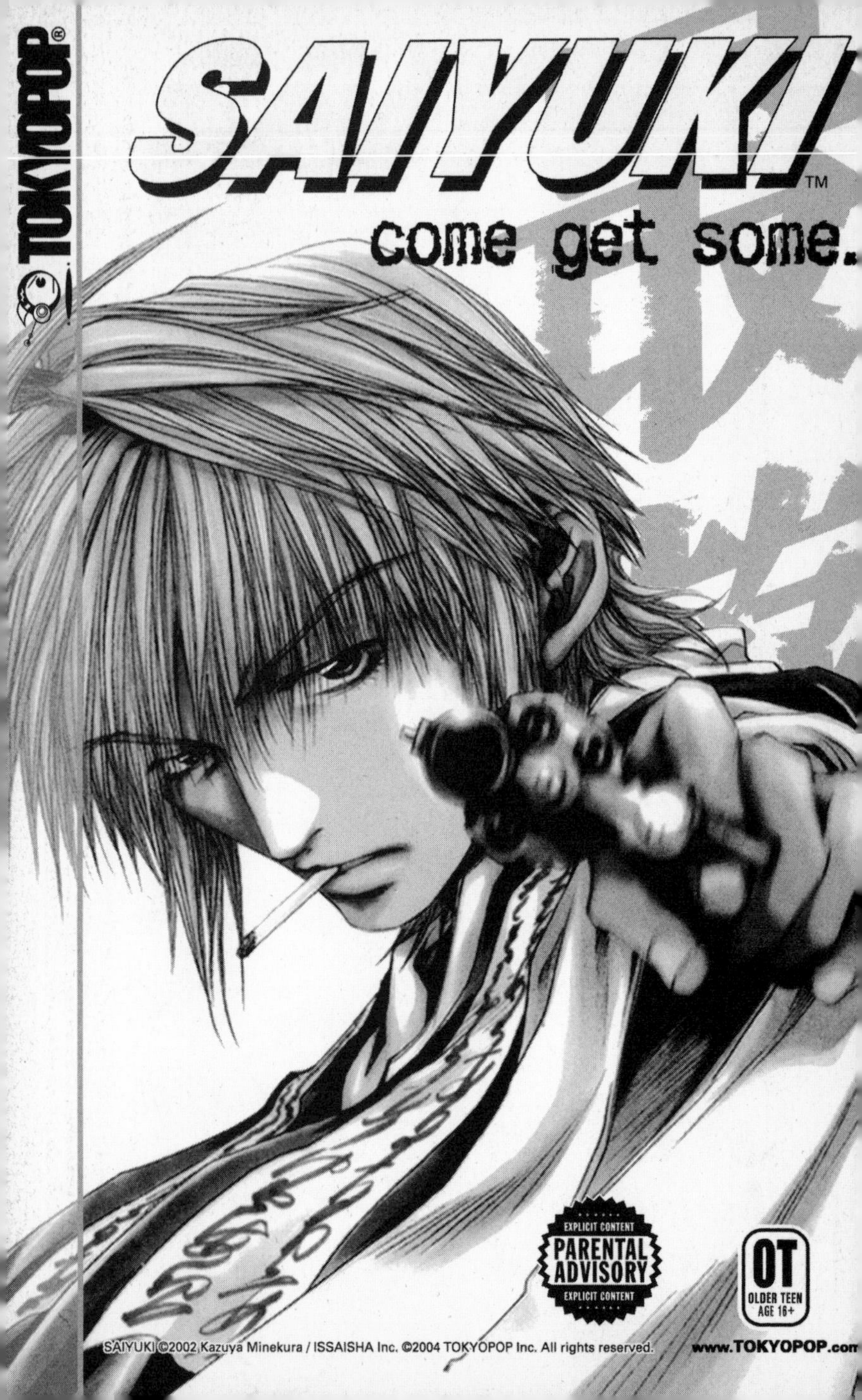
TOKYOPOP®
SAIYUKI™
come get some.
EXPLICIT CONTENT
PARENTAL ADVISORY
EXPLICIT CONTENT
OT
OLDER TEEN
AGE 16+
SAIYUKI ©2002 Kazuya Minekura / ISSAISHA Inc. ©2004 TOKYOPOP Inc. All rights reserved.
www.TOKYOPOP.com

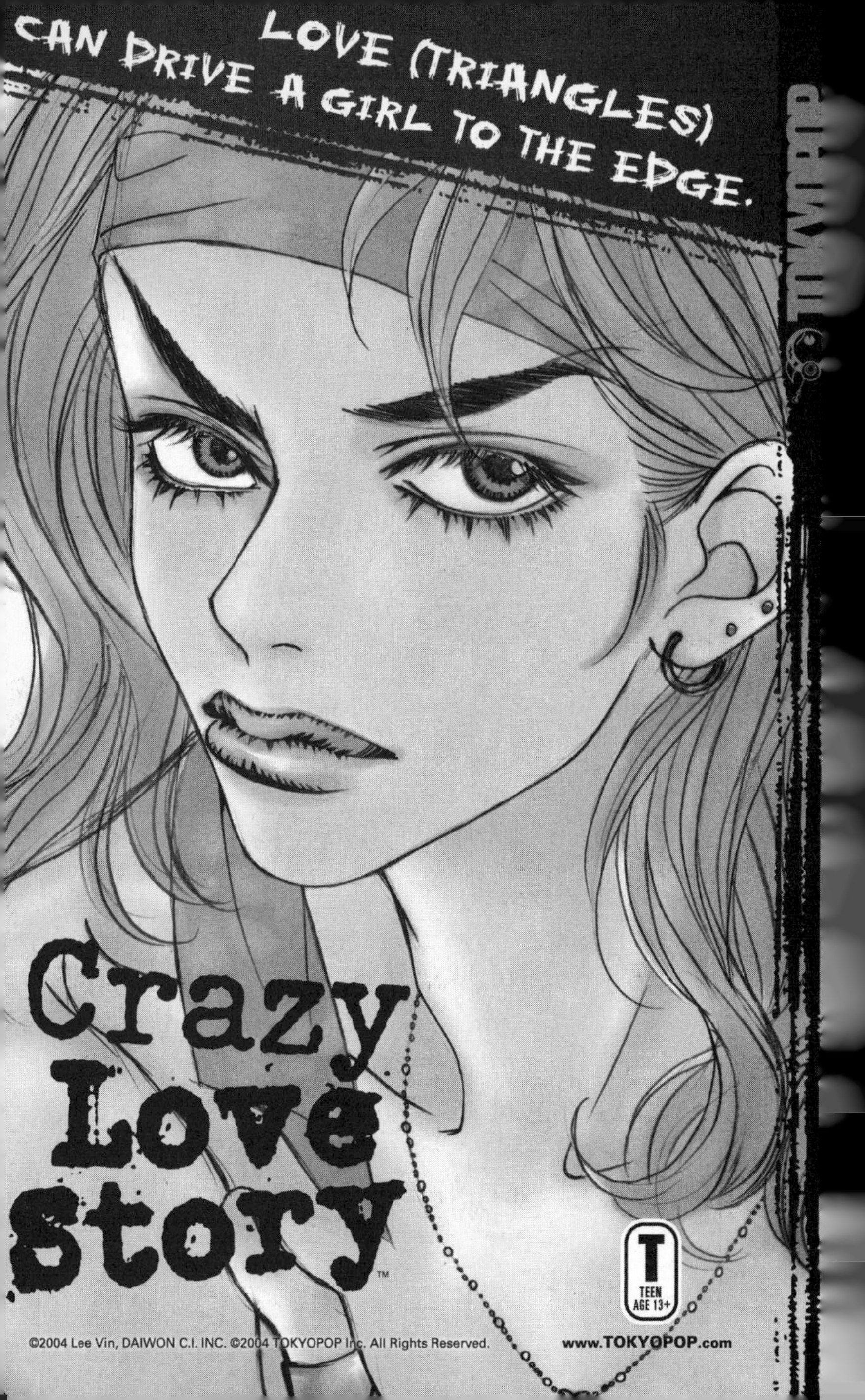
LOVE (TRIANGLES)
CAN DRIVE A GIRL TO THE EDGE.
TOKYOPOP
Crazy Love Story™
T TEEN AGE 13+
©2004 Lee Vin, DAIWON C.I. INC. ©2004 TOKYOPOP Inc. All Rights Reserved.
www.TOKYOPOP.com

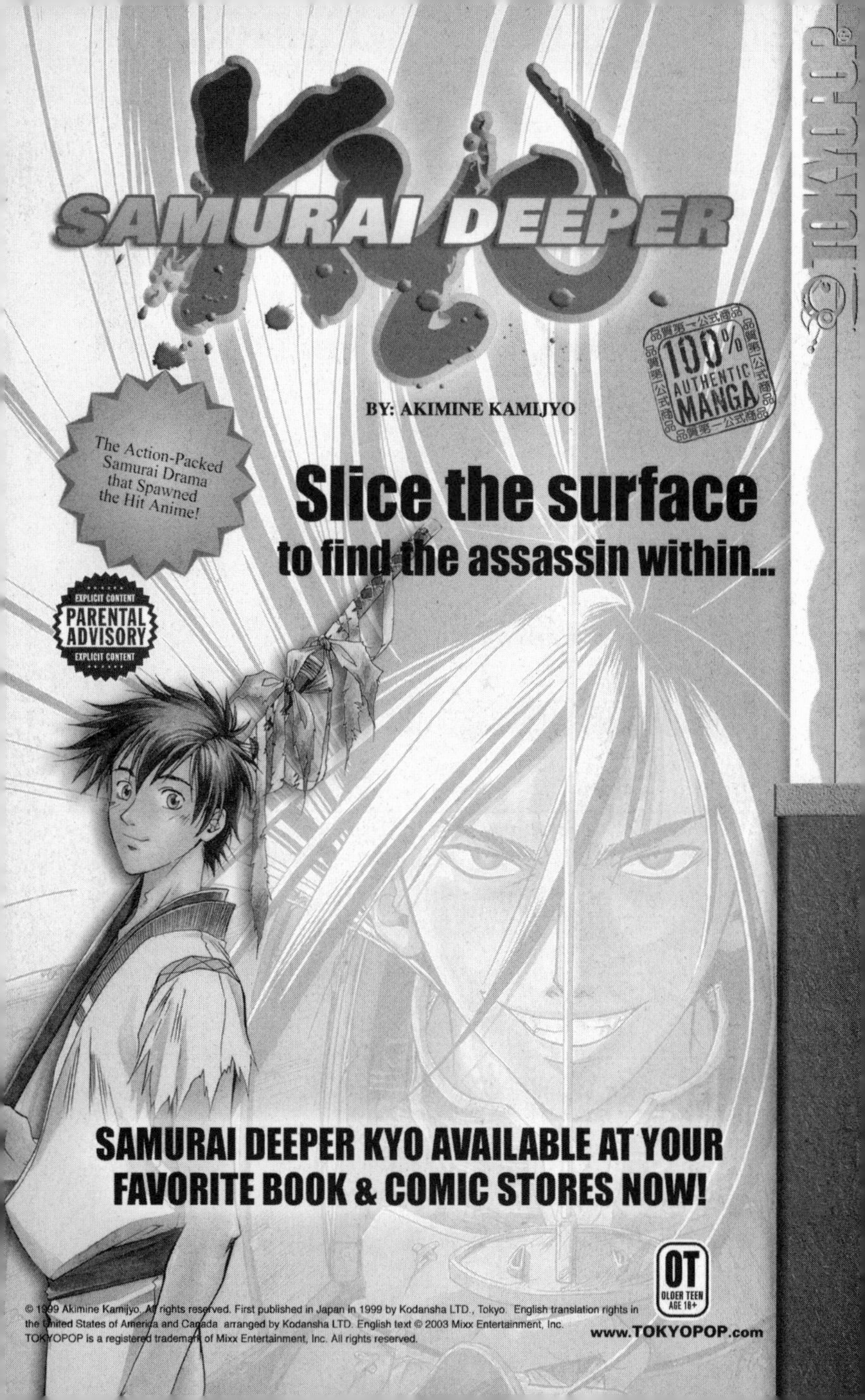

TOKYOPOP
SAMURAI DEEPER KYO
BY: AKIMINE KAMIJYO
100% AUTHENTIC MANGA
The Action-Packed Samurai Drama that Spawned the Hit Anime!
Slice the surface
to find the assassin within...
EXPLICIT CONTENT PARENTAL ADVISORY EXPLICIT CONTENT
SAMURAI DEEPER KYO AVAILABLE AT YOUR FAVORITE BOOK & COMIC STORES NOW!
OT OLDER TEEN AGE 18+
© 1999 Akimine Kamijyo. All rights reserved. First published in Japan in 1999 by Kodansha LTD., Tokyo. English translation rights in the United States of America and Canada arranged by Kodansha LTD. English text © 2003 Mixx Entertainment, Inc. TOKYOPOP is a registered trademark of Mixx Entertainment, Inc. All rights reserved.
www.TOKYOPOP.com

ALSO AVAILABLE FROM  TOKYOPOP®

08.20.04

ALSO AVAILABLE FROM TOKYOPOP

PLANETES
PRESIDENT DAD
PRIEST
PRINCESS AI
PSYCHIC ACADEMY
QUEEN'S KNIGHT, THE
RAGNAROK
RAVE MASTER
REALITY CHECK
REBIRTH
REBOUND
REMOTE
RISING STARS OF MANGA
SABER MARIONETTE J
SAILOR MOON
SAINT TAIL
SAIYUKI
SAMURAI DEEPER KYO
SAMURAI GIRL REAL BOUT HIGH SCHOOL
SCRYED
SEIKAI TRILOGY, THE
SGT. FROG
SHAOLIN SISTERS
SHIRAHIME-SYO: SNOW GODDESS TALES
SHUTTERBOX
SKULL MAN, THE
SNOW DROP
SORCERER HUNTERS
STONE
SUIKODEN III
SUKI
TAROT CAFÉ, THE
THREADS OF TIME
TOKYO BABYLON
TOKYO MEW MEW
TOKYO TRIBES
TRAMPS LIKE US
UNDER THE GLASS MOON
VAMPIRE GAME
VISION OF ESCAFLOWNE, THE
WARCRAFT
WARRIORS OF TAO
WILD ACT
WISH
WORLD OF HARTZ
X-DAY
ZODIAC P.I.

NOVELS

CLAMP SCHOOL PARANORMAL INVESTIGATORS
SAILOR MOON

ART BOOKS

ART OF CARDCAPTOR SAKURA
ART OF MAGIC KNIGHT RAYEARTH, THE
PEACH: MIWA UEDA ILLUSTRATIONS
CLAMP NORTHSIDE
CLAMP SOUTHSIDE

ANIME GUIDES

COWBOY BEBOP
GUNDAM TECHNICAL MANUALS
SAILOR MOON SCOUT GUIDES

TOKYOPOP KIDS

STRAY SHEEP

CINE-MANGA™

ALADDIN
CARDCAPTORS
DUEL MASTERS
FAIRLY ODDPARENTS, THE
FAMILY GUY
FINDING NEMO
G.I. JOE SPY TROOPS
GREATEST STARS OF THE NBA: SHAQUILLE O'NEAL
GREATEST STARS OF THE NBA: TIM DUNCAN
JACKIE CHAN ADVENTURES
JIMMY NEUTRON: BOY GENIUS, THE ADVENTURES OF
KIM POSSIBLE
LILO & STITCH: THE SERIES
LIZZIE MCGUIRE
LIZZIE MCGUIRE MOVIE, THE
MALCOLM IN THE MIDDLE
POWER RANGERS: DINO THUNDER
POWER RANGERS: NINJA STORM
PRINCESS DIARIES 2
RAVE MASTER
SHREK 2
SIMPLE LIFE, THE
SPONGEBOB SQUAREPANTS
SPY KIDS 2
SPY KIDS 3-D: GAME OVER
TEENAGE MUTANT NINJA TURTLES
THAT'S SO RAVEN
TOTALLY SPIES
TRANSFORMERS: ARMADA
TRANSFORMERS: ENERGON

**You want it? We got it!
A full range of TOKYOPOP
products are available now at:
www.TOKYOPOP.com/shop**

08.20.04T

Suikoden III

幻想水滸伝

A legendary hero.
A war with no future.
An epic for today.

TOKYOPOP

T TEEN
AGE 13+

www.TOKYOPOP.com